Photographs have a life of their own;
captured moments in eternity
that warm the viewer's soul.

Also by Fabrice Poussin

In Absentia, (Silver Bow Publishing (2021)
If I Had a Gun, (Silver Bow Publishing (2022)
Half Past Life (Silver Bow Publishing (2023)
The Temptation of Silence (Silver Bow Publishing (2024)
Forgive Me For Dreaming (Silver Bow Publishing (2025)

Through The Eye
Of
Solitude

by

Fabrice Poussin

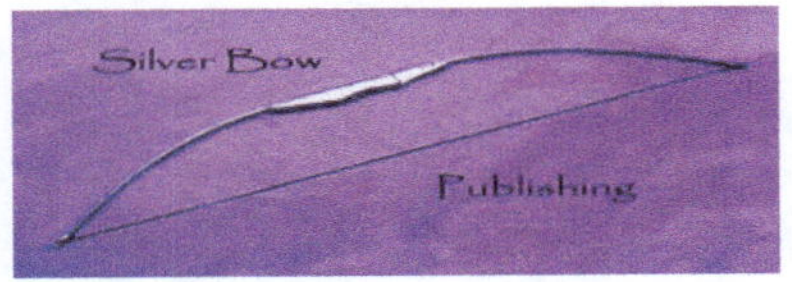

720 –Sixth Street, Box # 5
New Westminster, BC V3C 3C5
CANADA

Title: Through The Eye Of Solitude
Author: Fabrice Poussin
Cover Painting: "Stained Glass " Photograph by Fabrice Poussin
Layout Design: Candice James
Editor: Candice James
All artwork/paintings in the book are by Fabrice Poussin

© Silver Bow Publishing
978177403 368-5 print
978177403 369-2 eBook

Library and Archives Canada Cataloguing in Publication

Title: Through the eye of solitude / by Fabrice Poussin.
Names: Poussin, Fabrice, photographer
Identifiers: Canadiana (print) 20250231670 | Canadiana (ebook) 20250232901 | ISBN 9781774033685
   (softcover) | ISBN 9781774033692 (Kindle)
Subjects: LCSH: Photography, Artistic. | LCSH: Poussin, Fabrice. | LCGFT: Photobooks.
Classification: LCC TR655 .P687 2025 | DDC 779.092—dc23

Foreword

All photographs in this book are by Fabrice Poussin. They have been sized, minimally, to fit the page for the best viewing advantage to the viewer..

Dedication

To all the shutterbugs, big and small, famous or not, who have inspired me to photograph the world.

**PHOTOGRAPHS
by Fabrice Poussin**

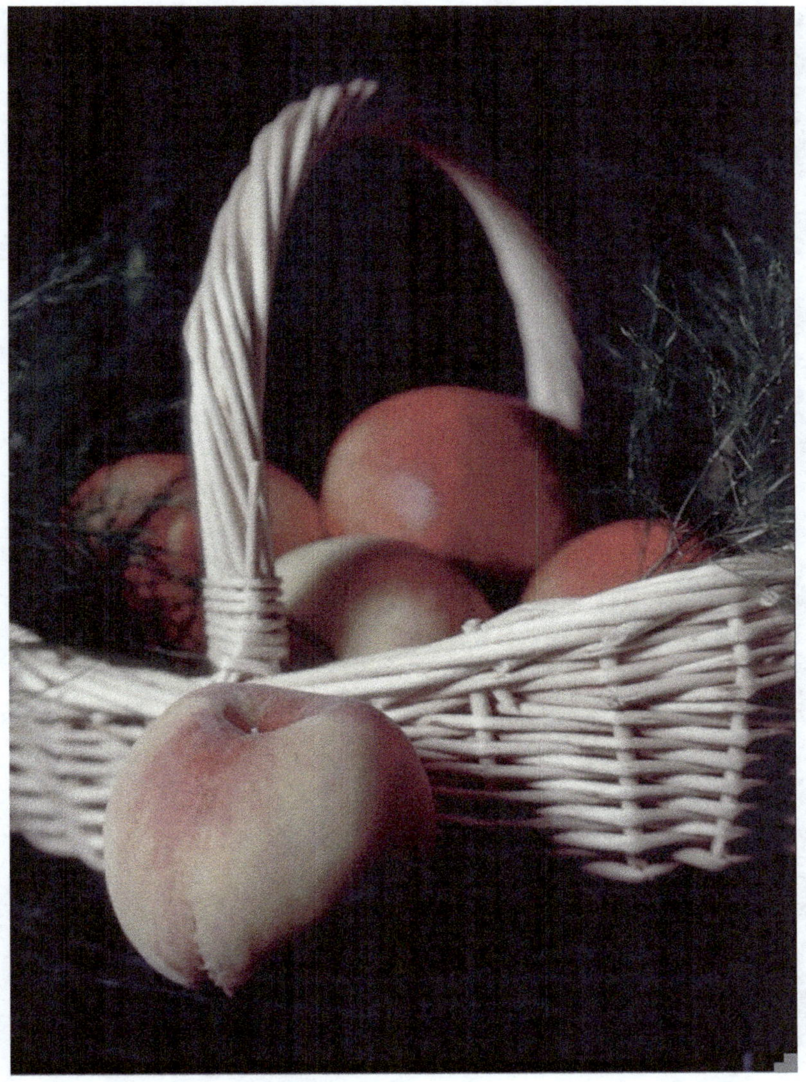

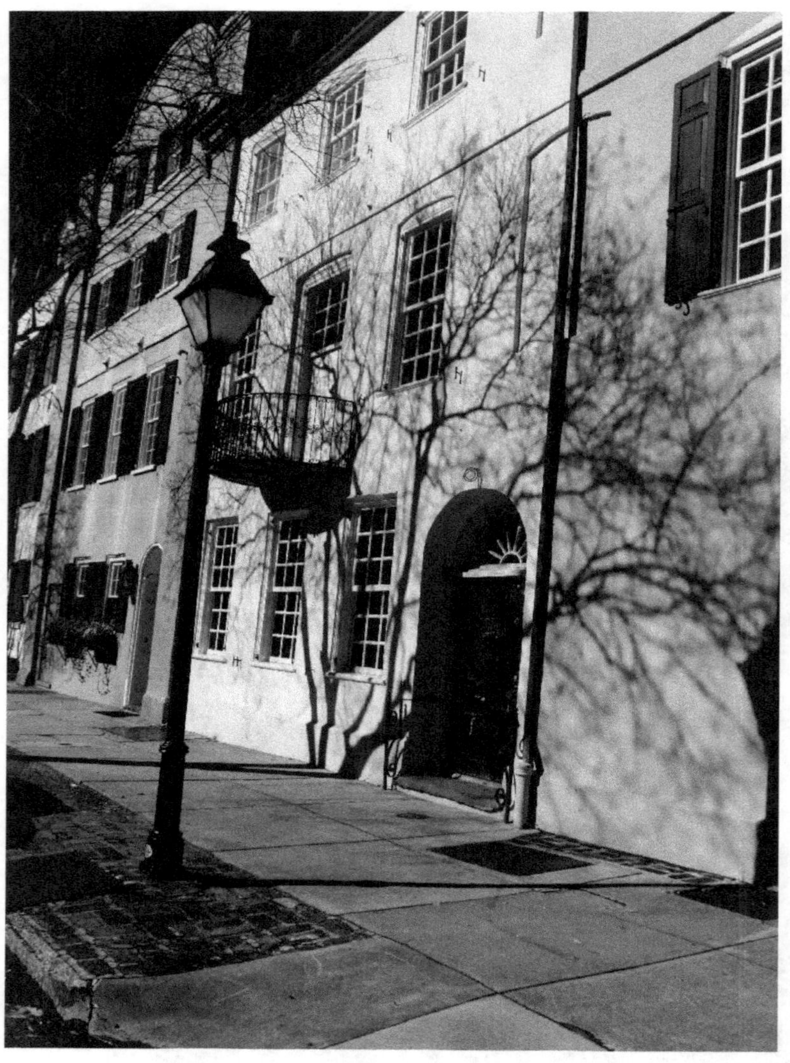

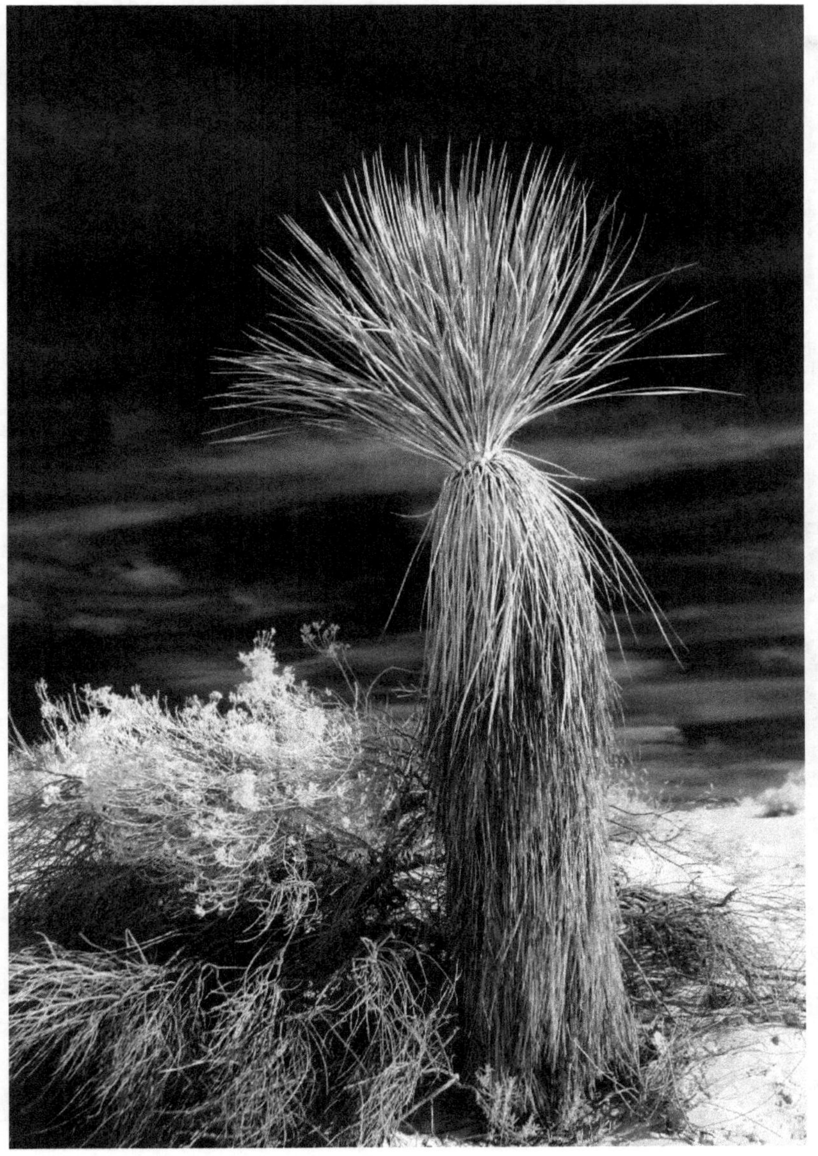

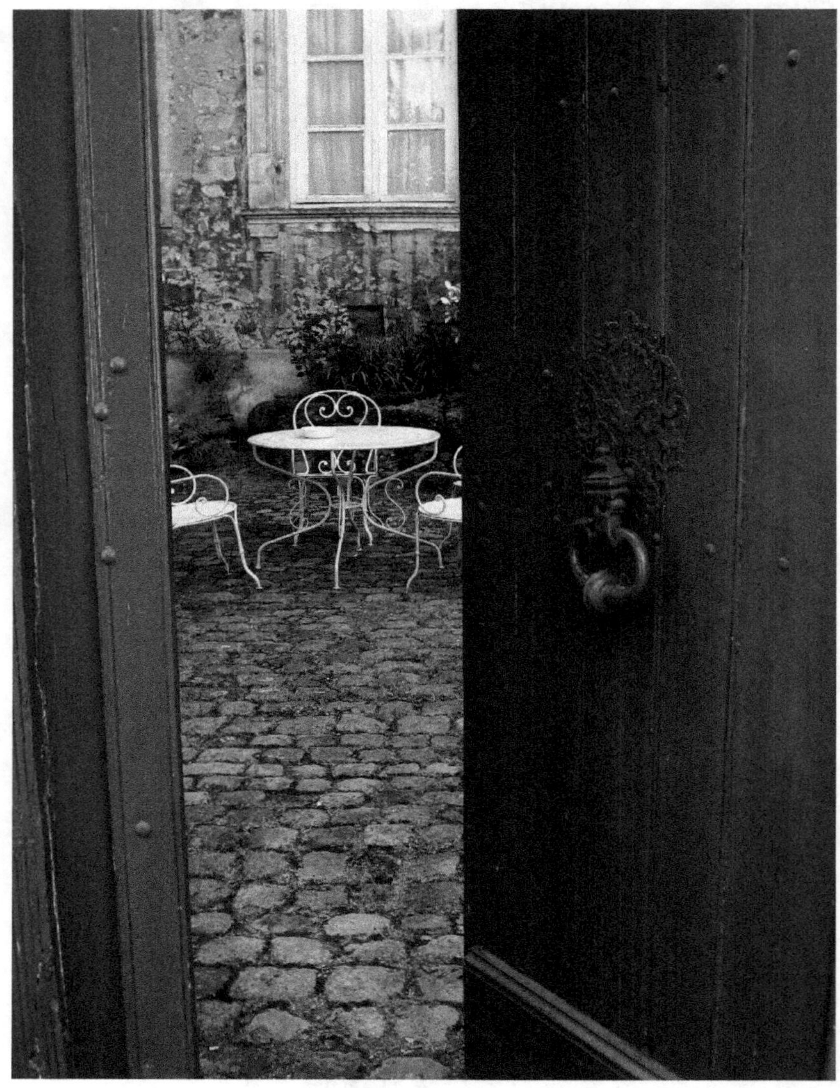

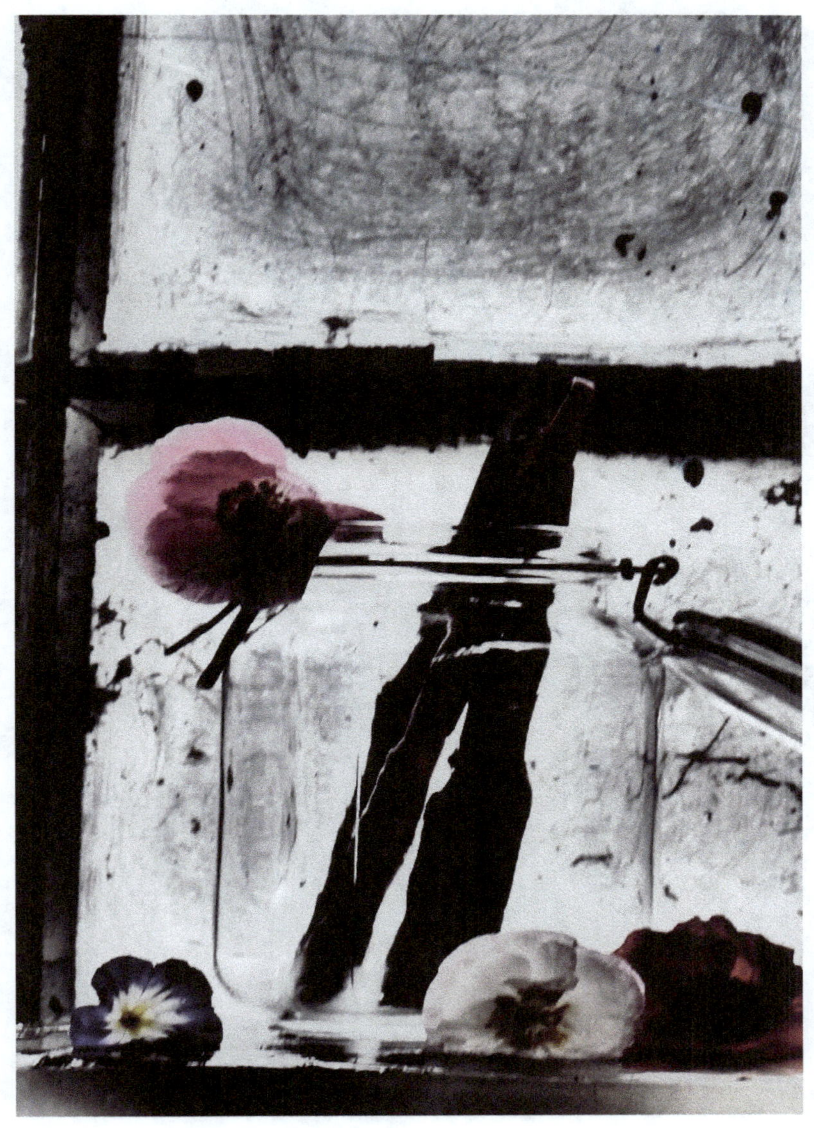

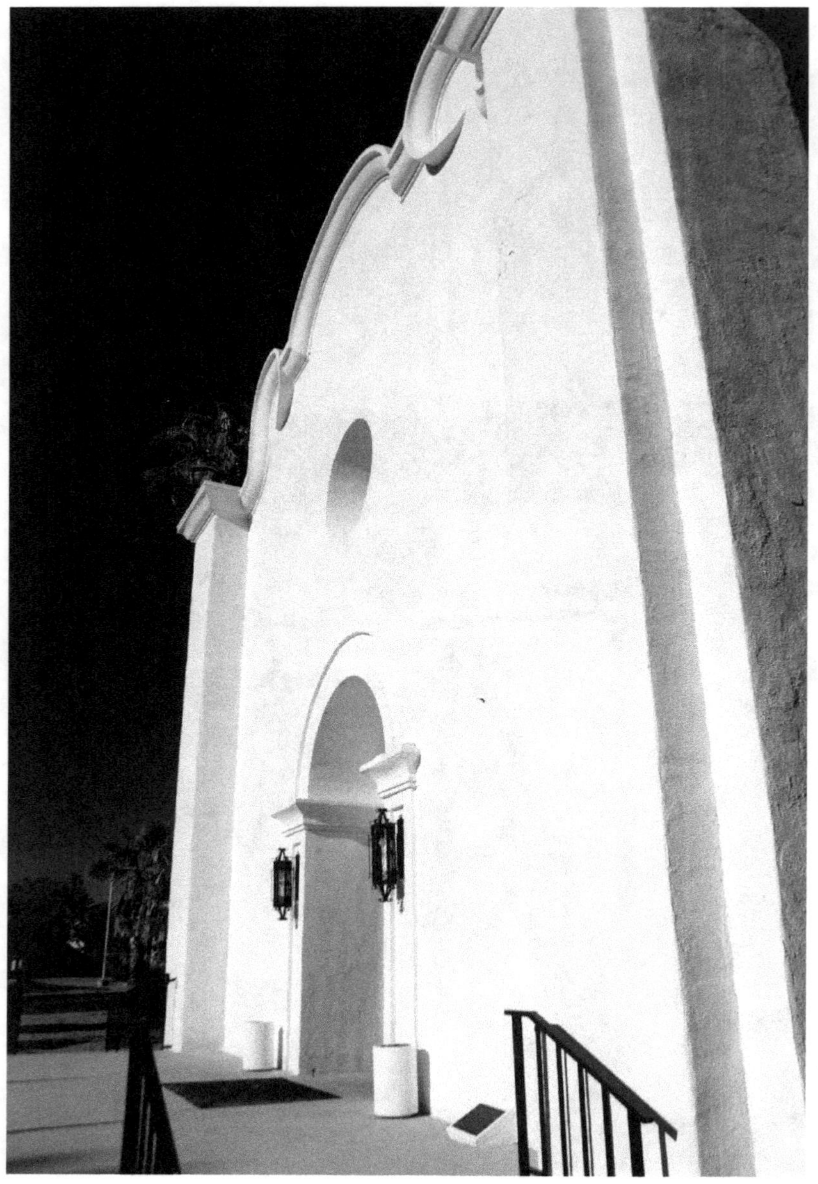

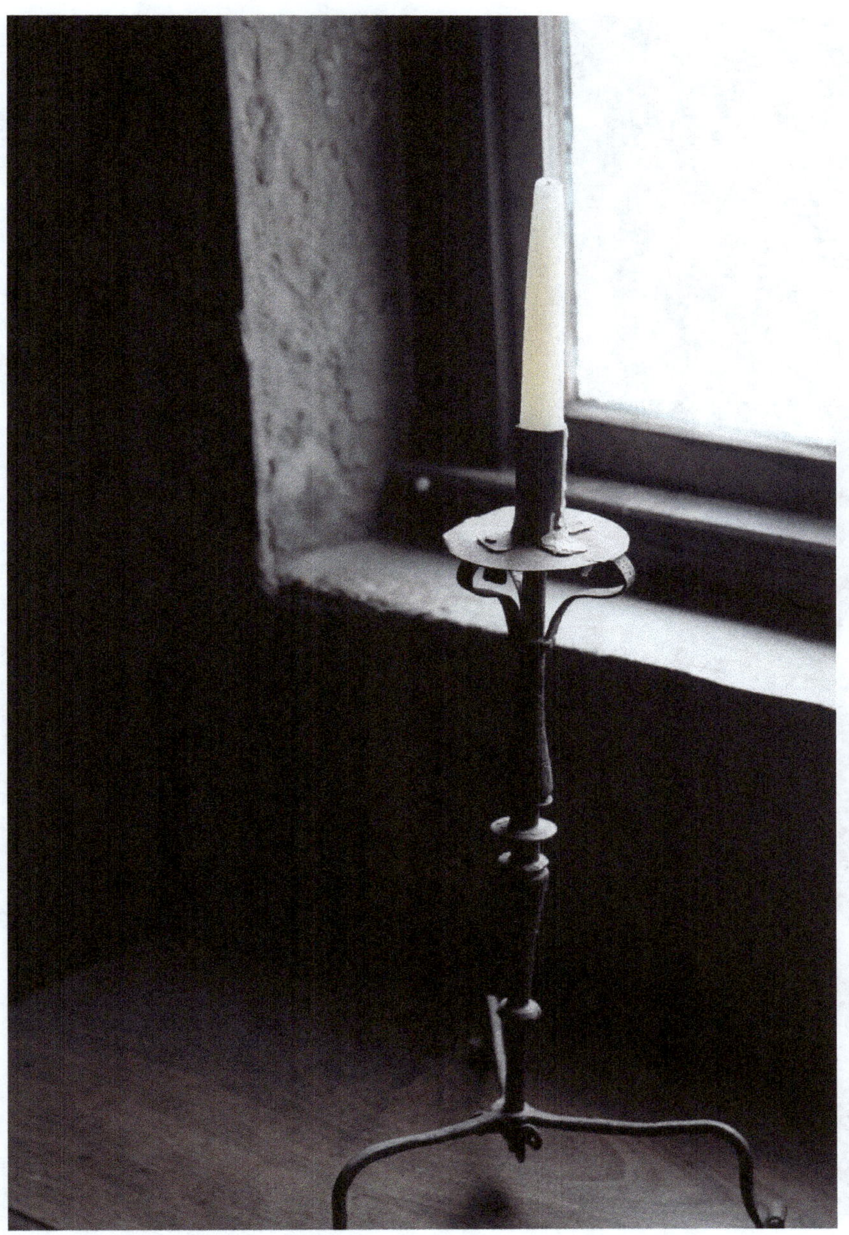

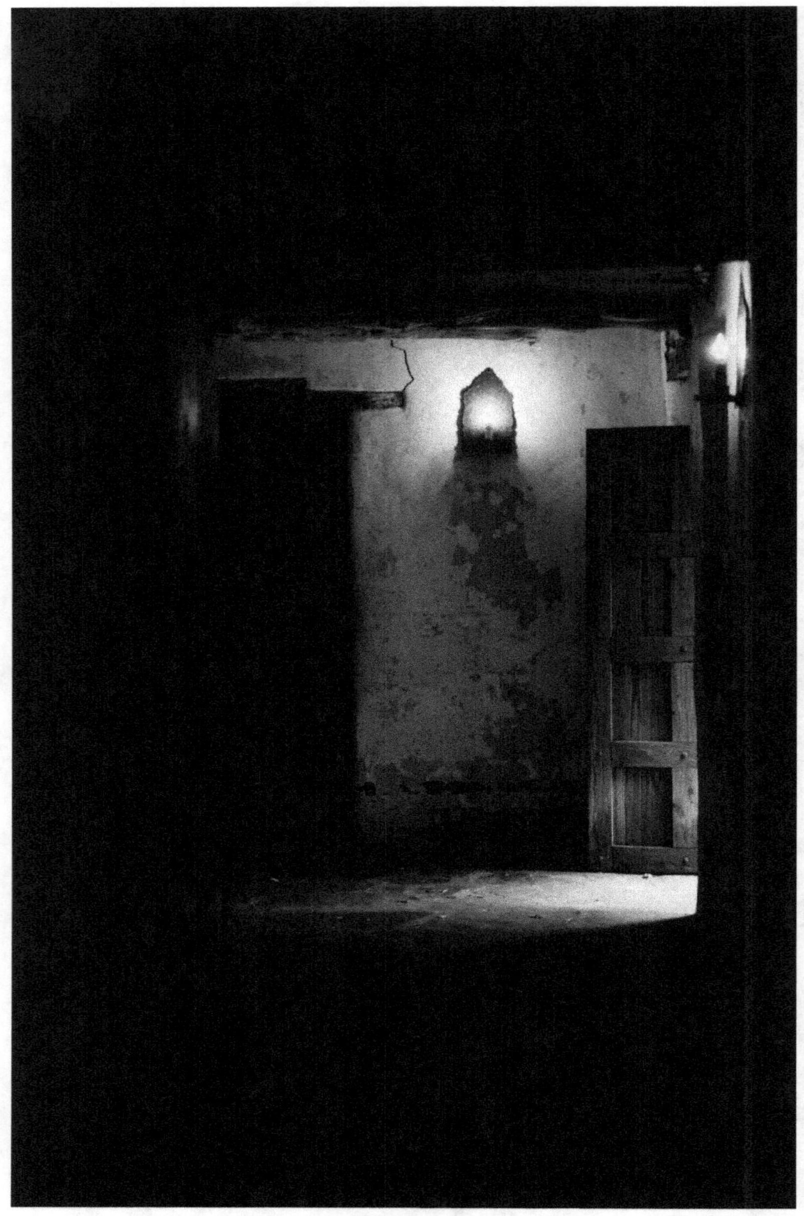

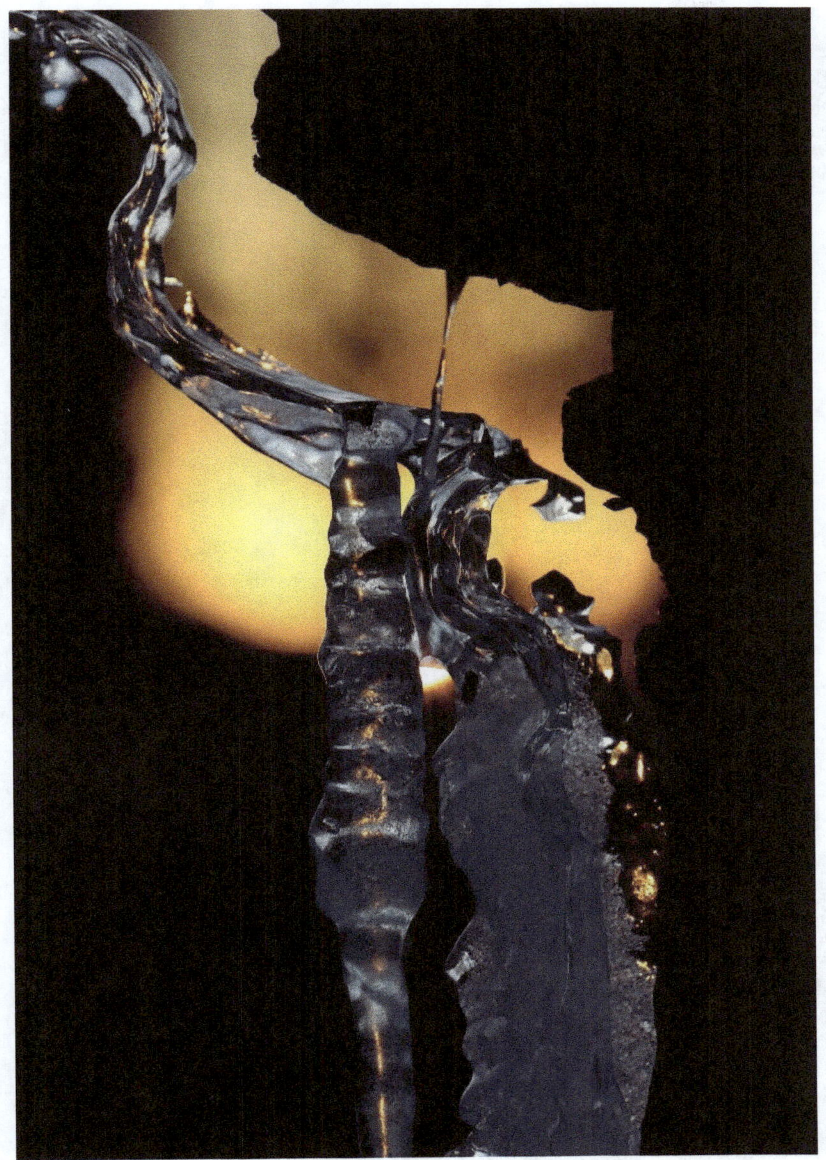

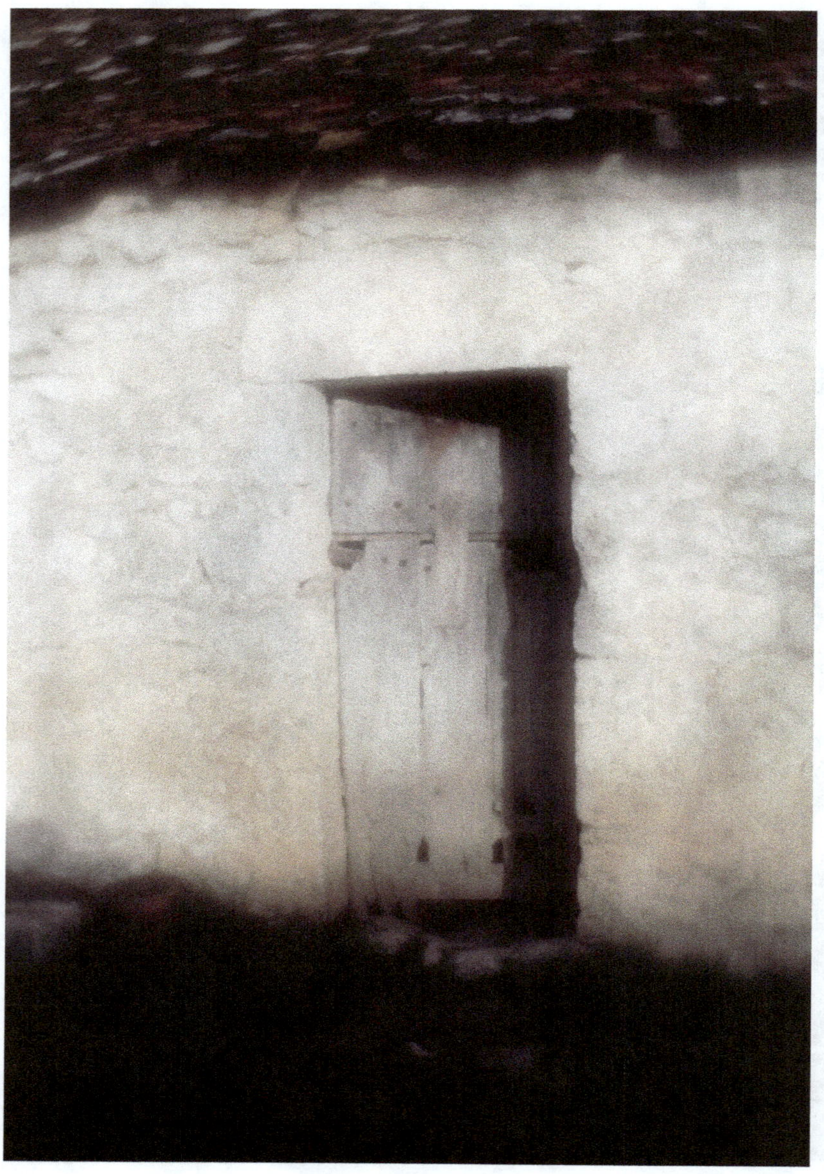

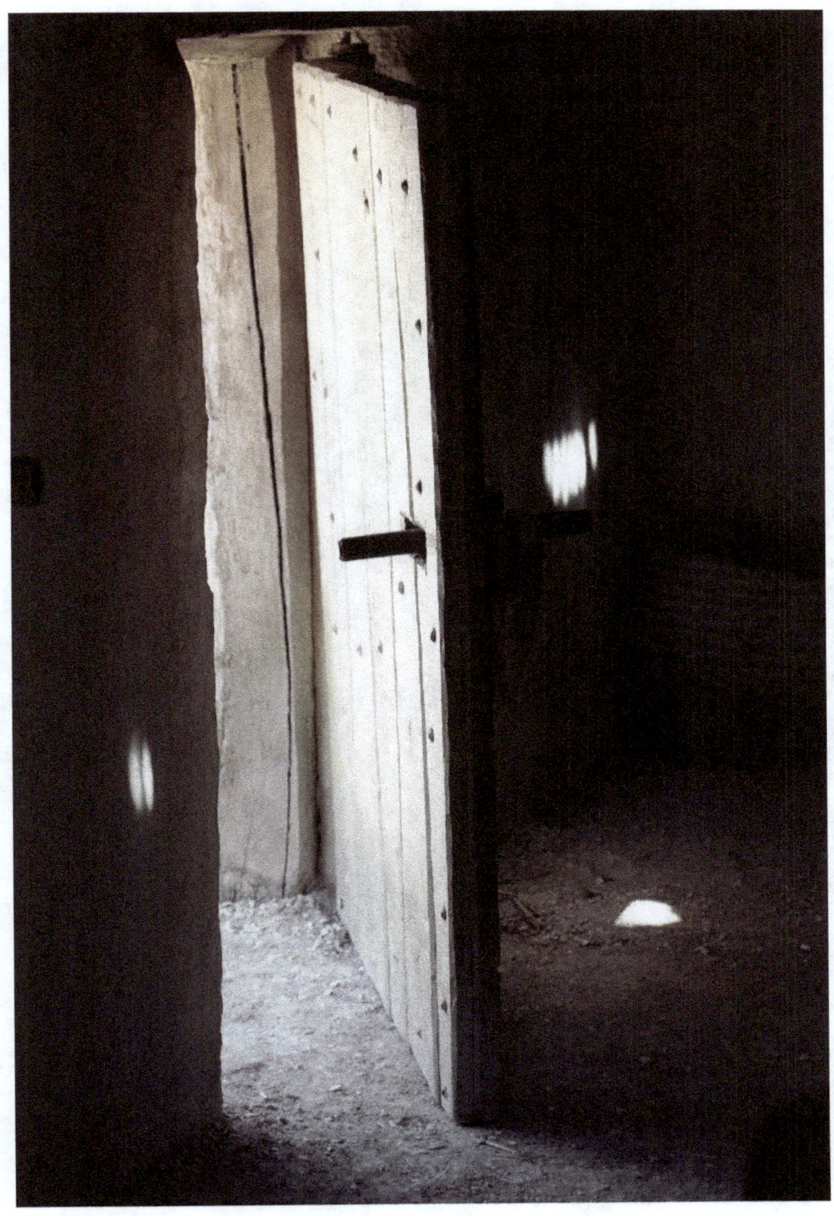

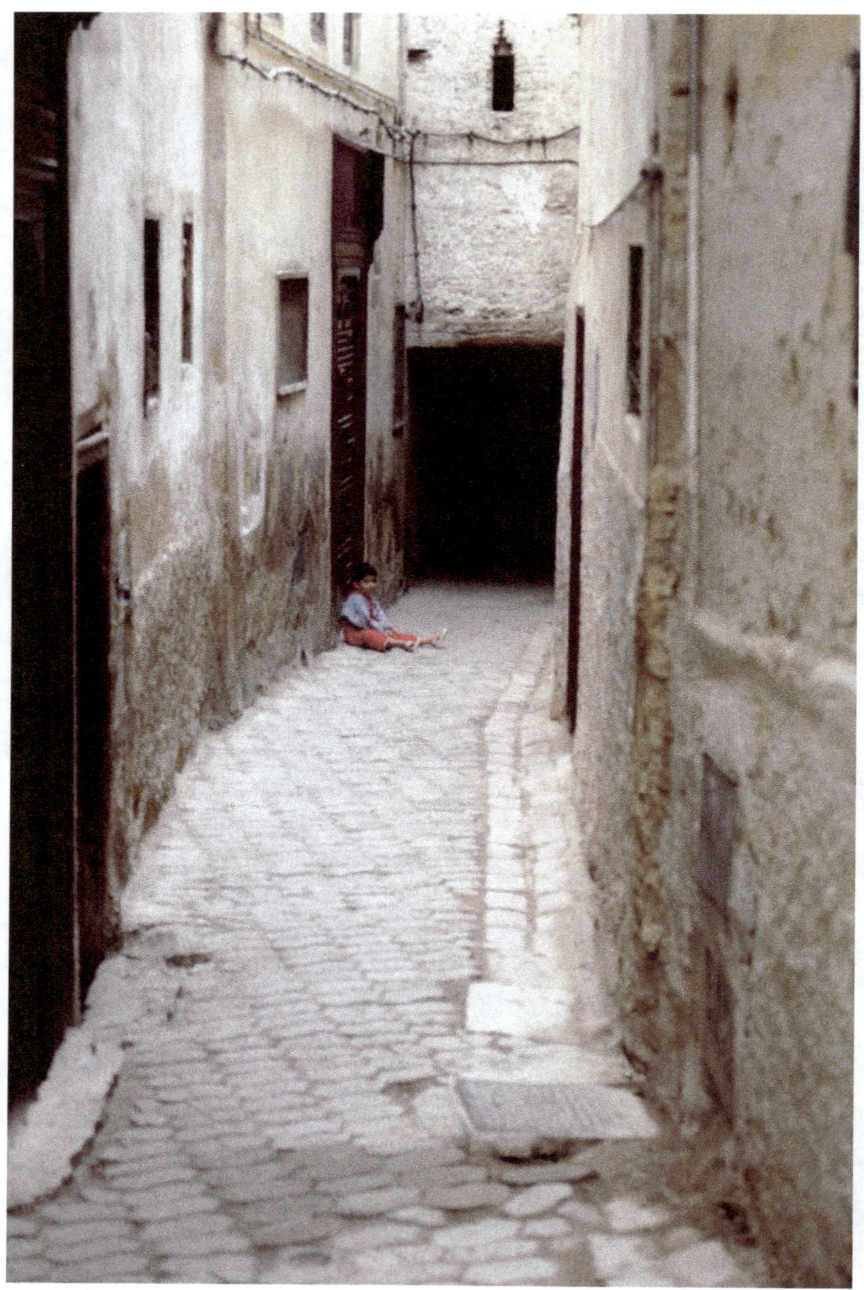

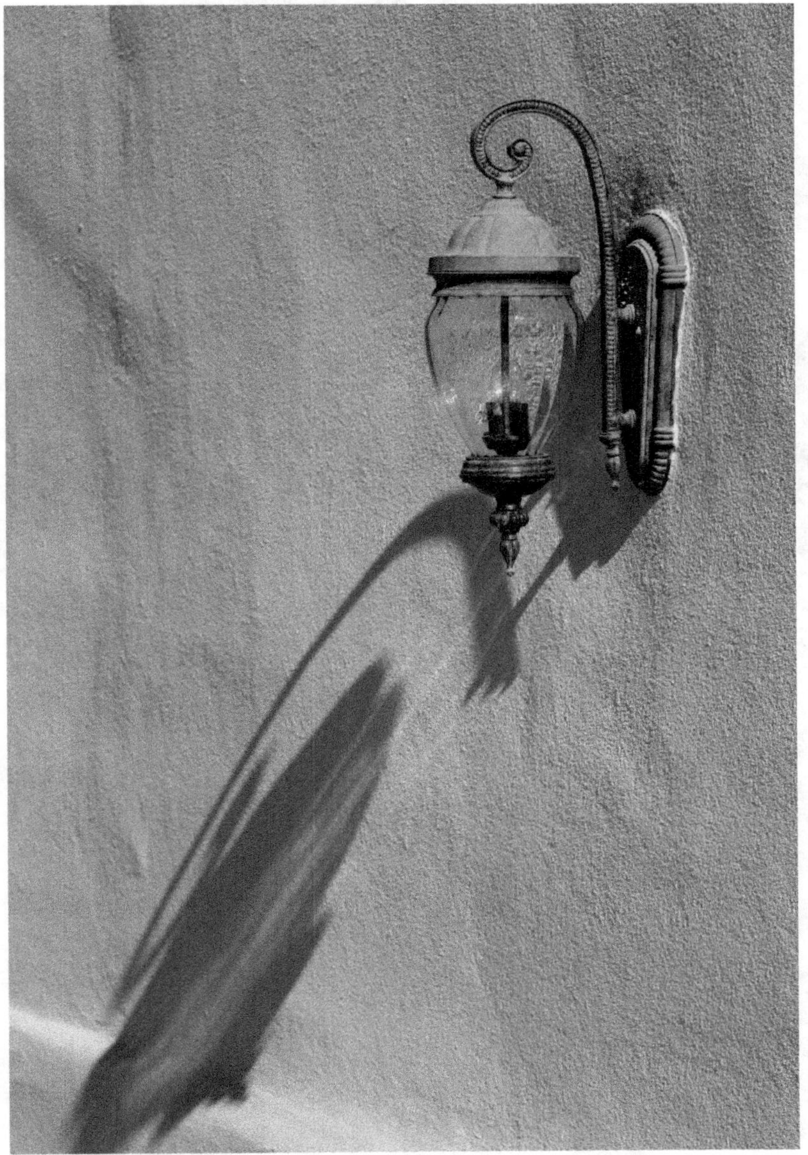

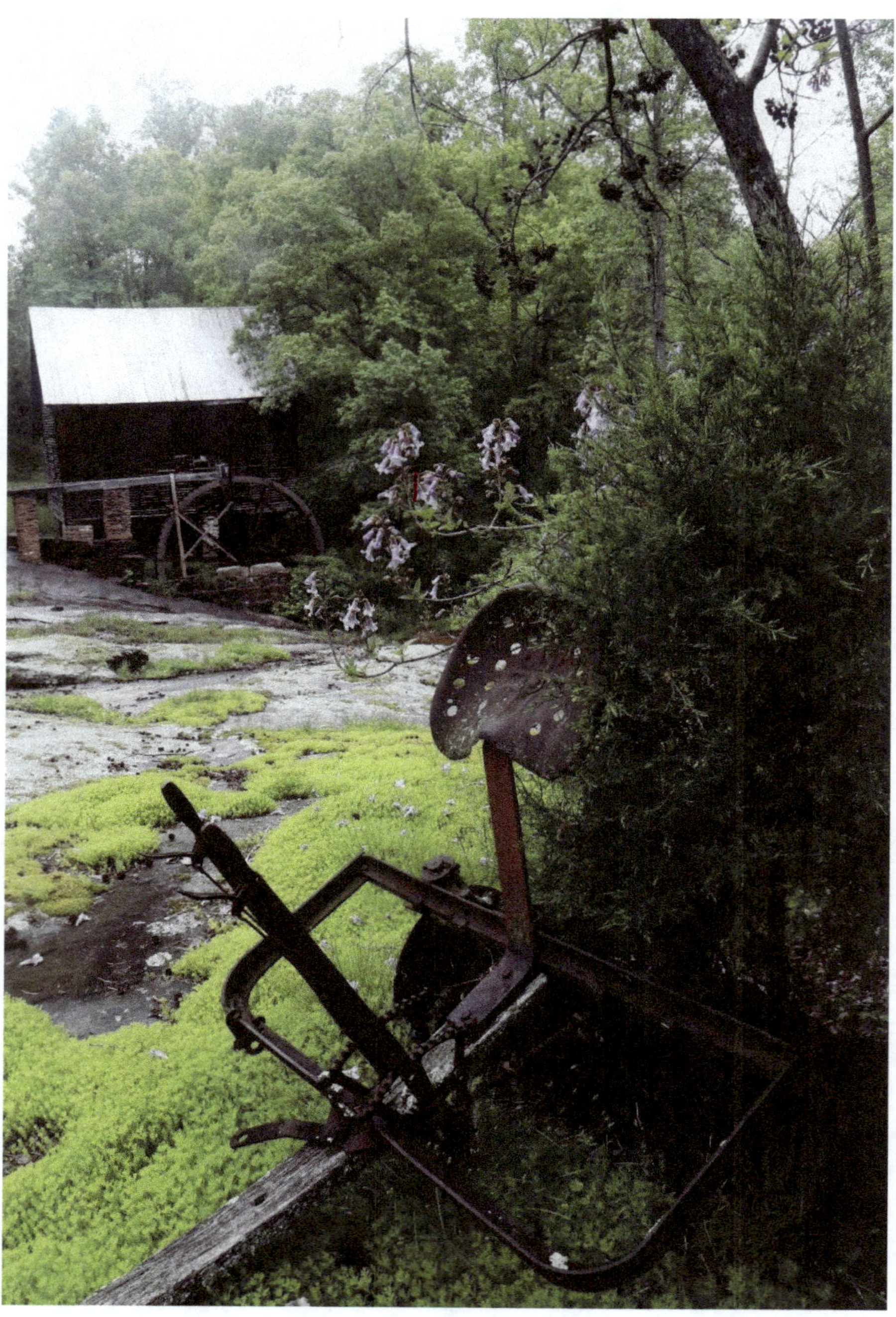

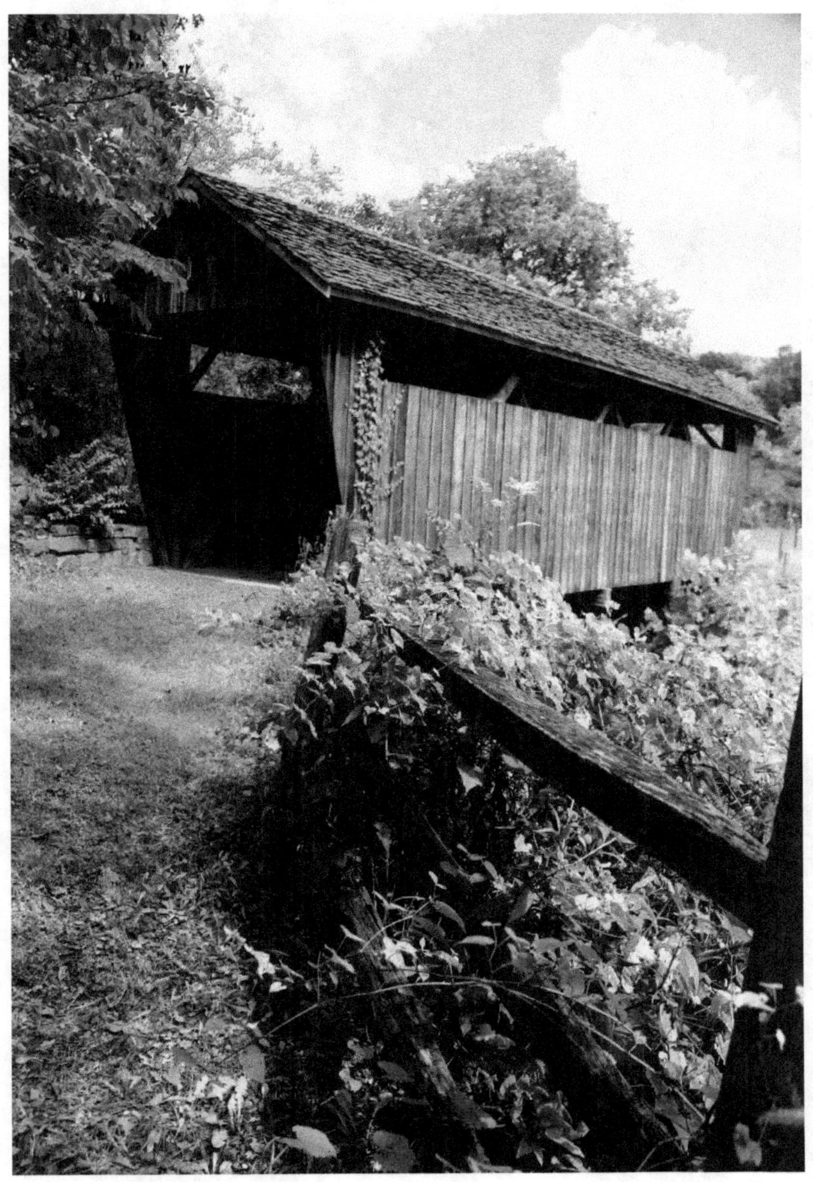

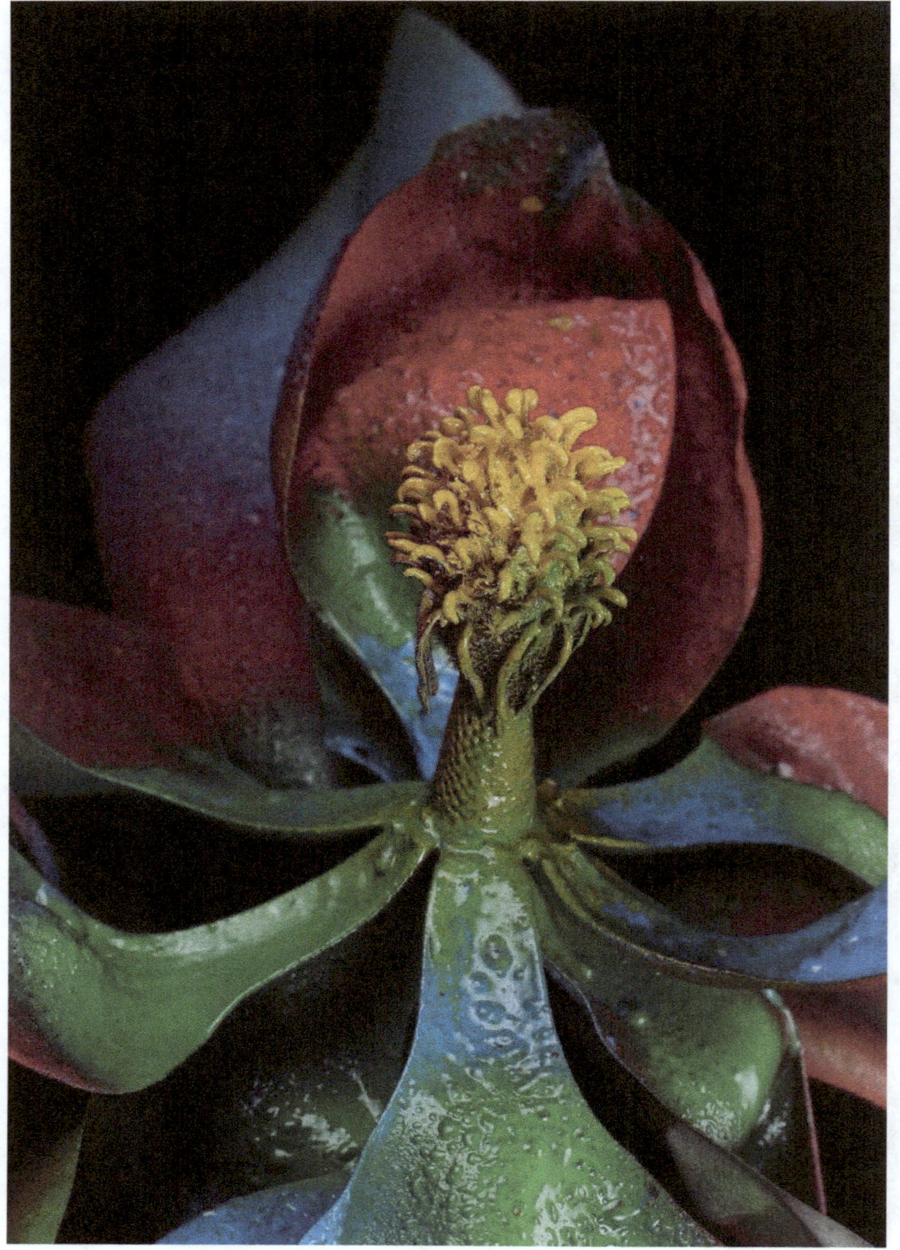

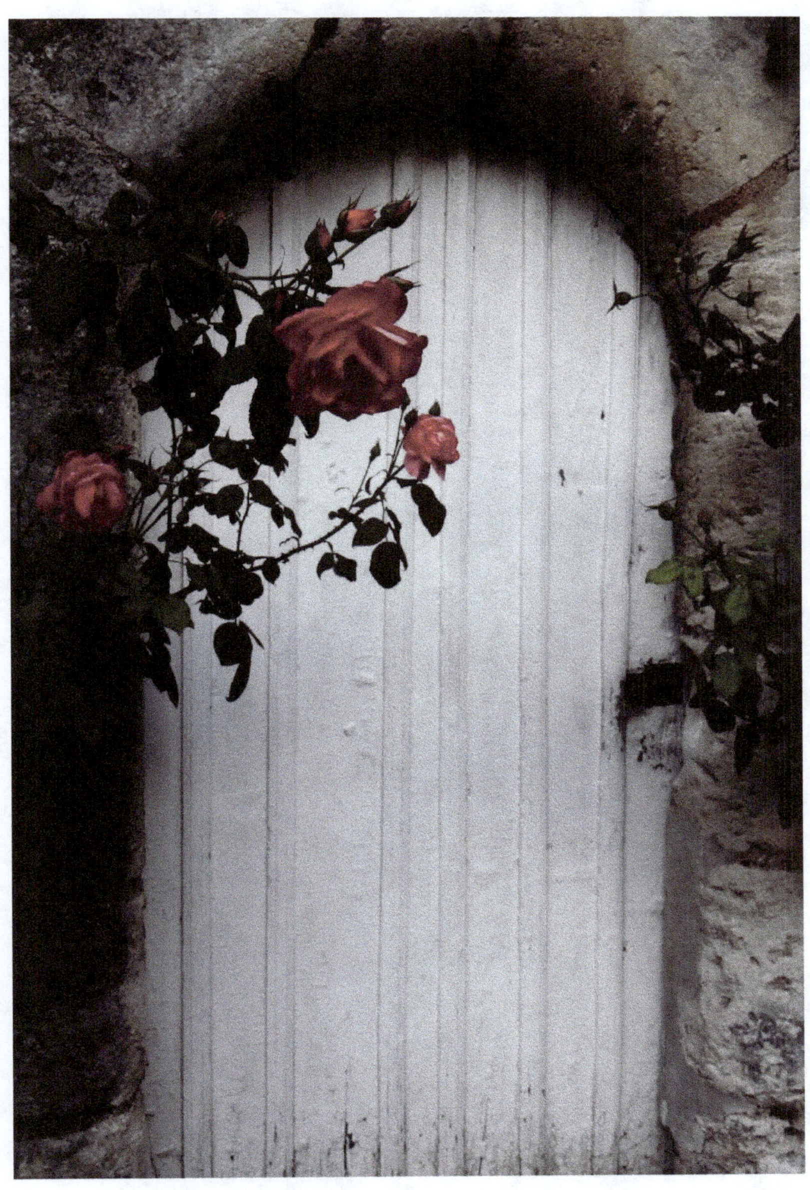

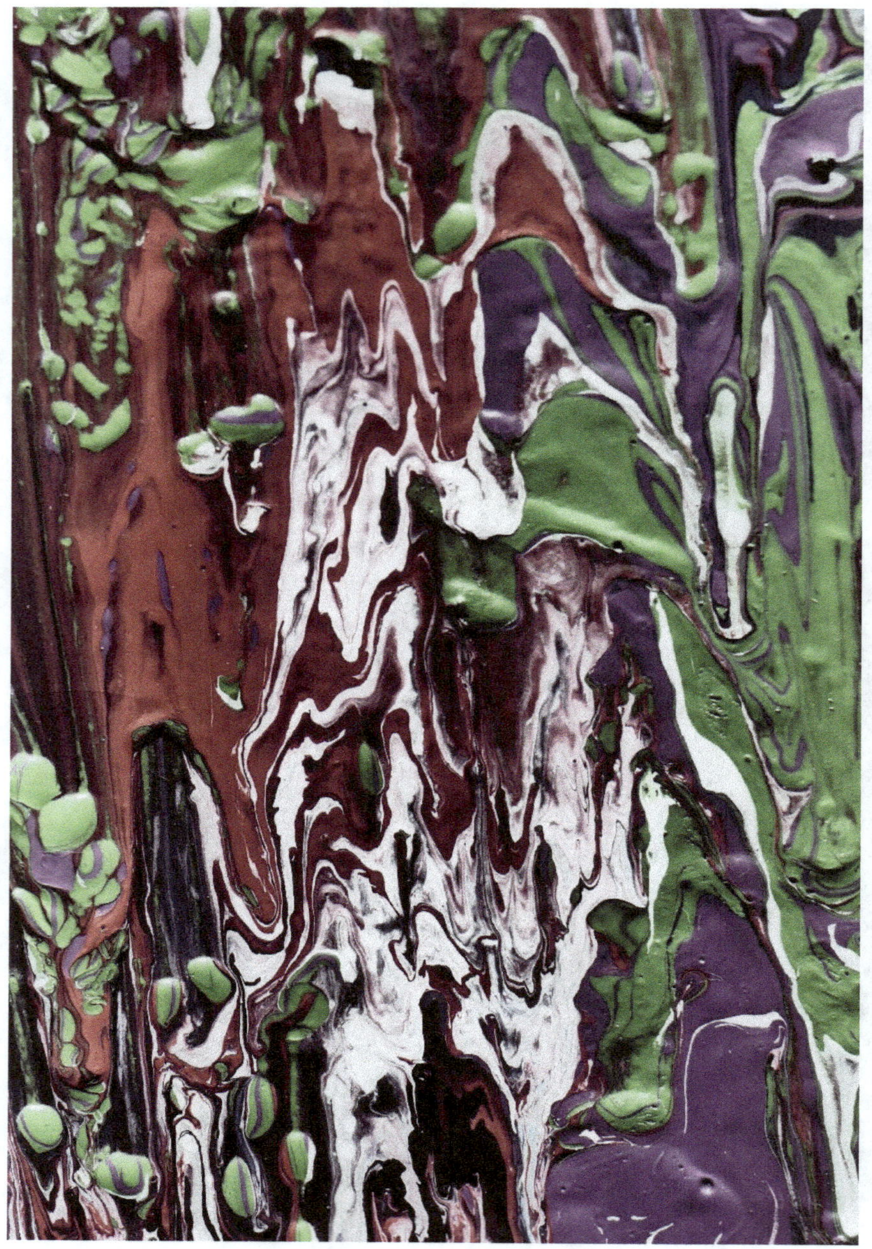

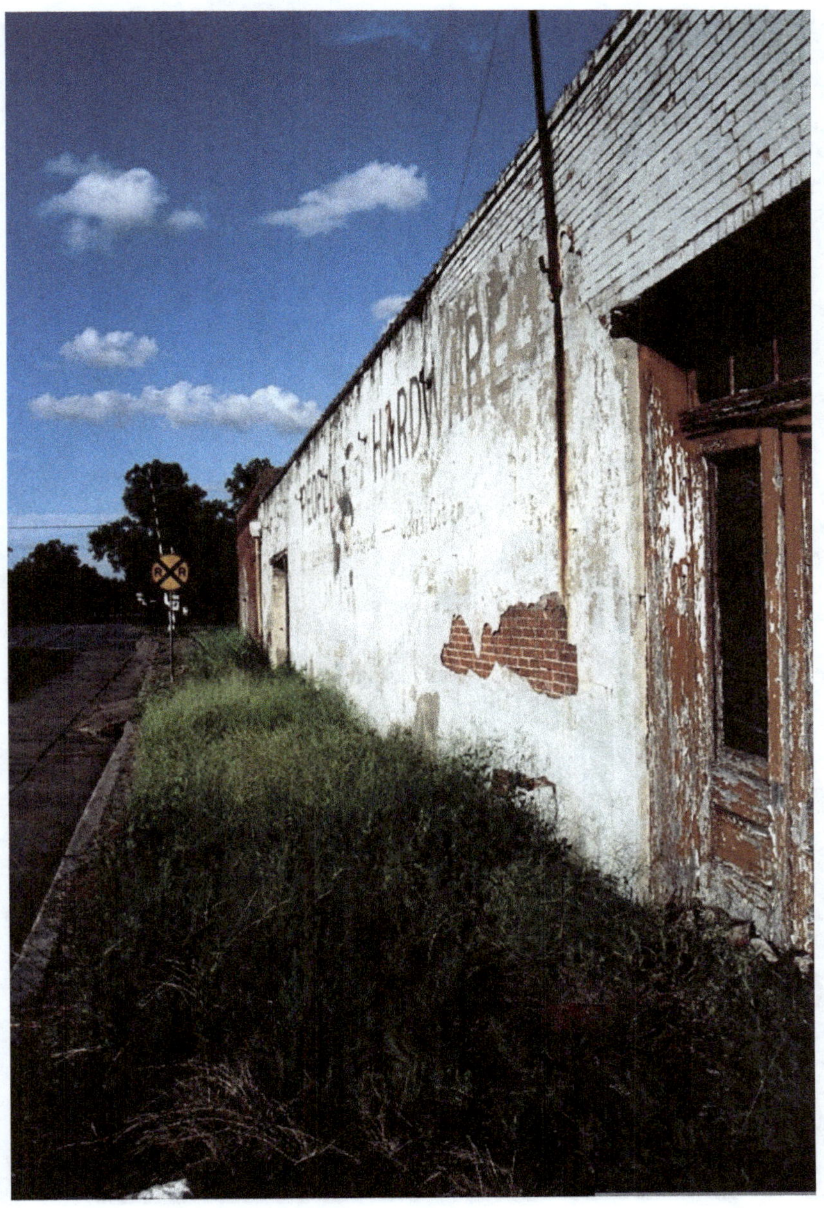

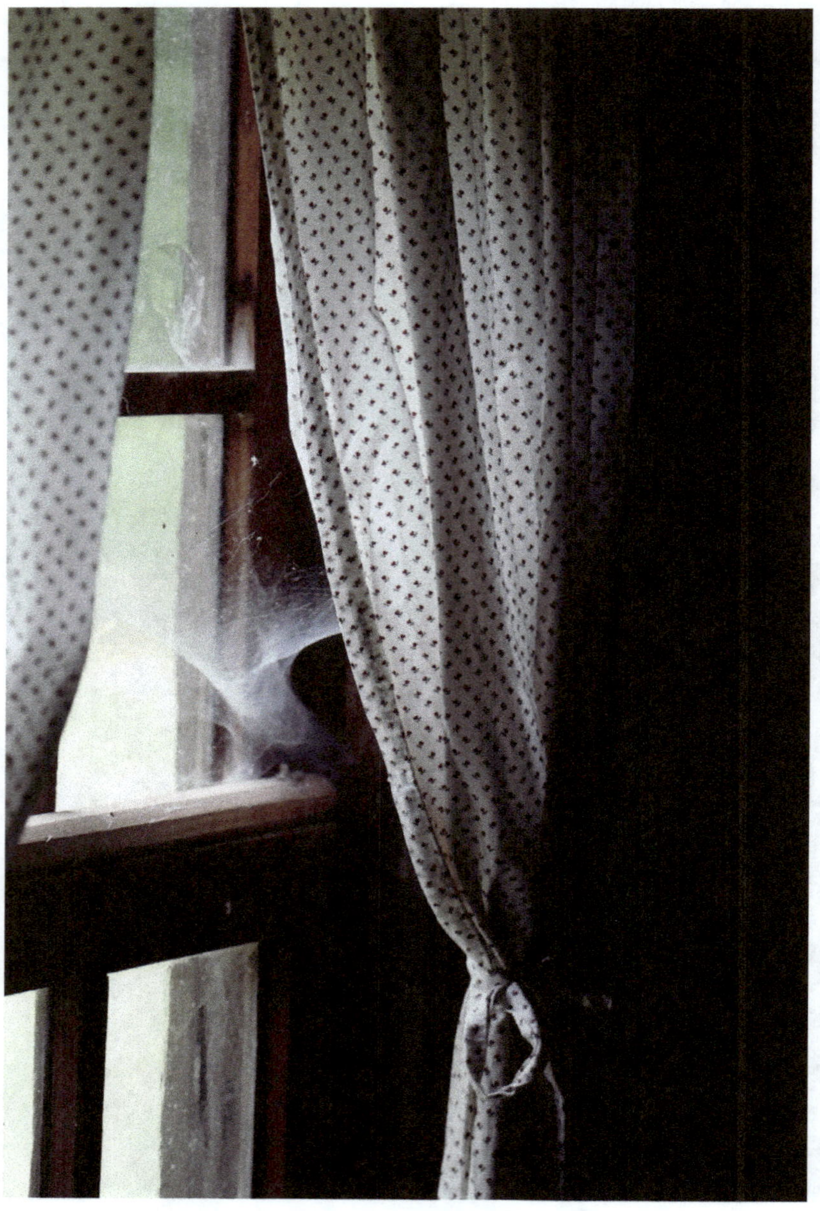

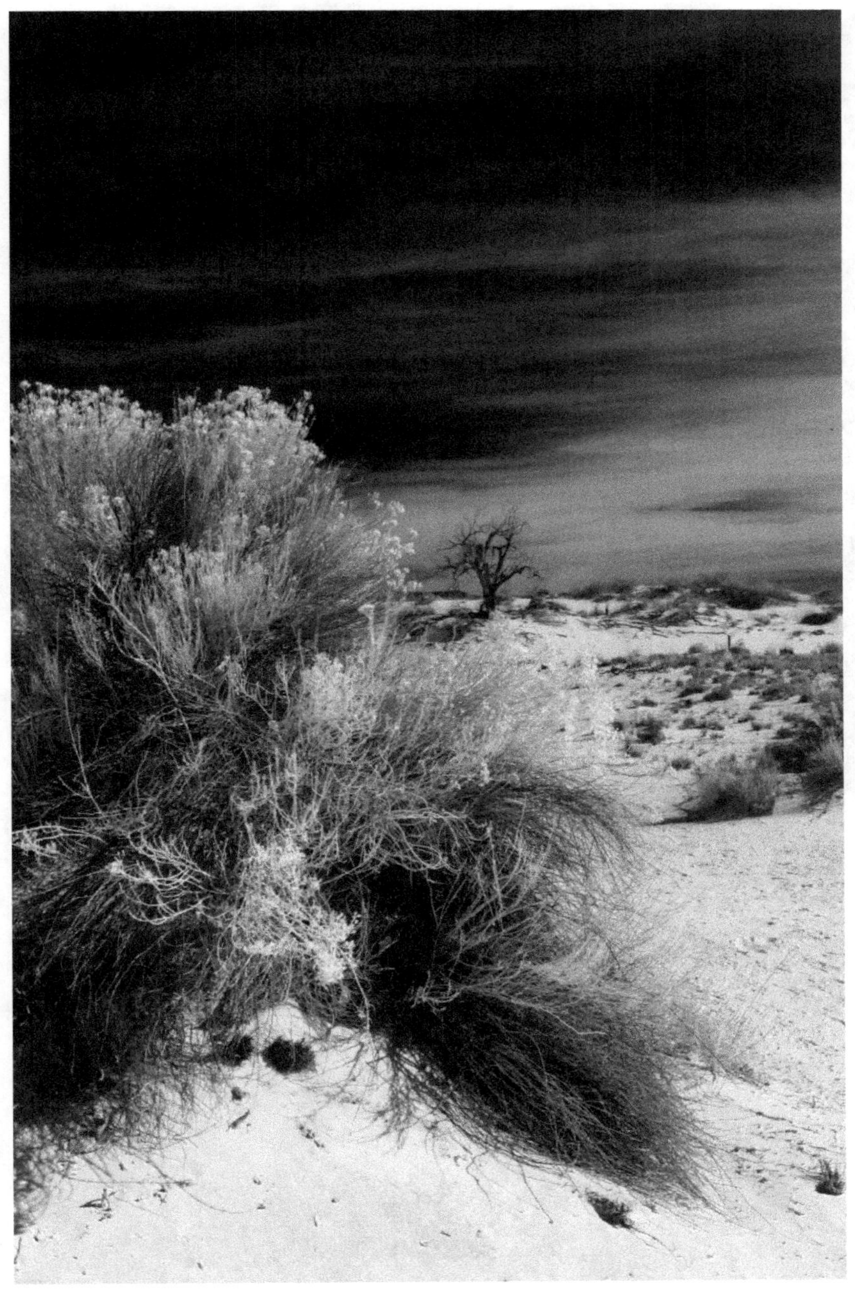

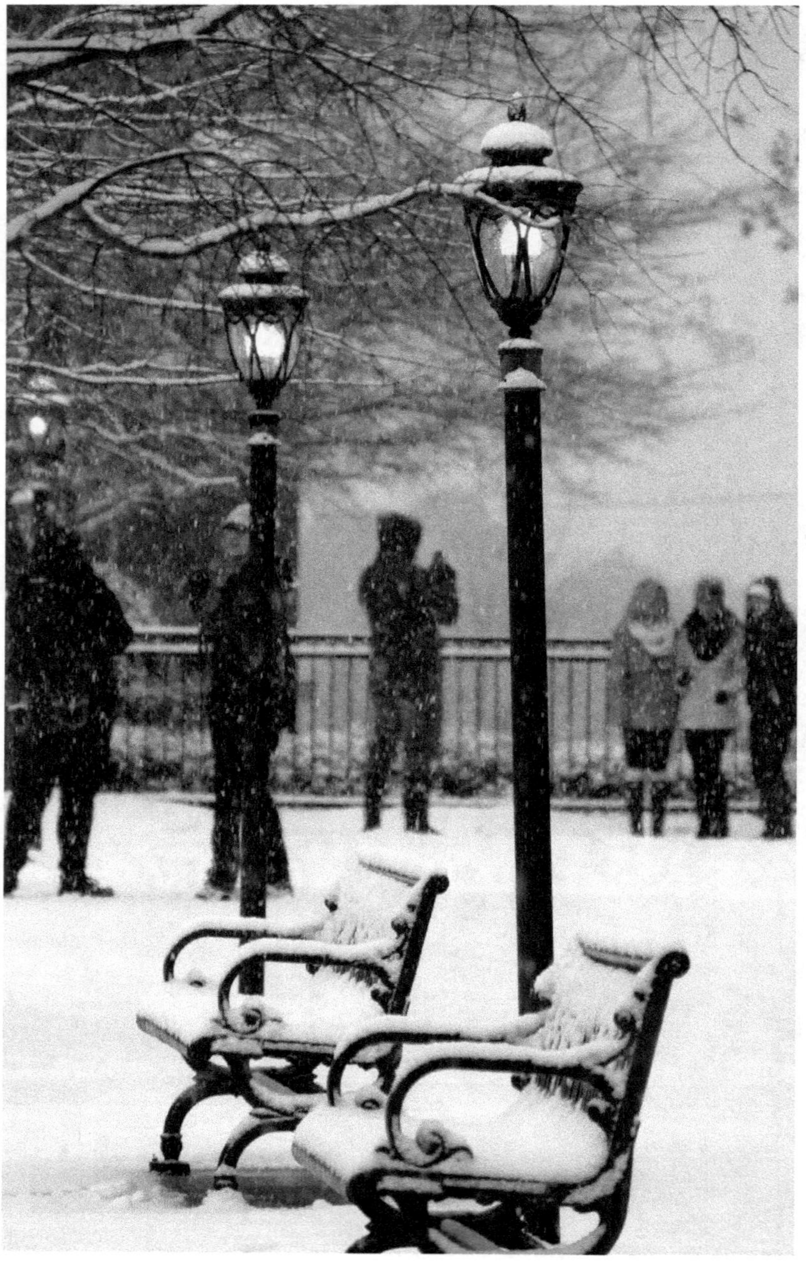

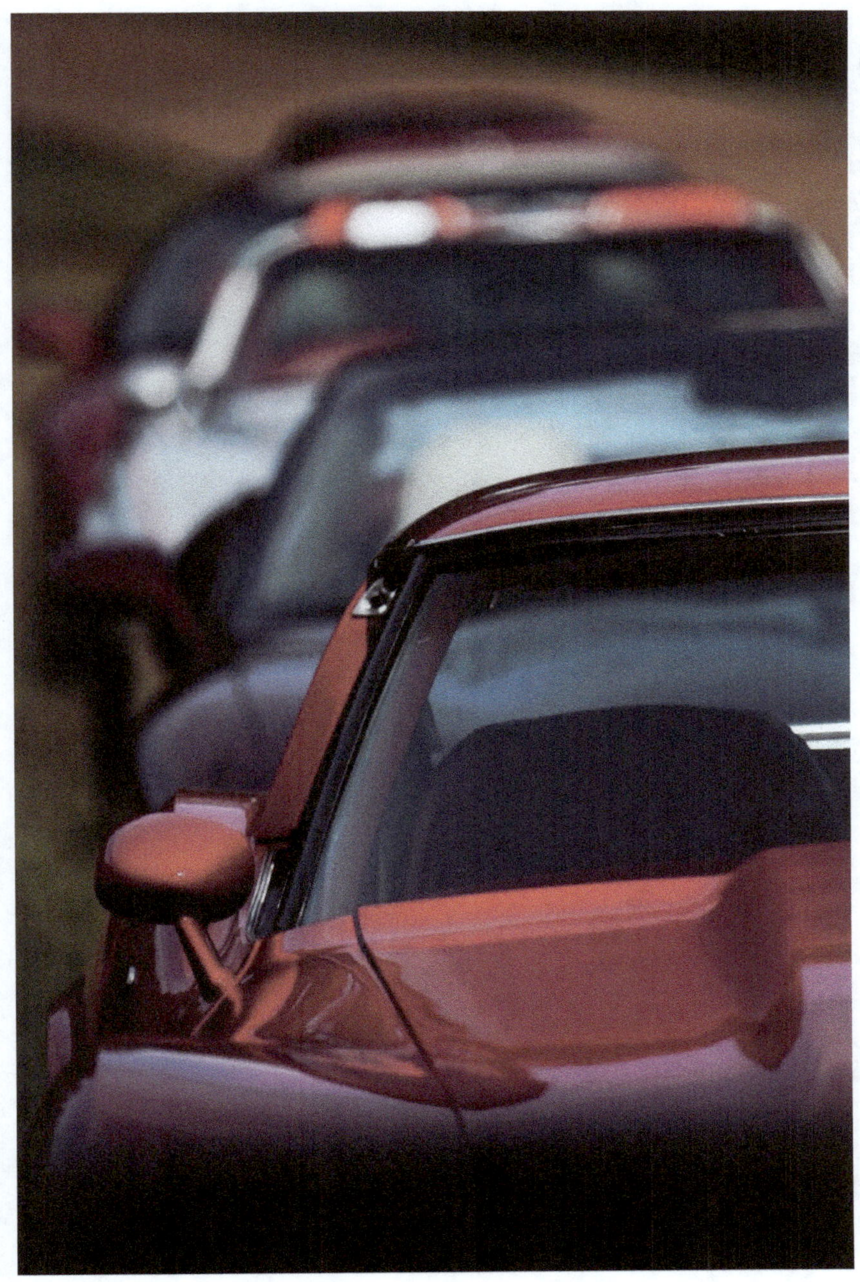

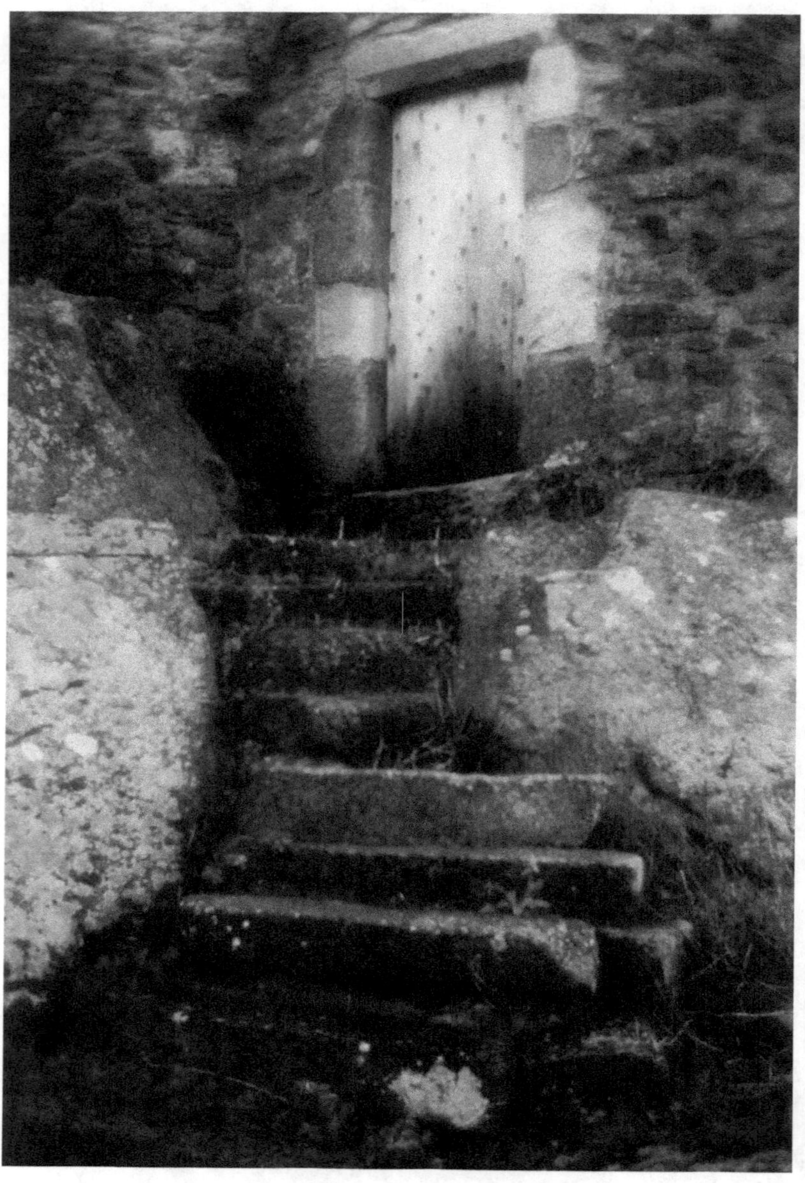

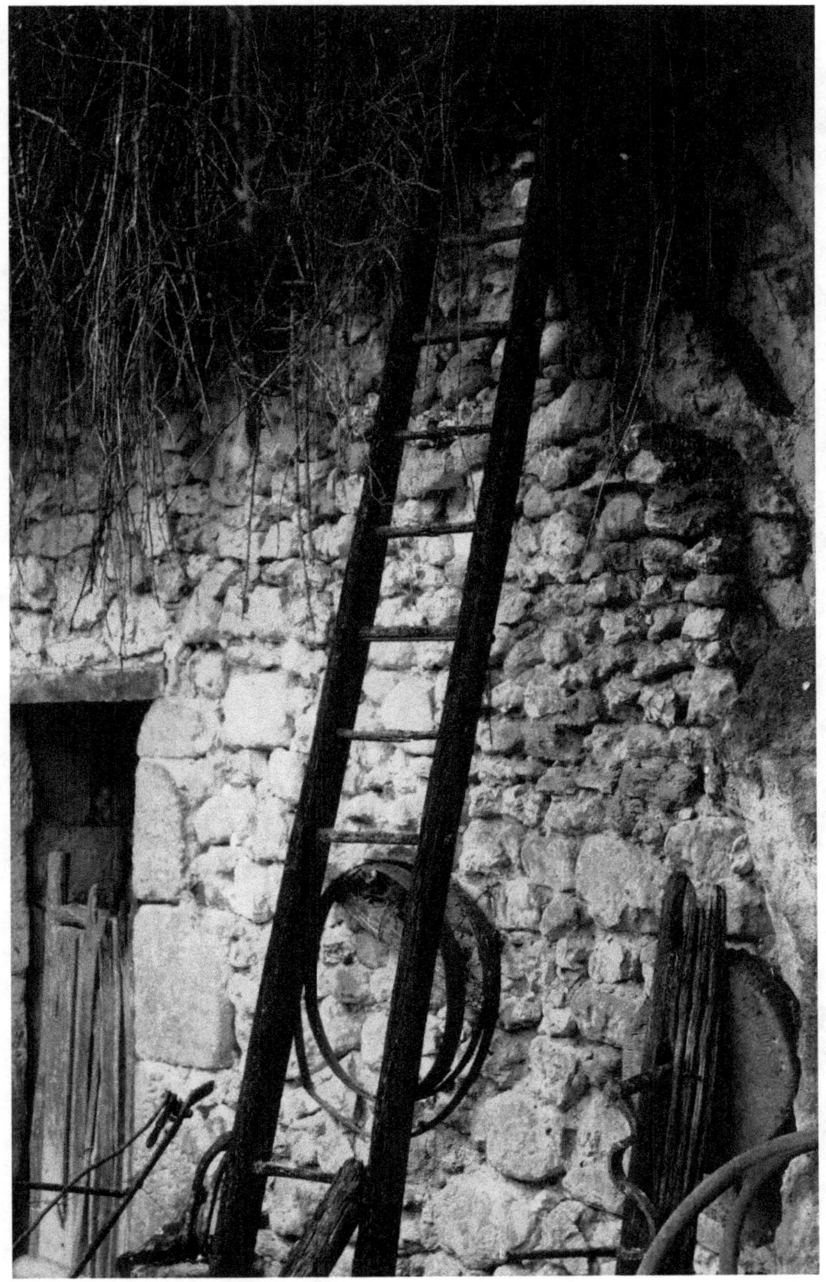

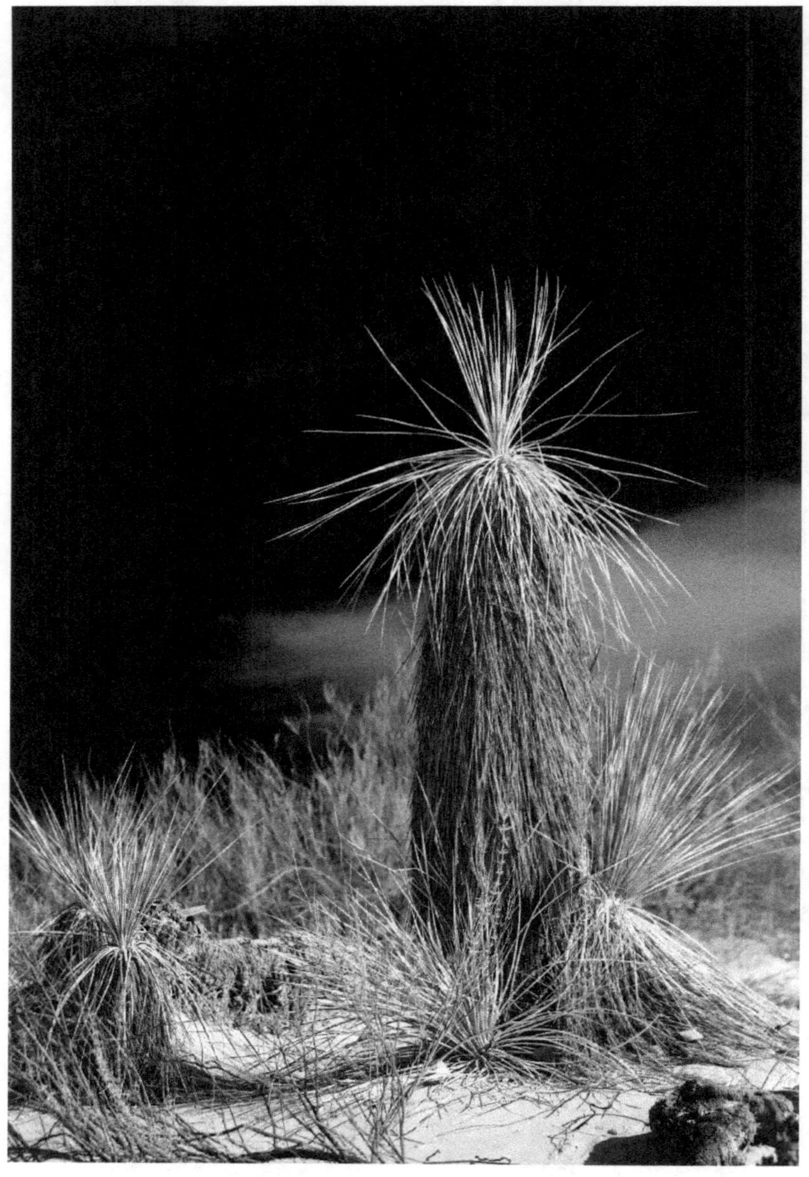

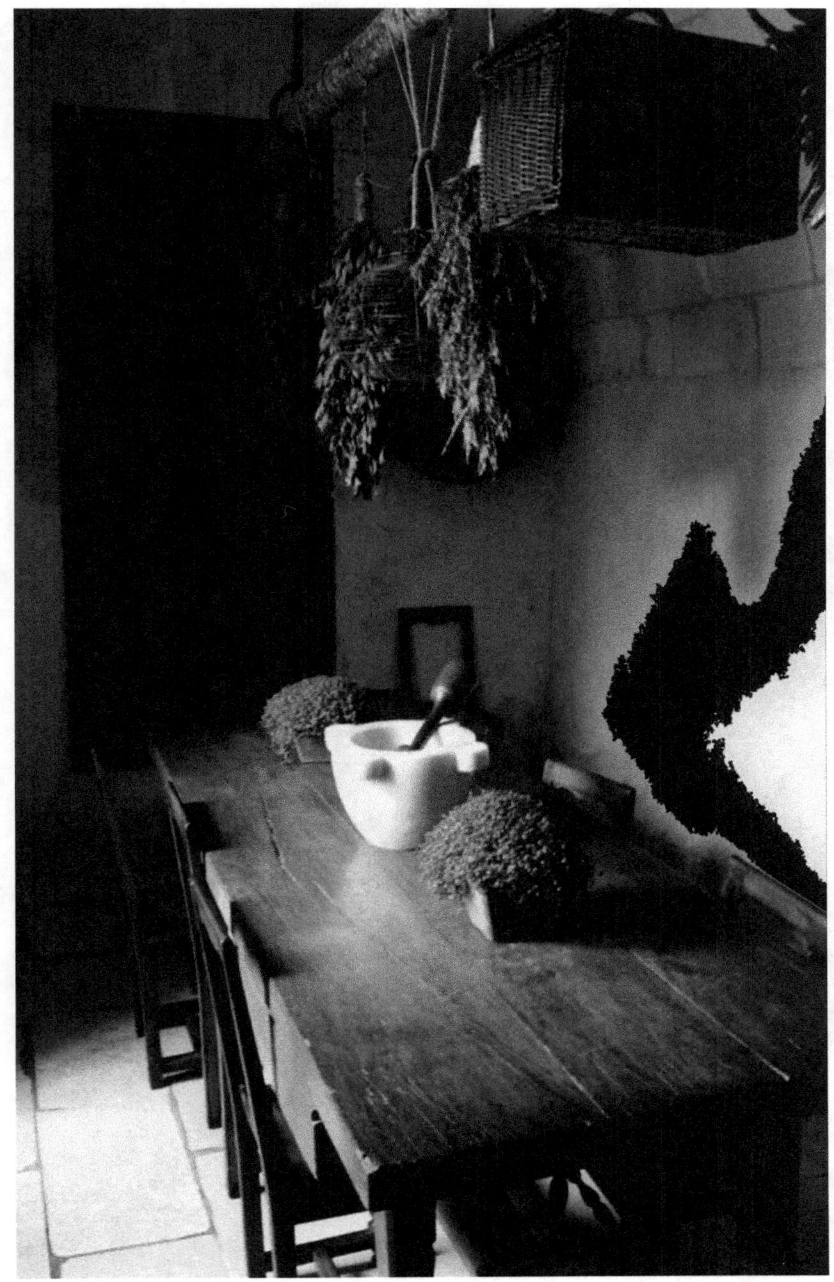

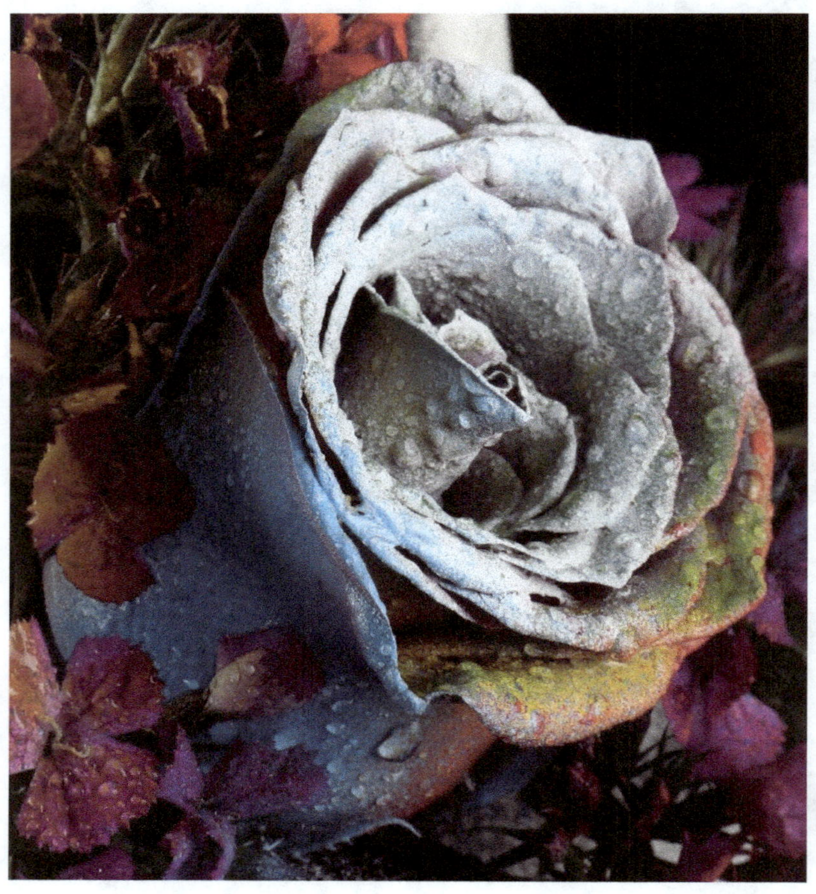

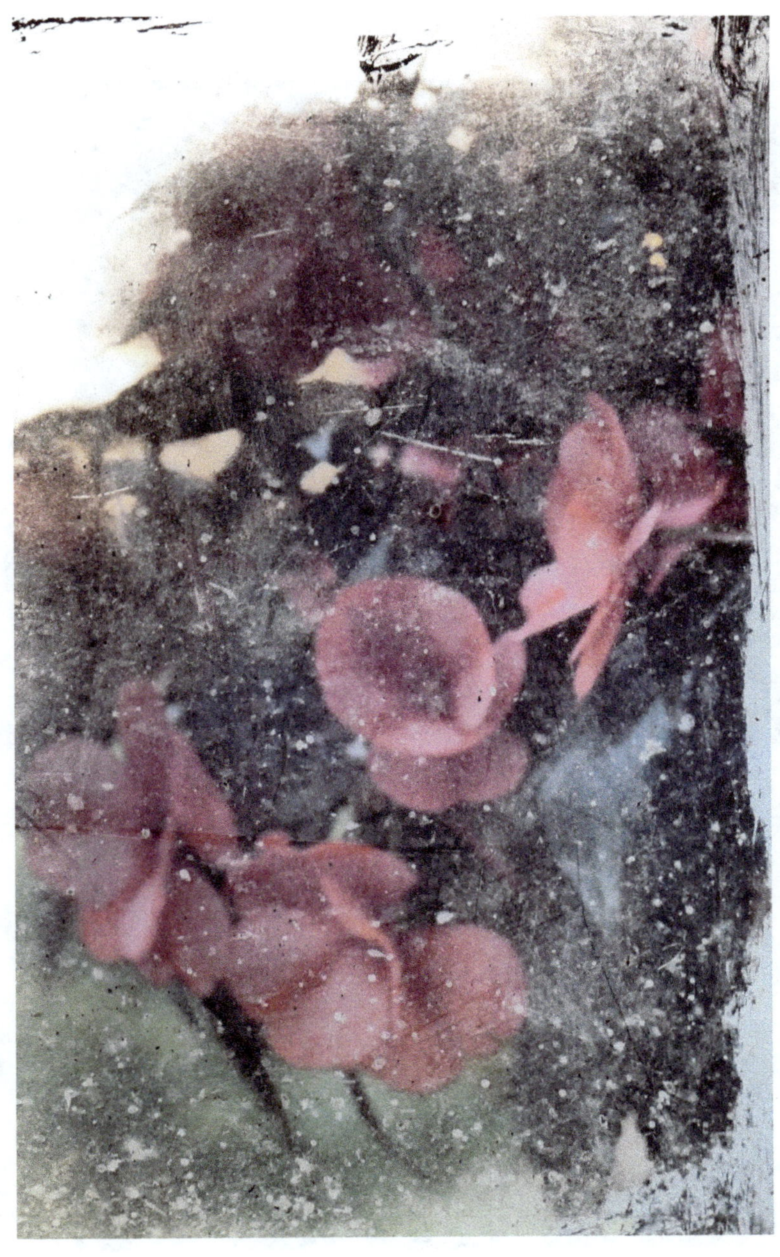

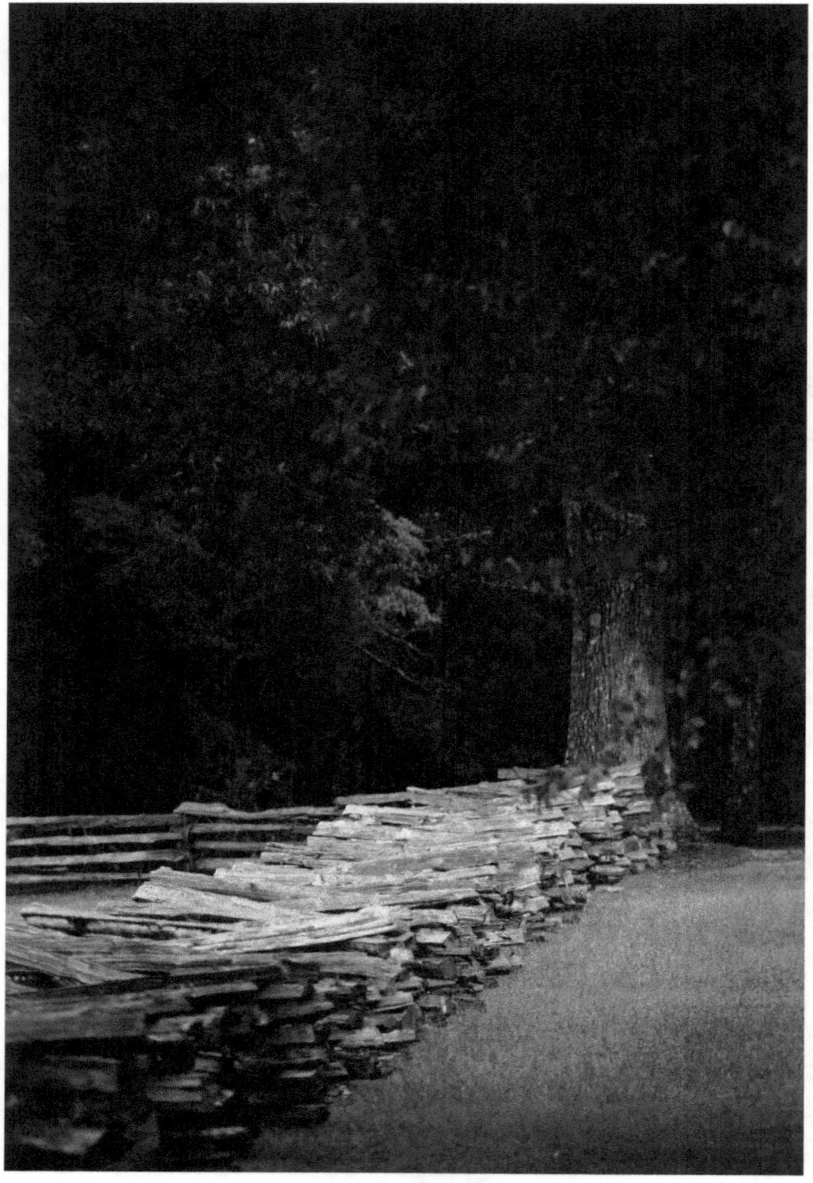

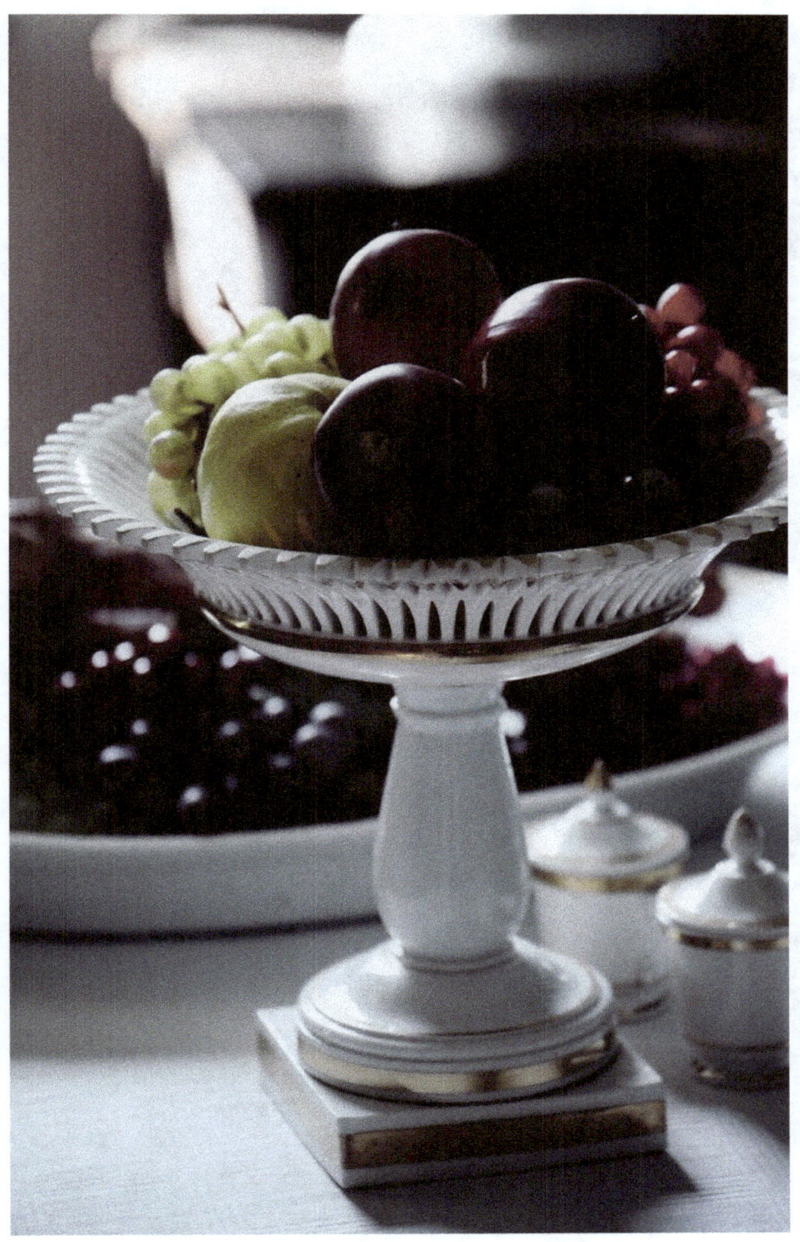

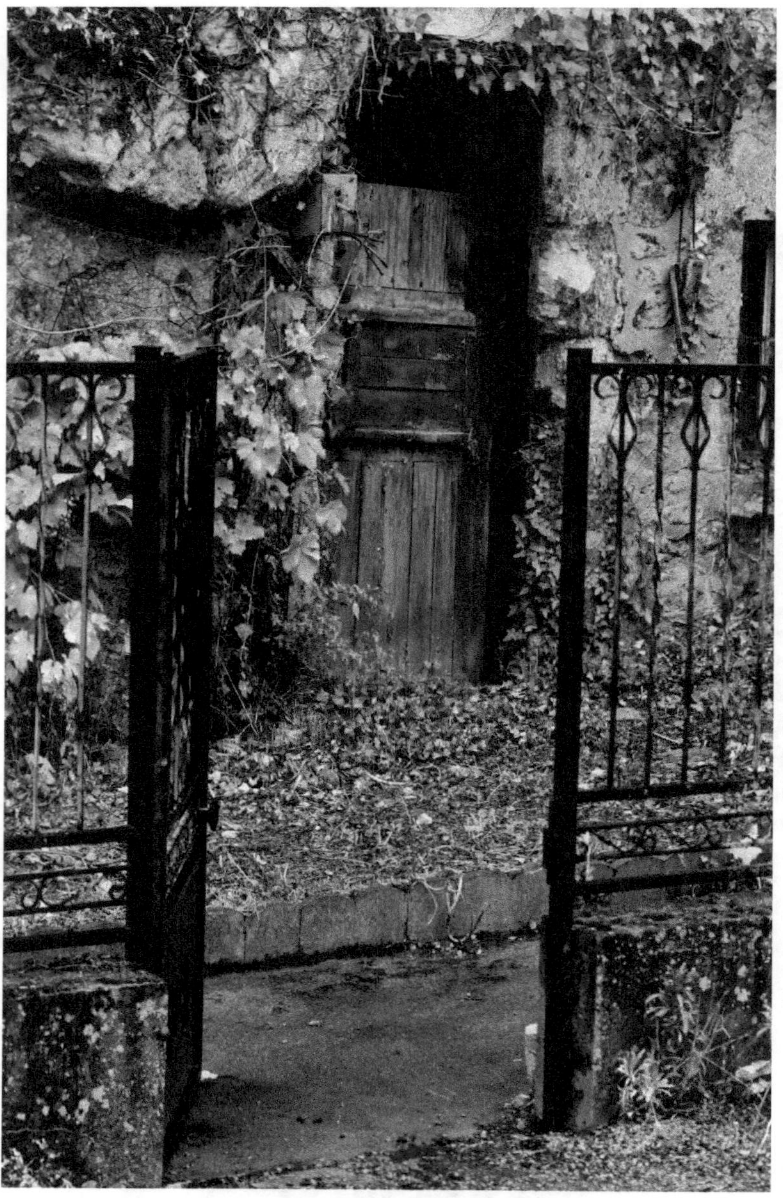

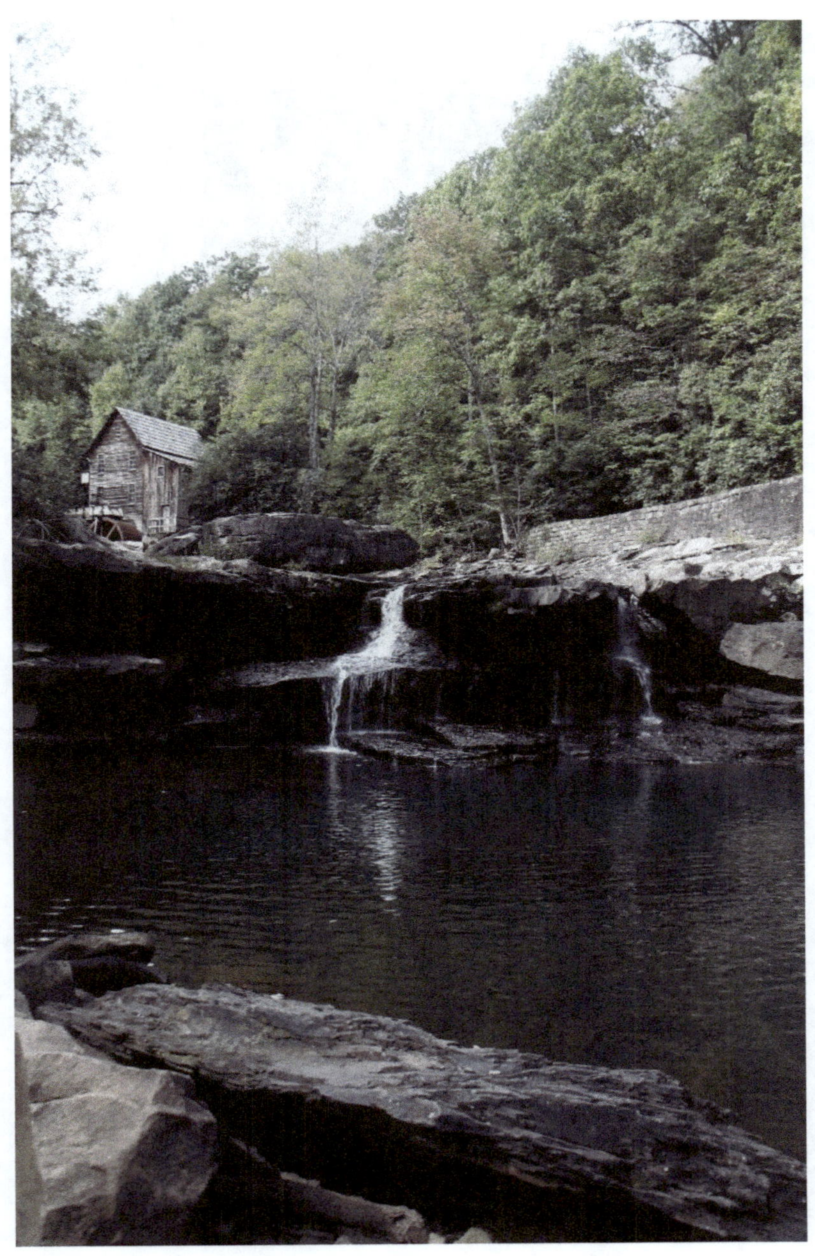

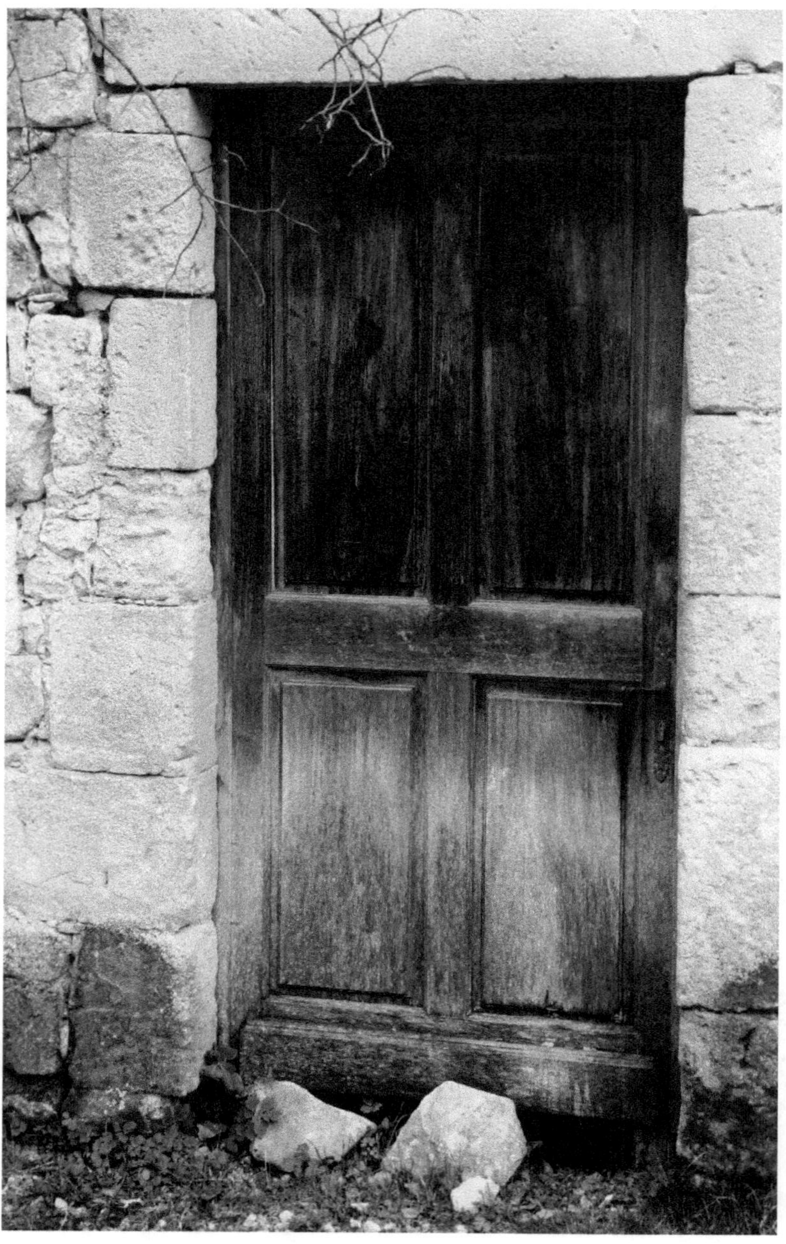

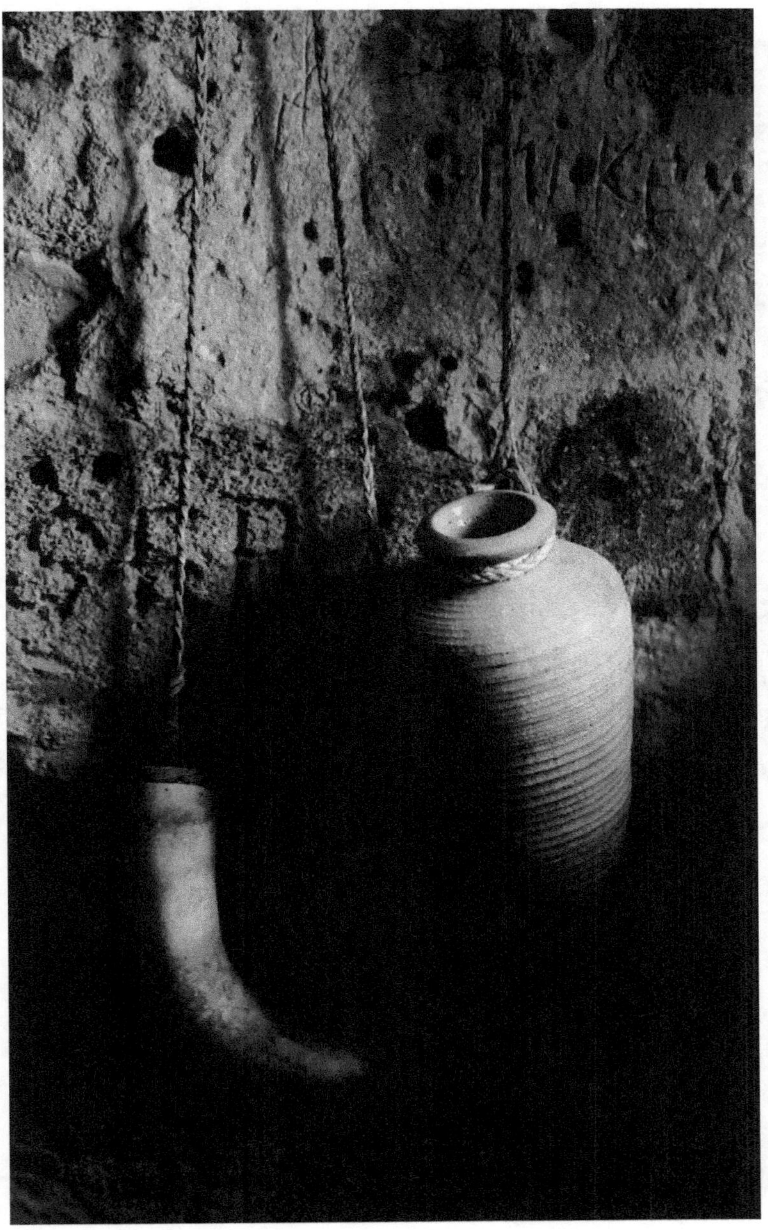

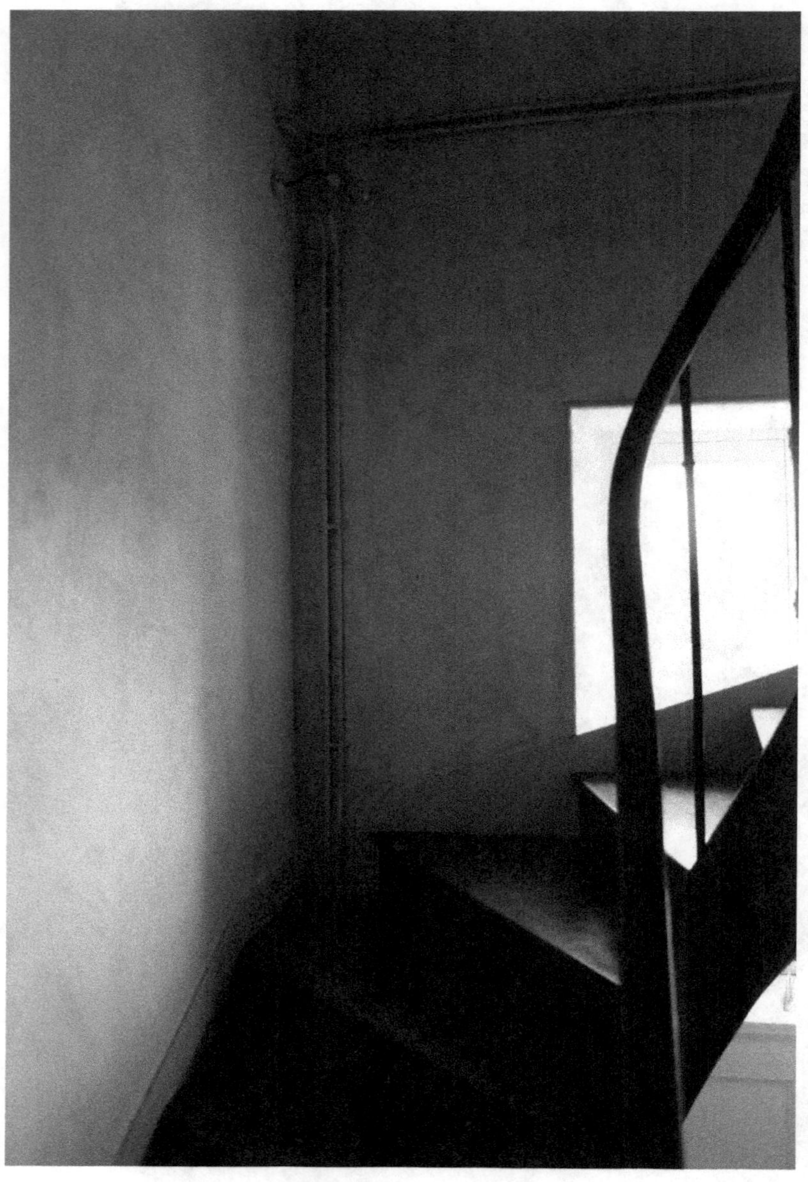

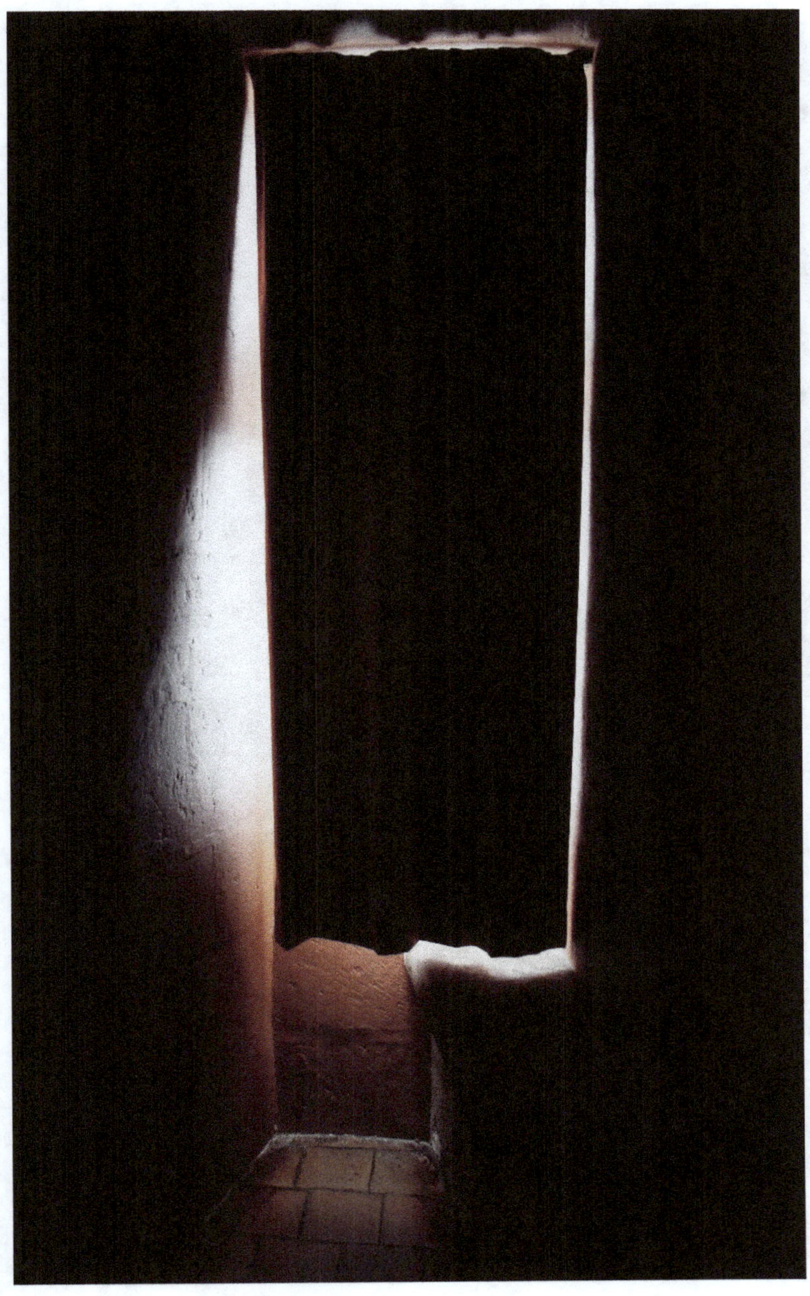

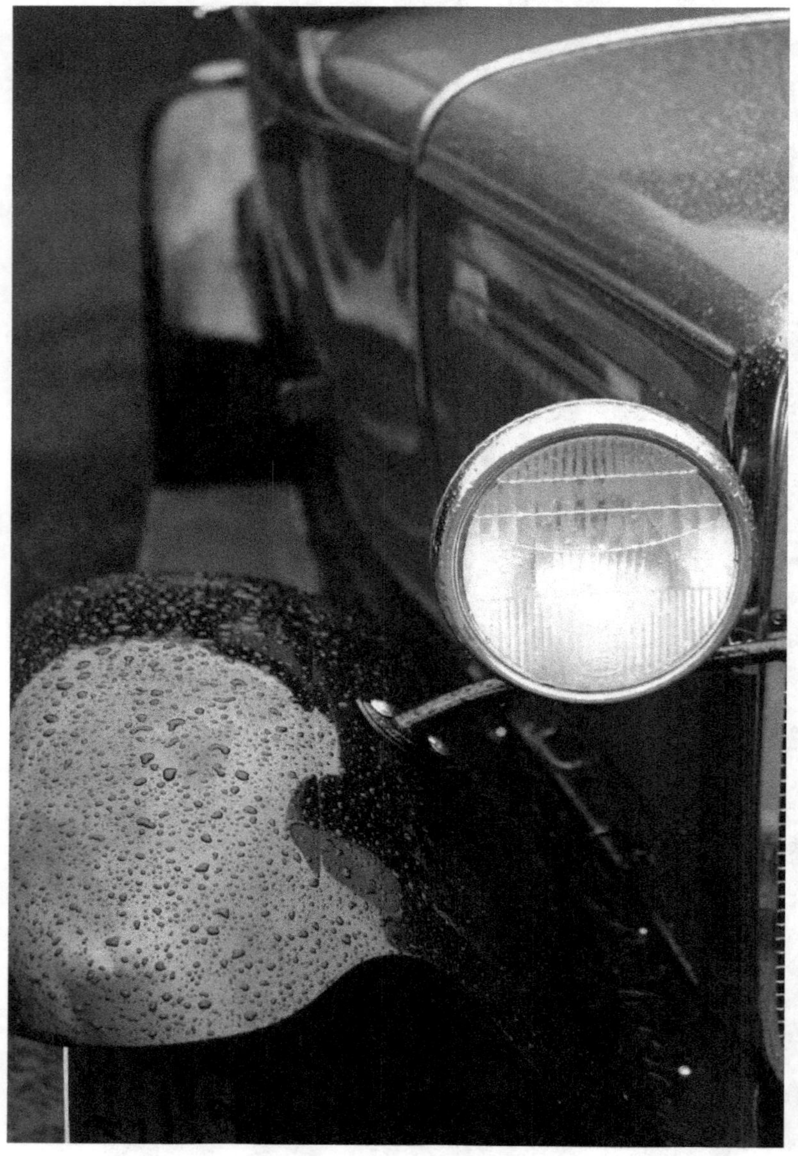

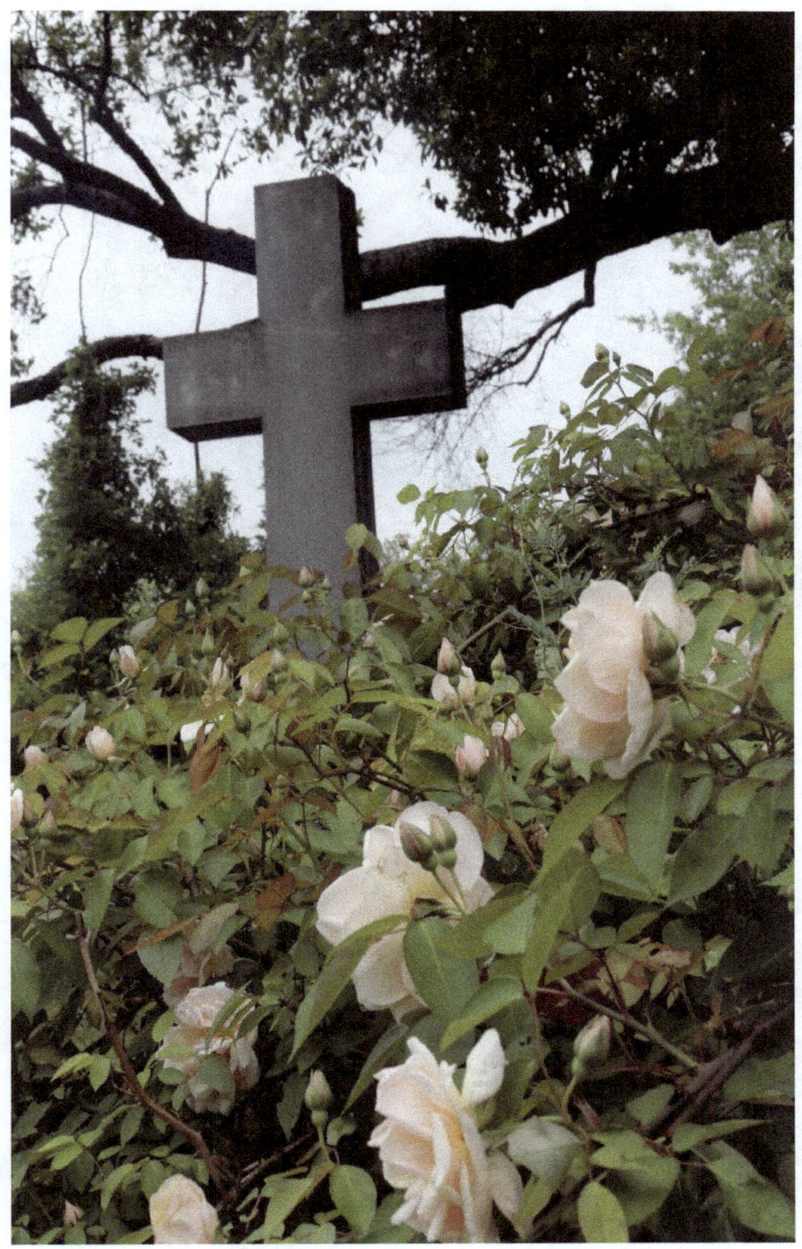

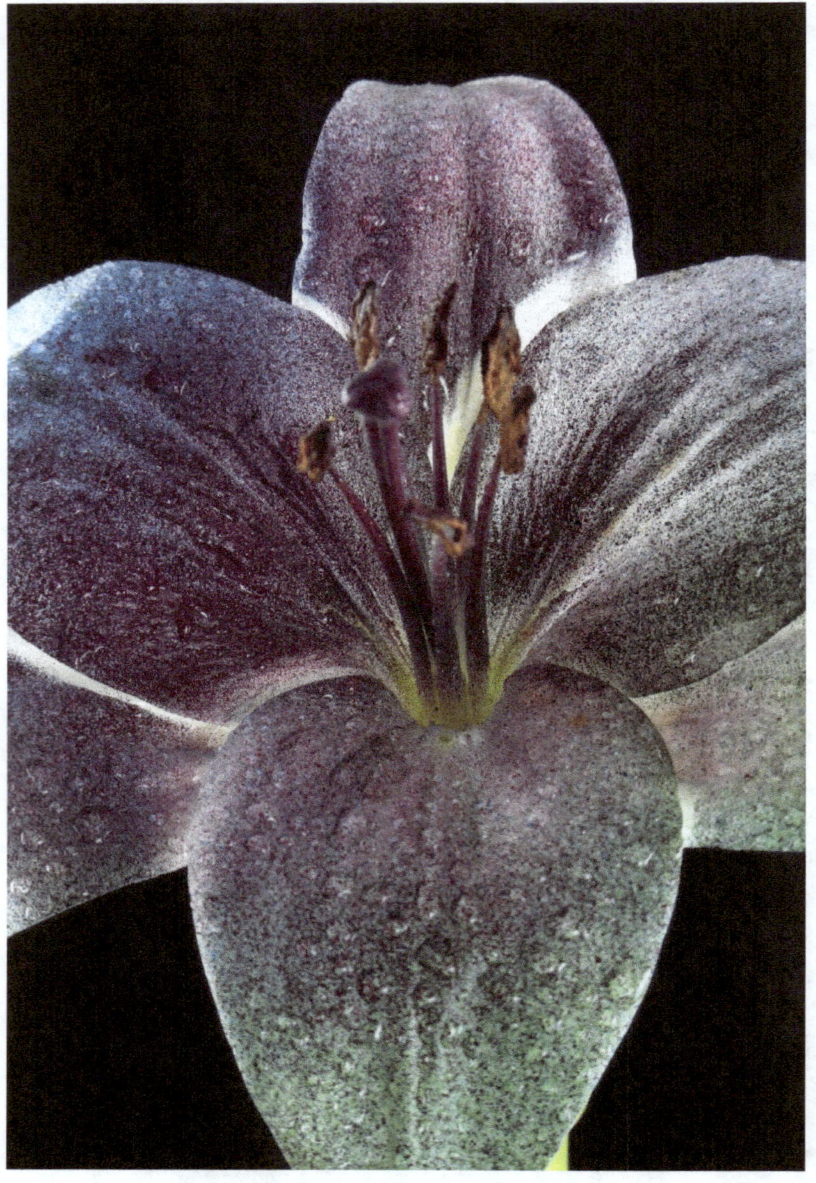

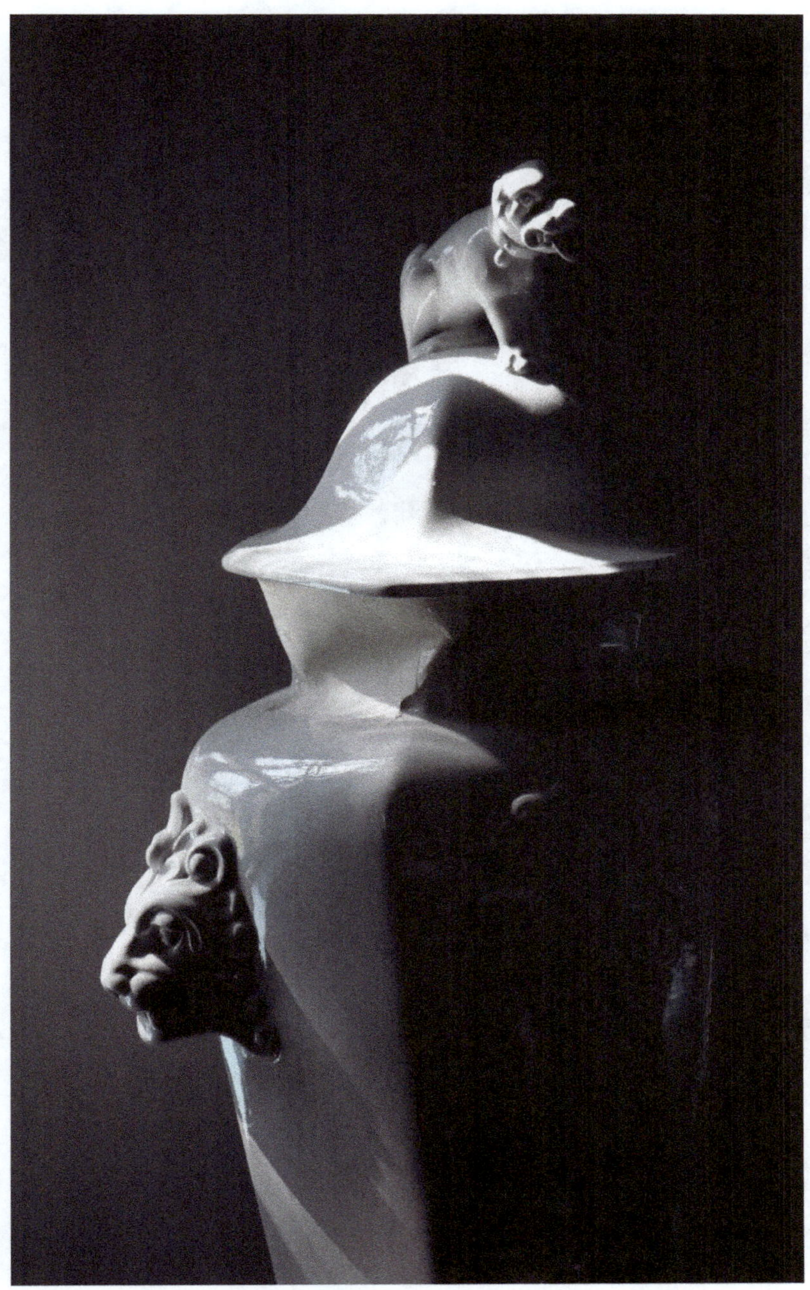

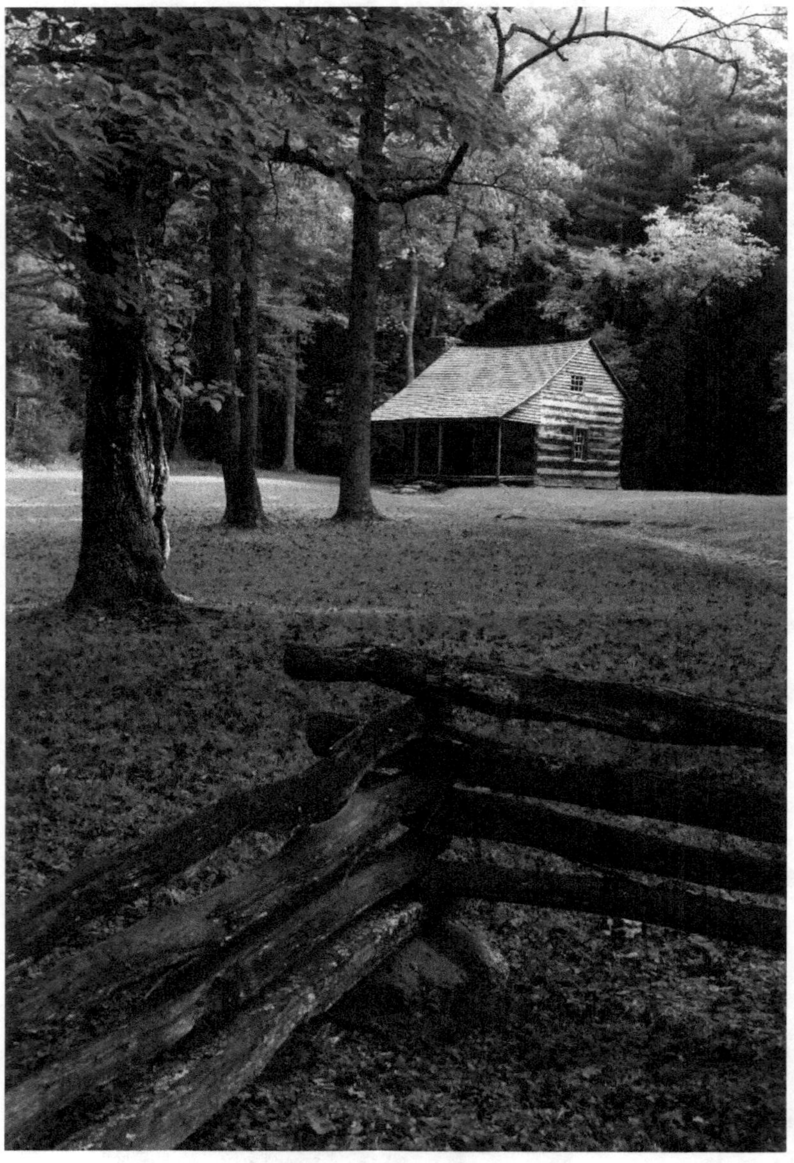

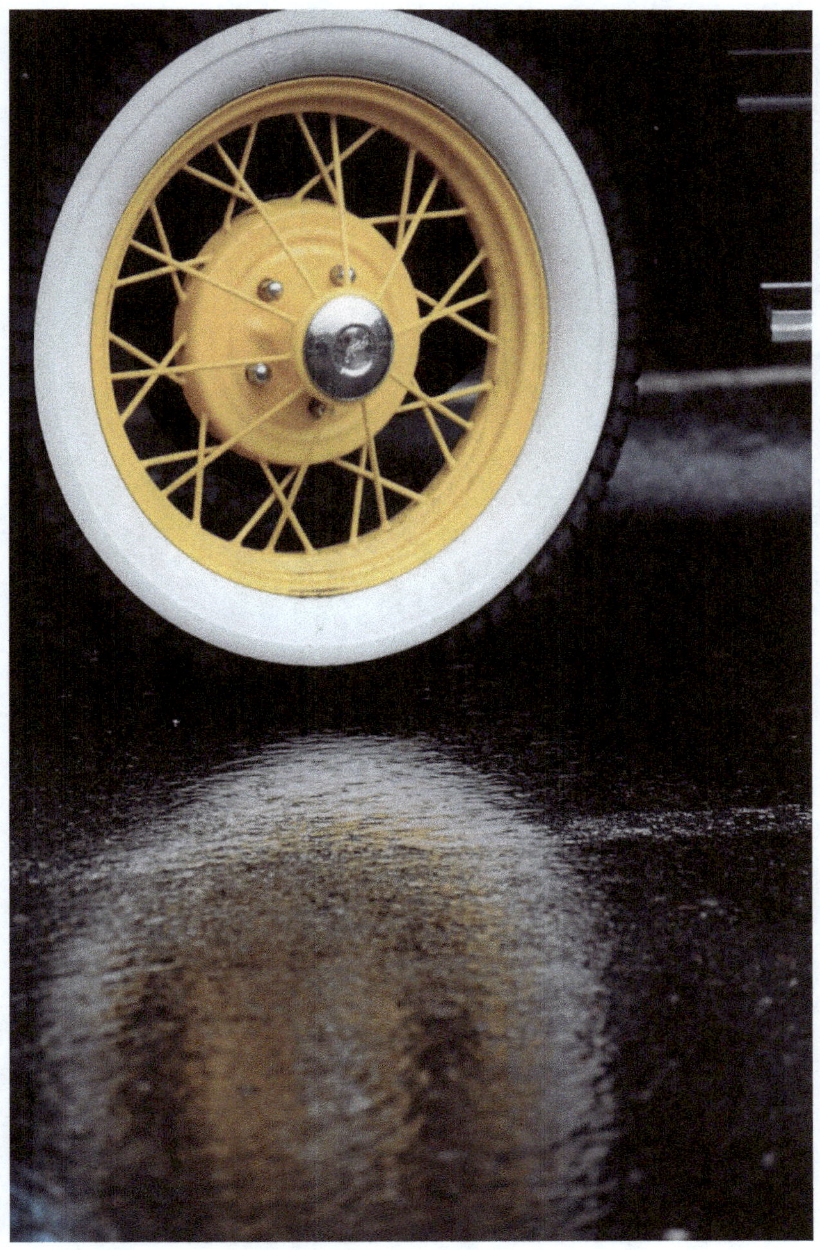

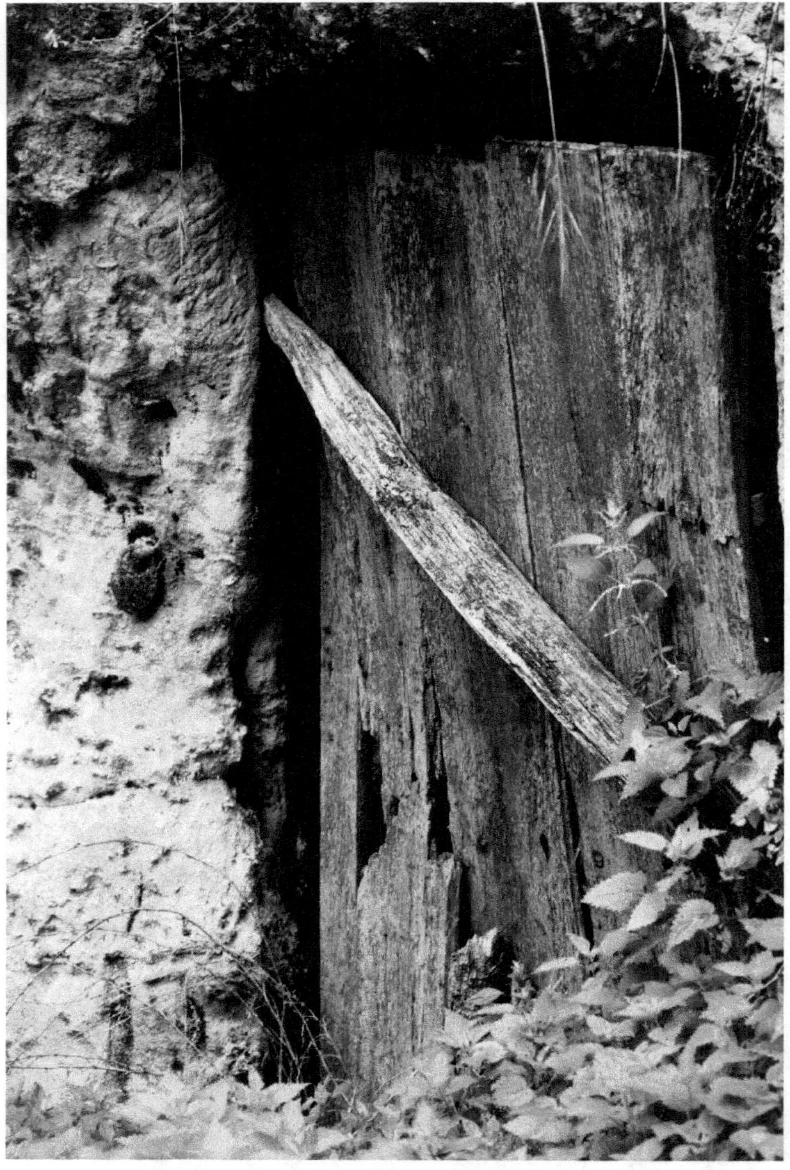

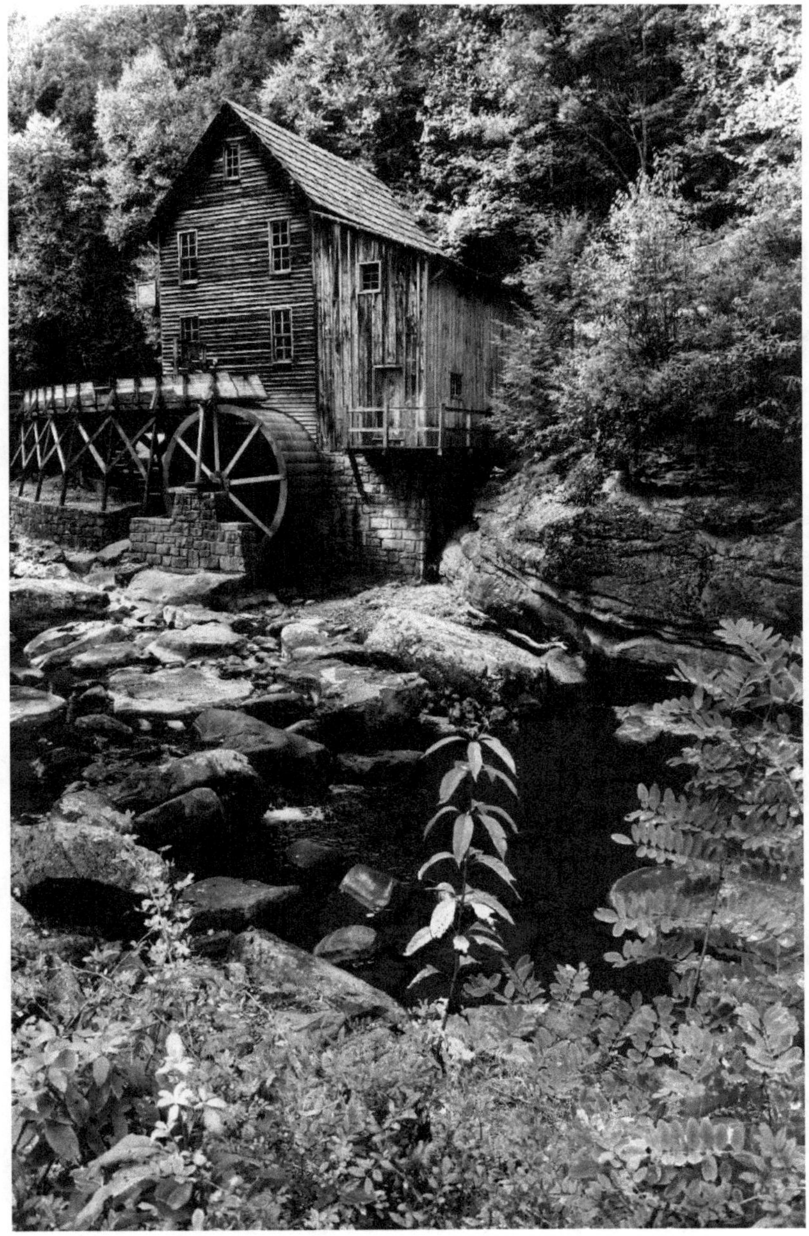

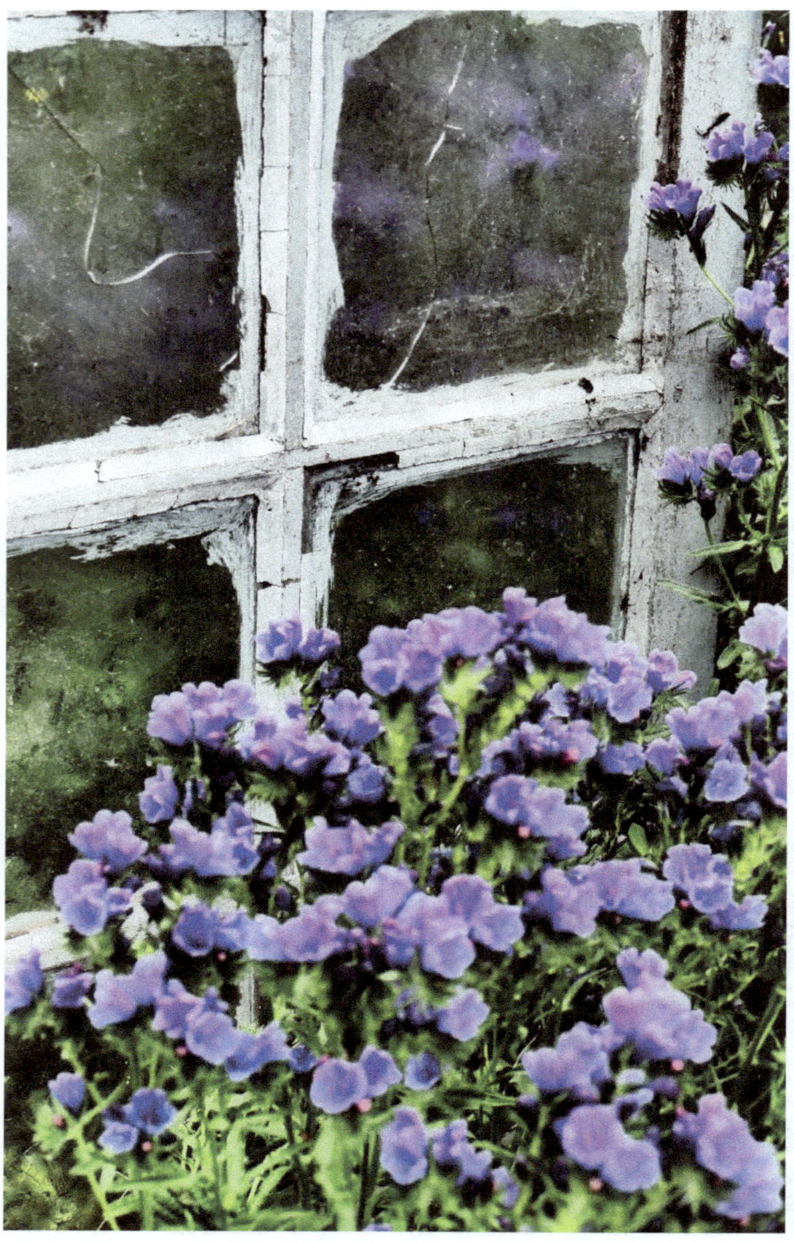

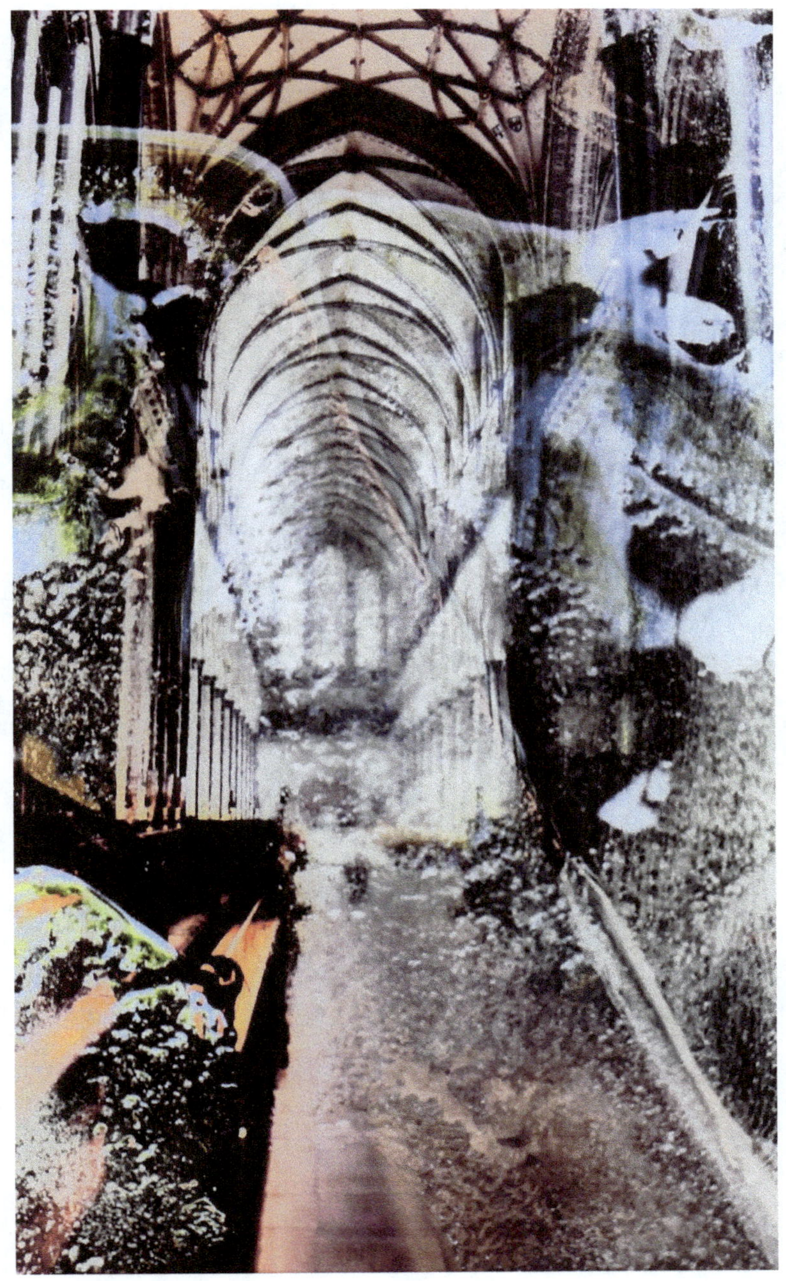

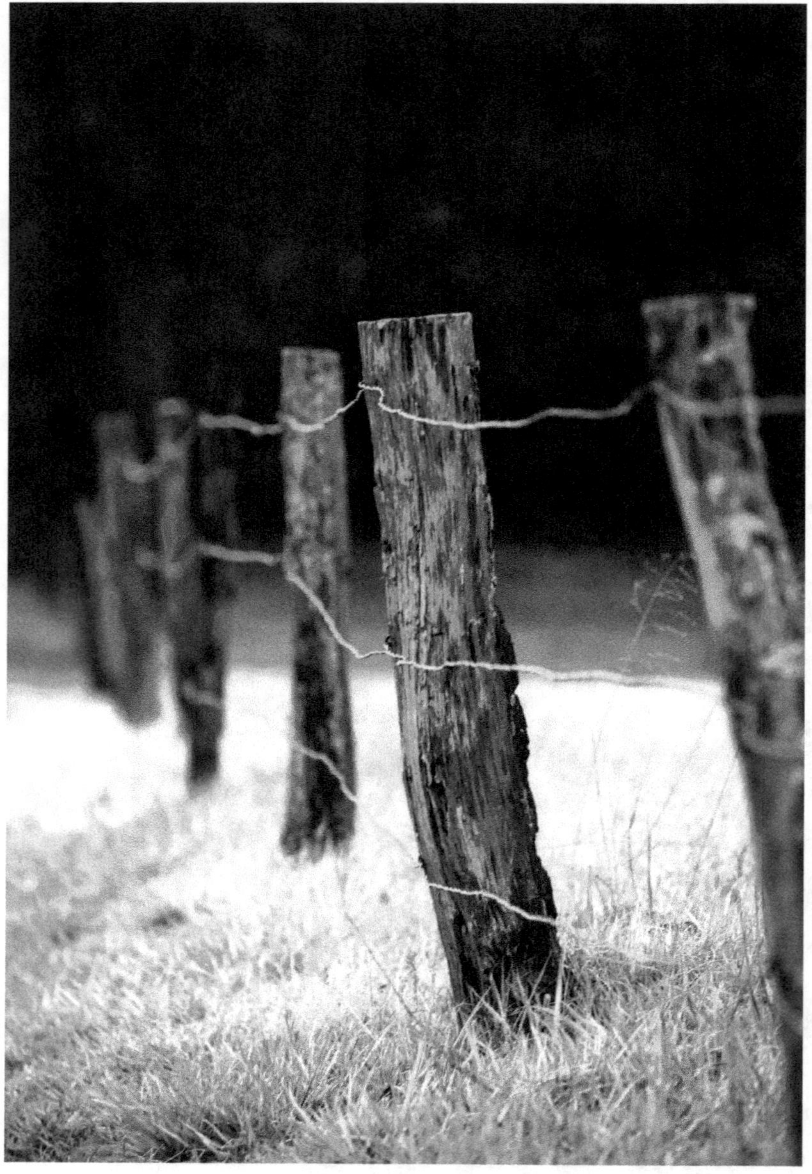

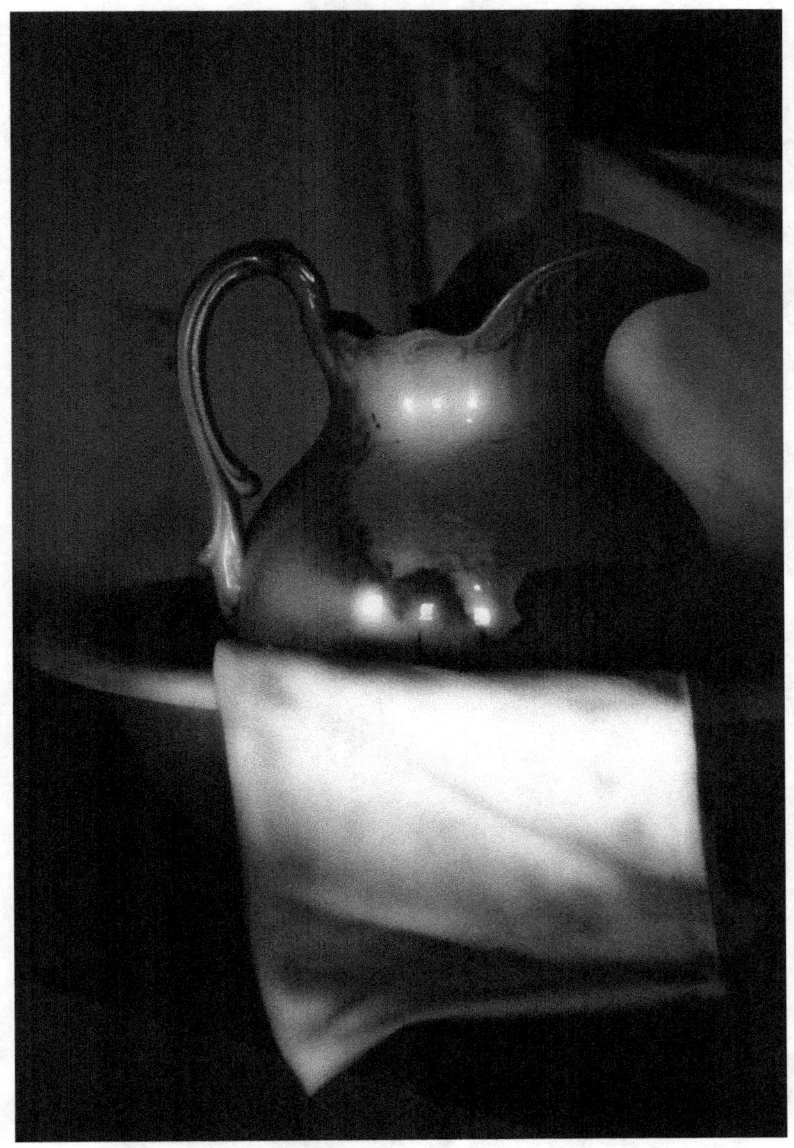

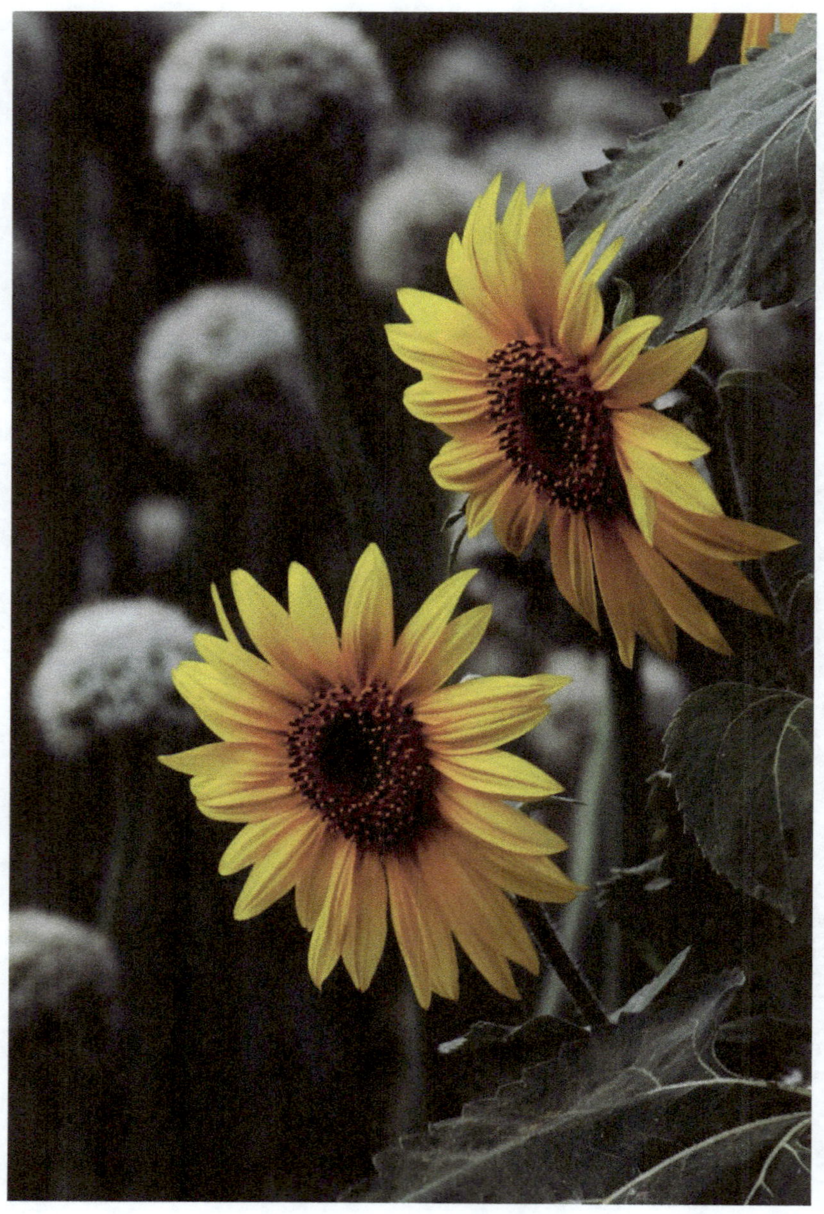

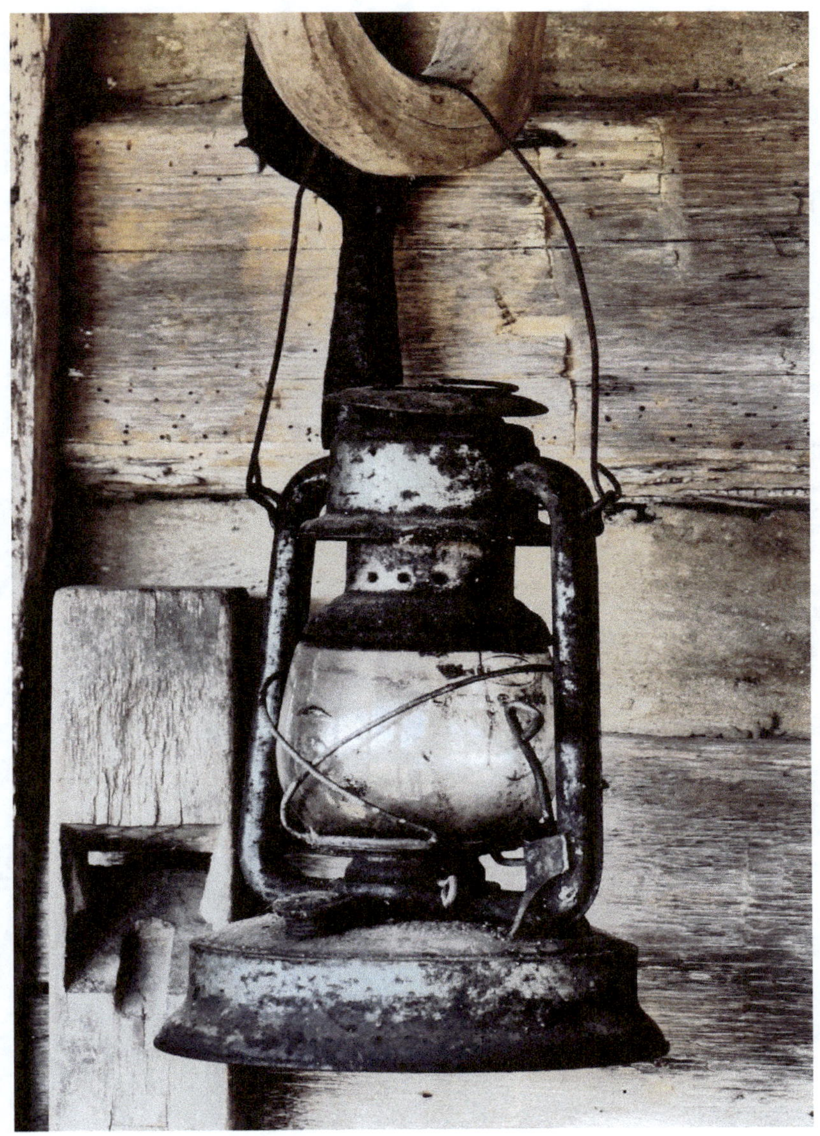

62

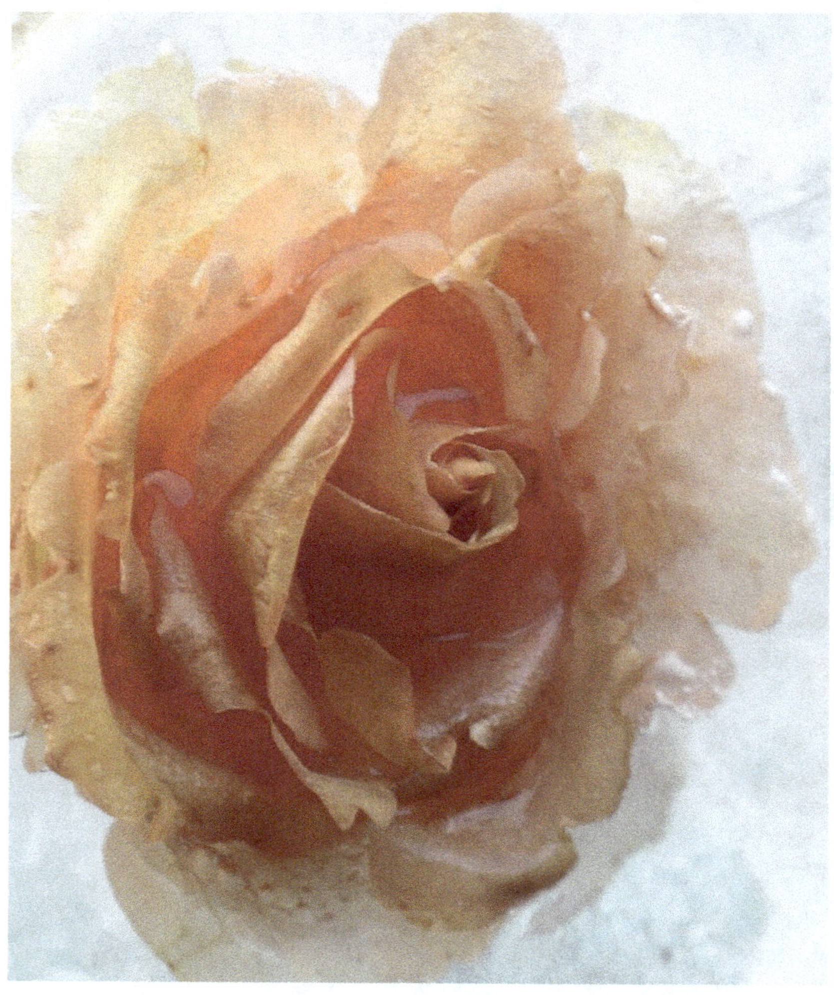

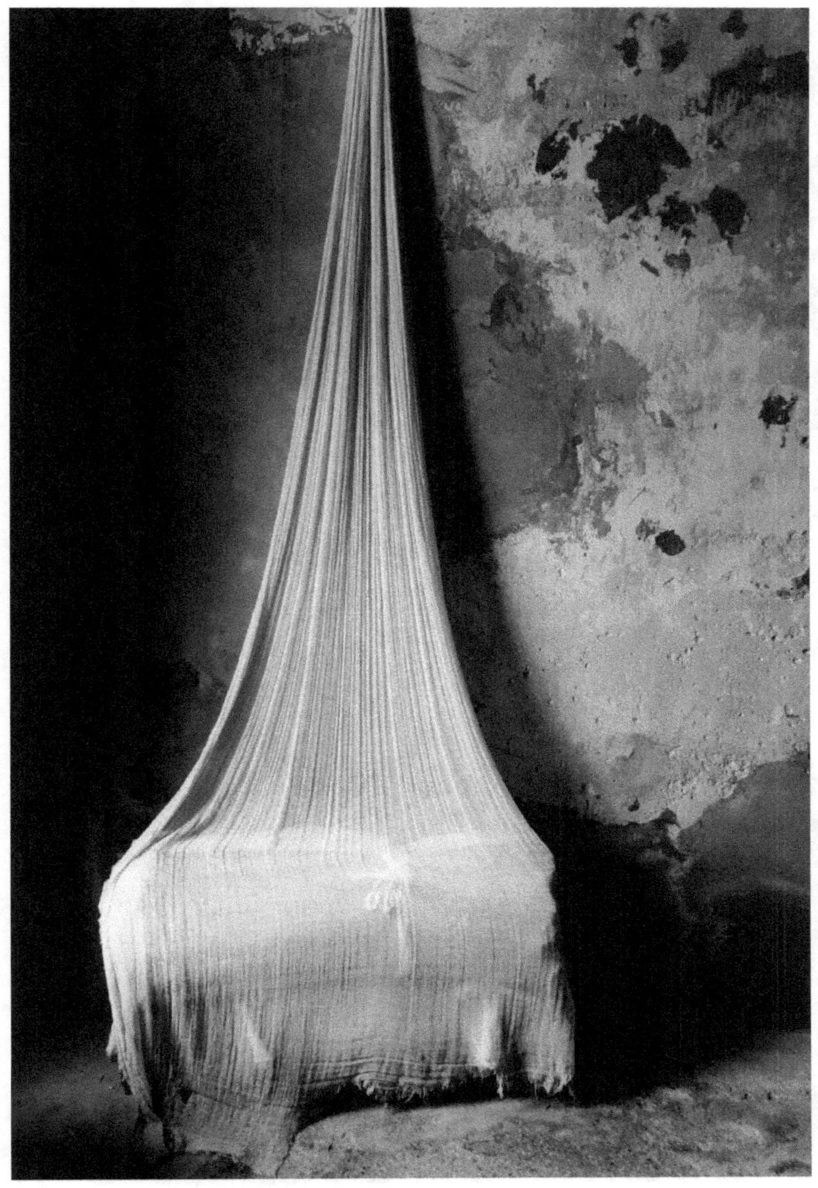

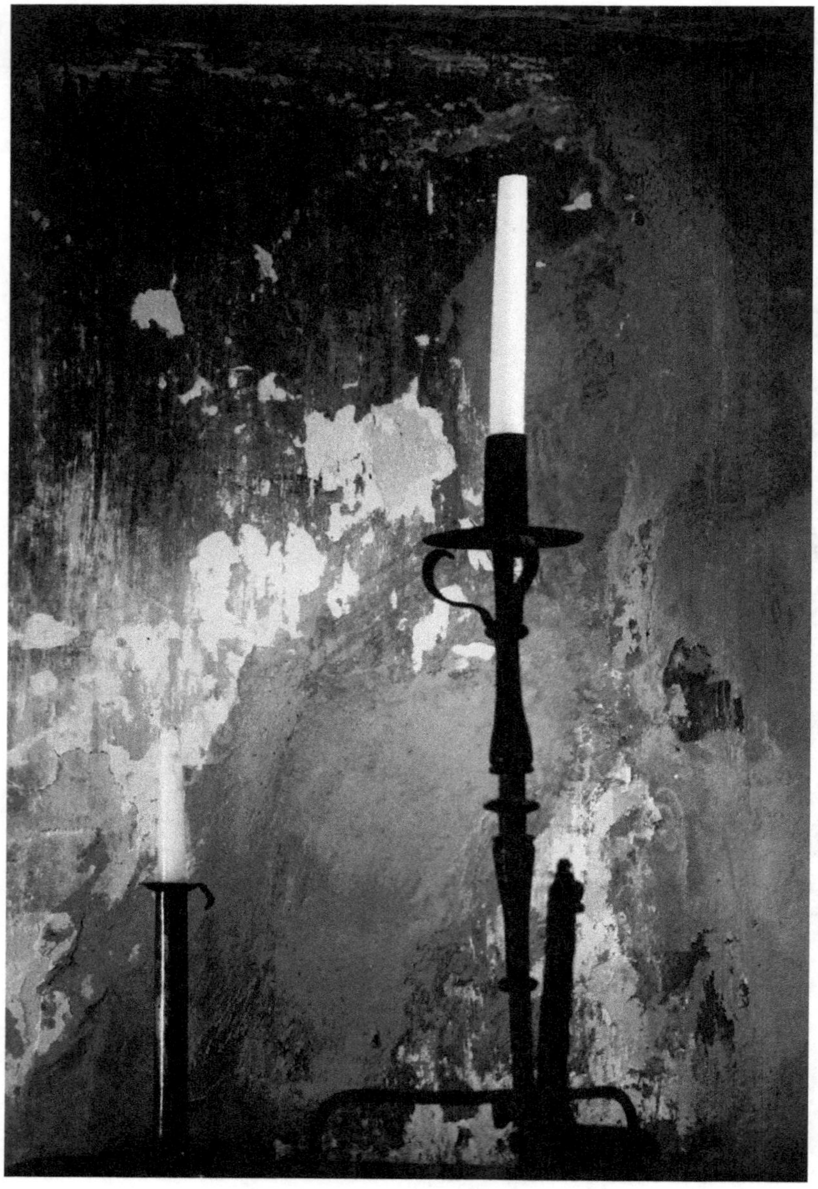

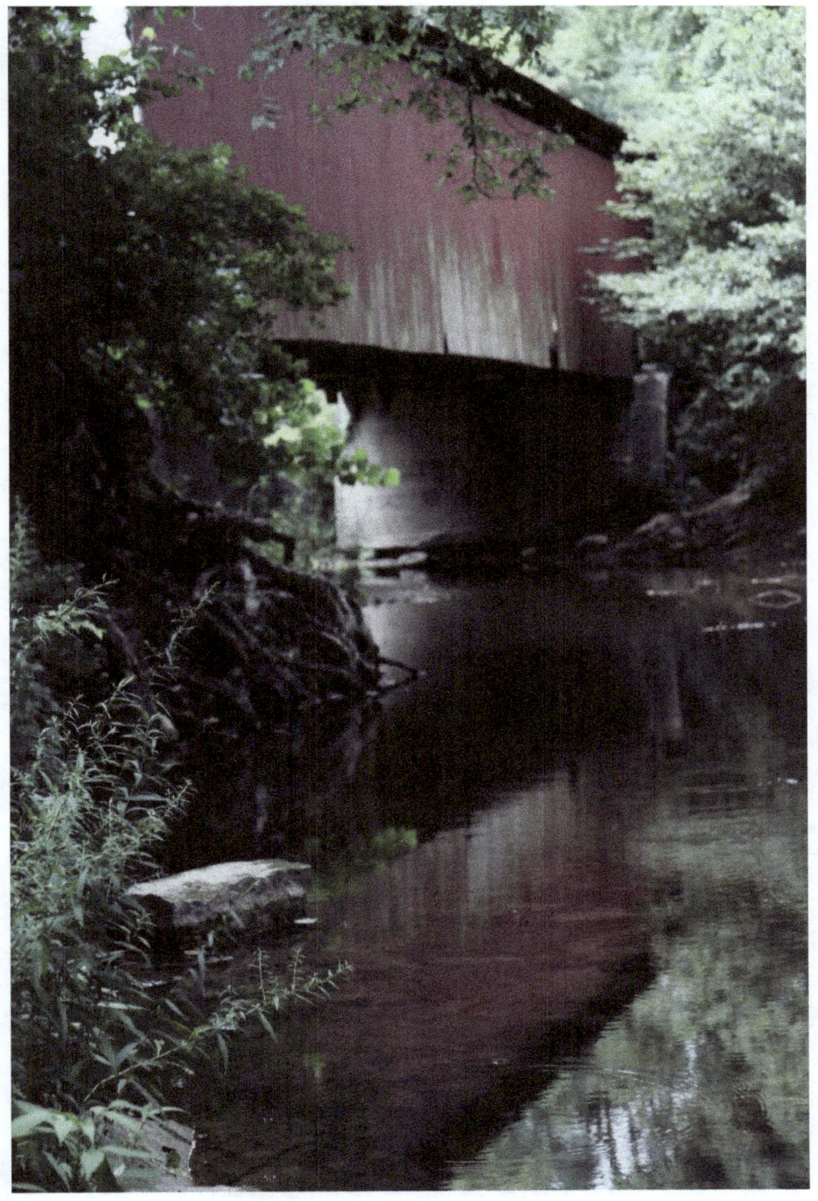

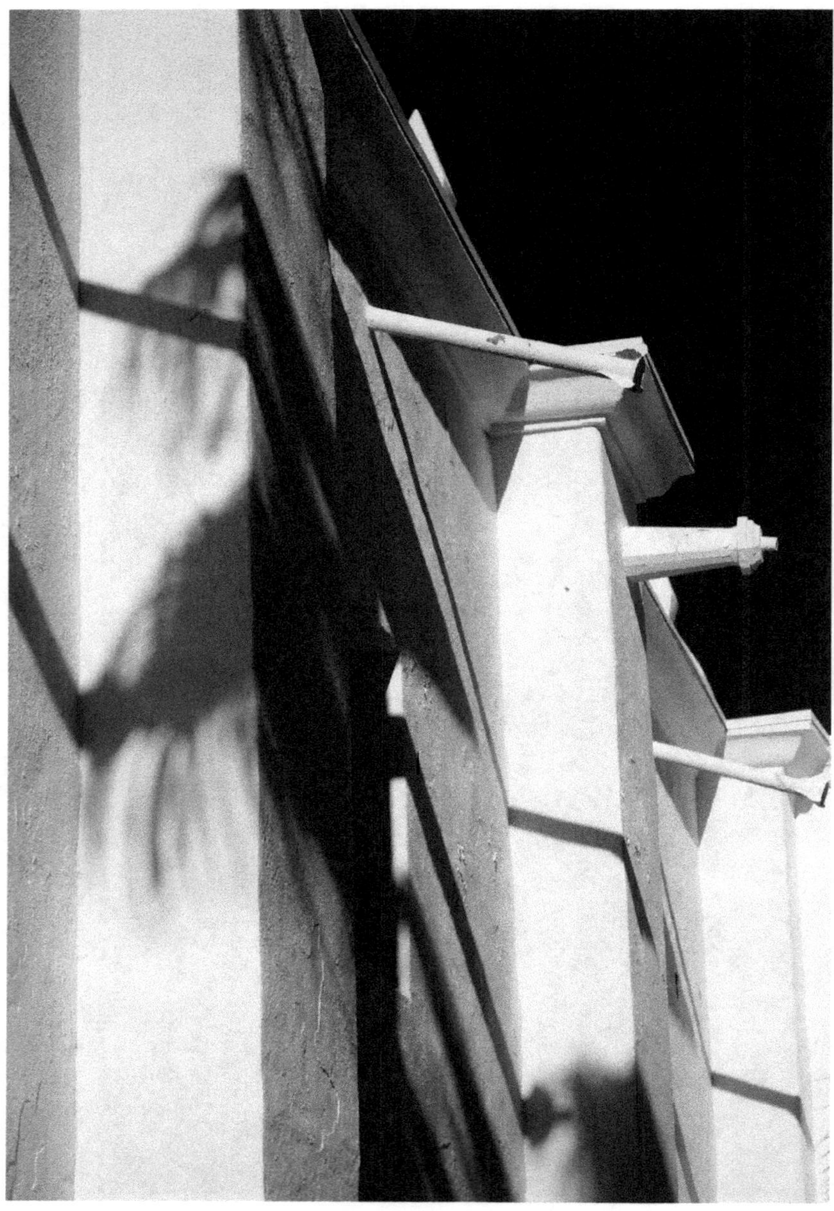

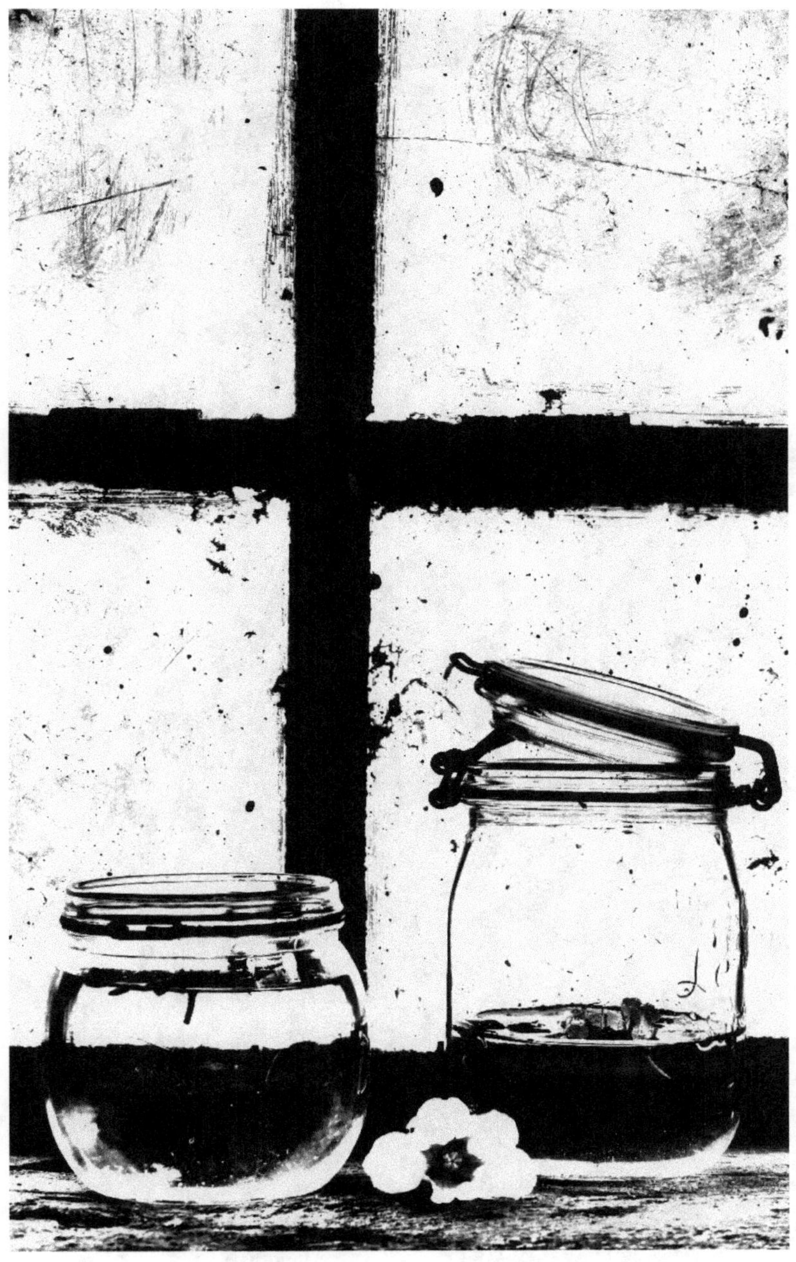

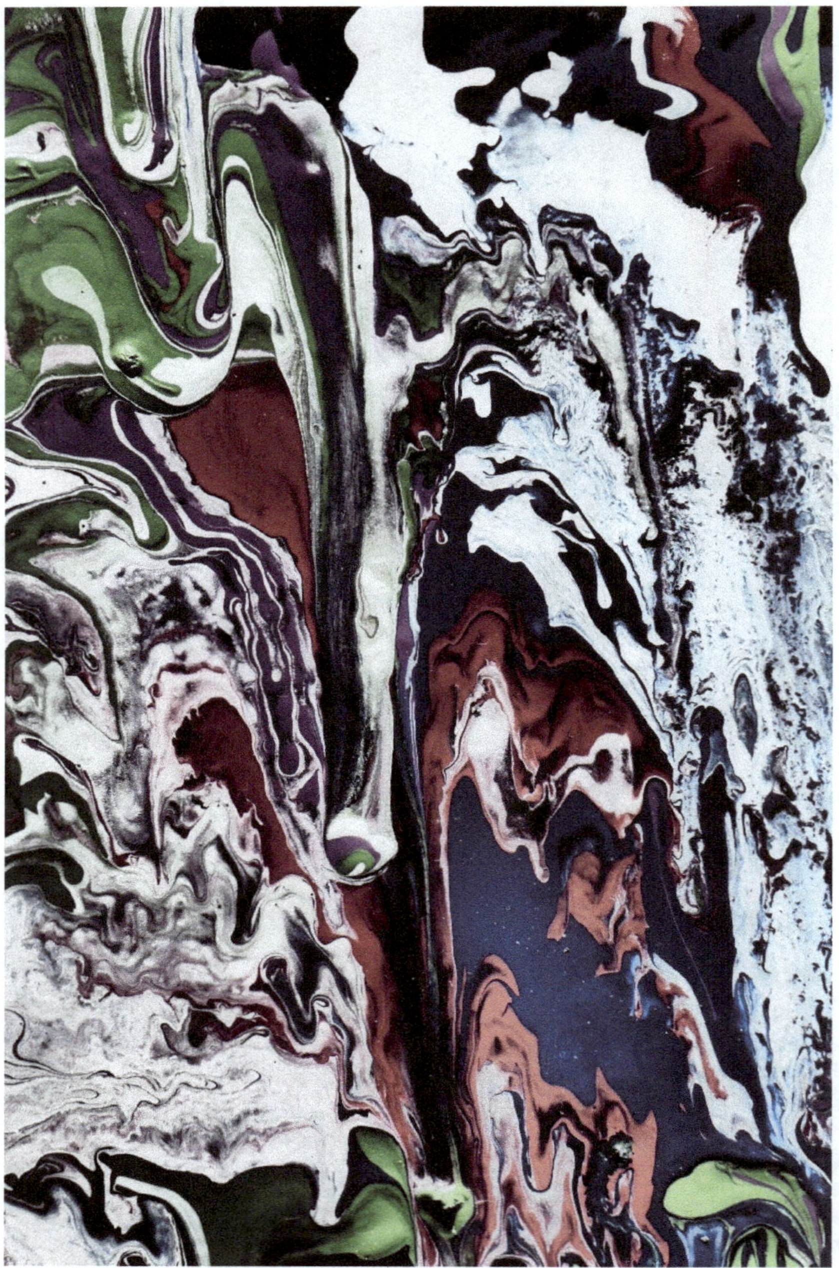

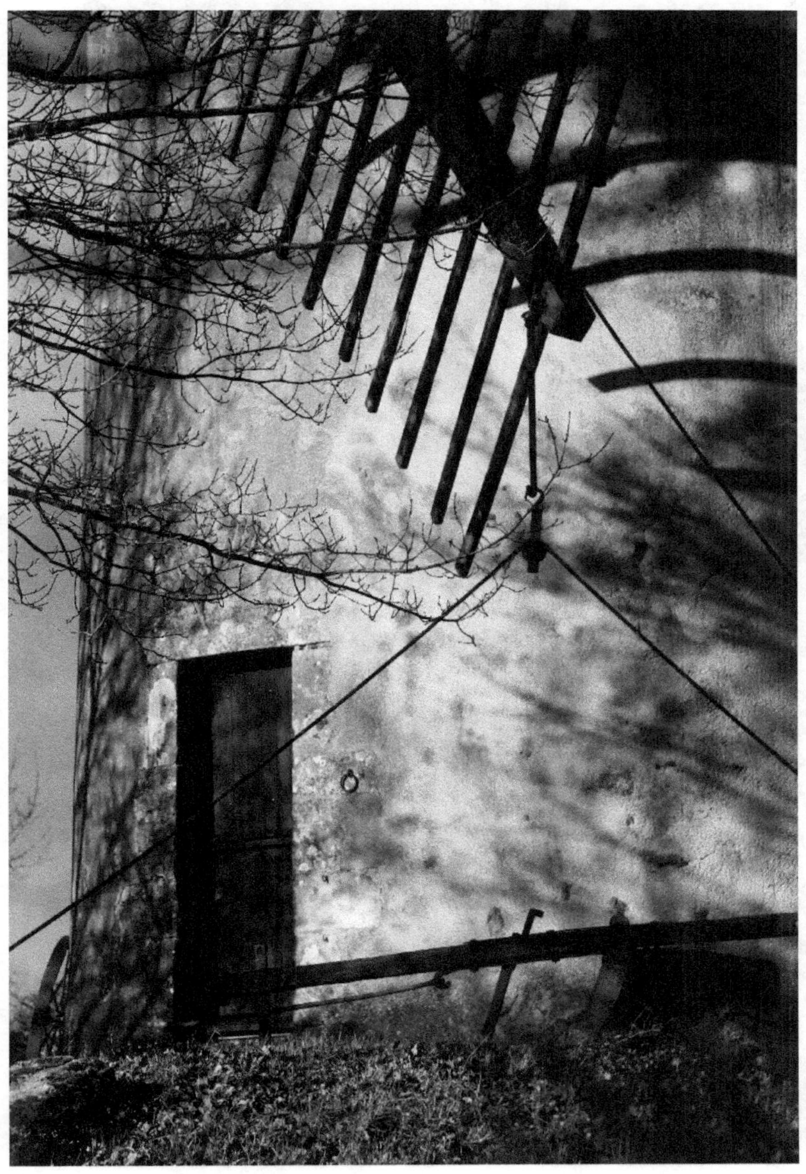

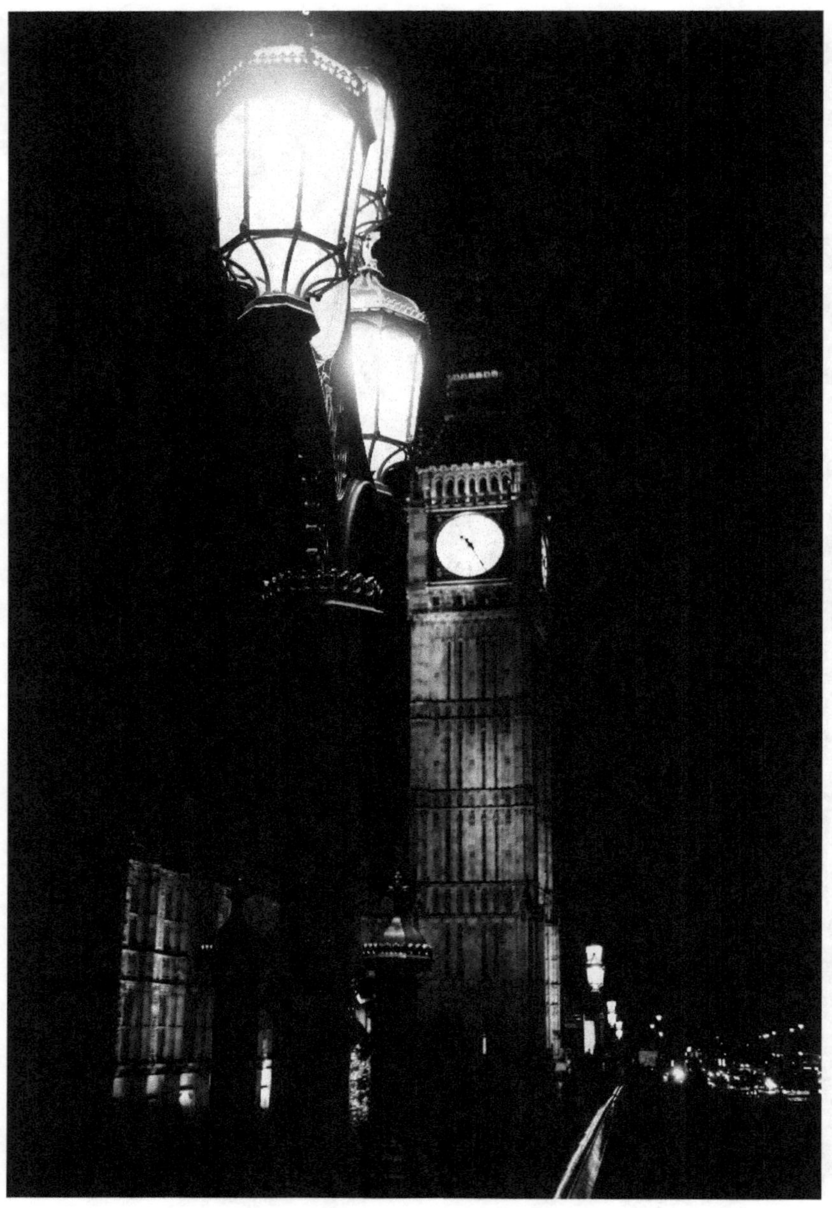

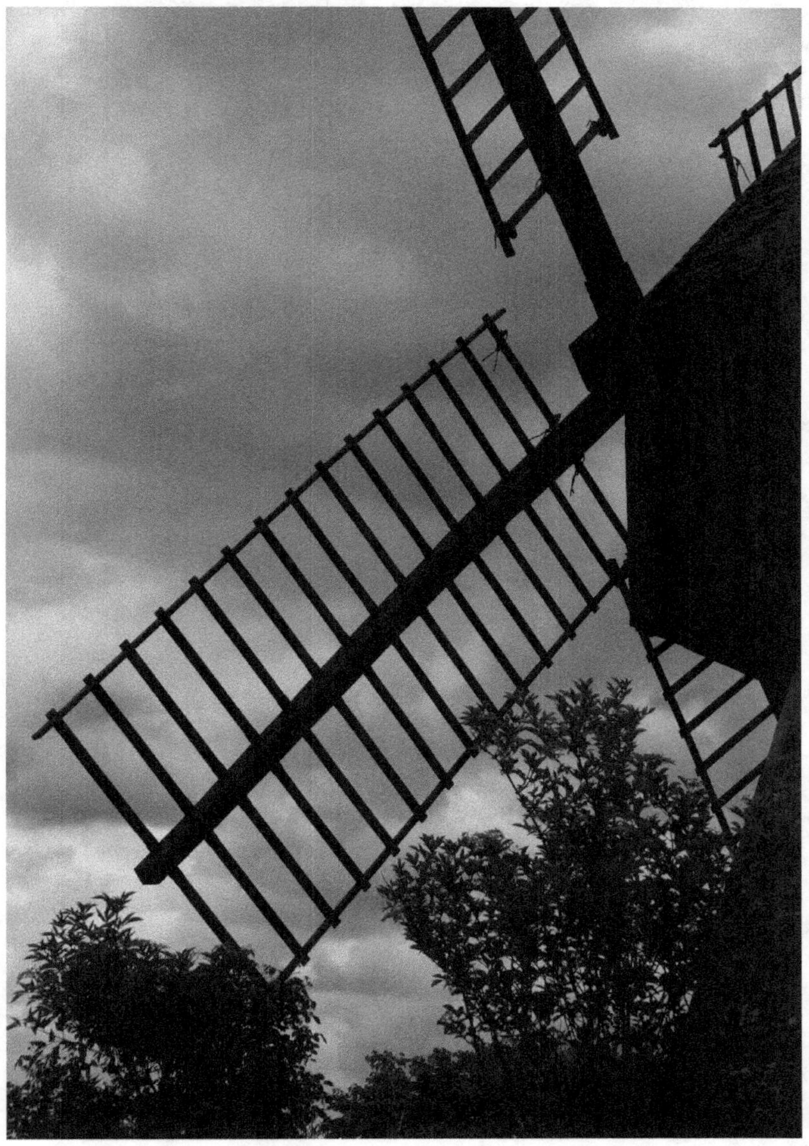

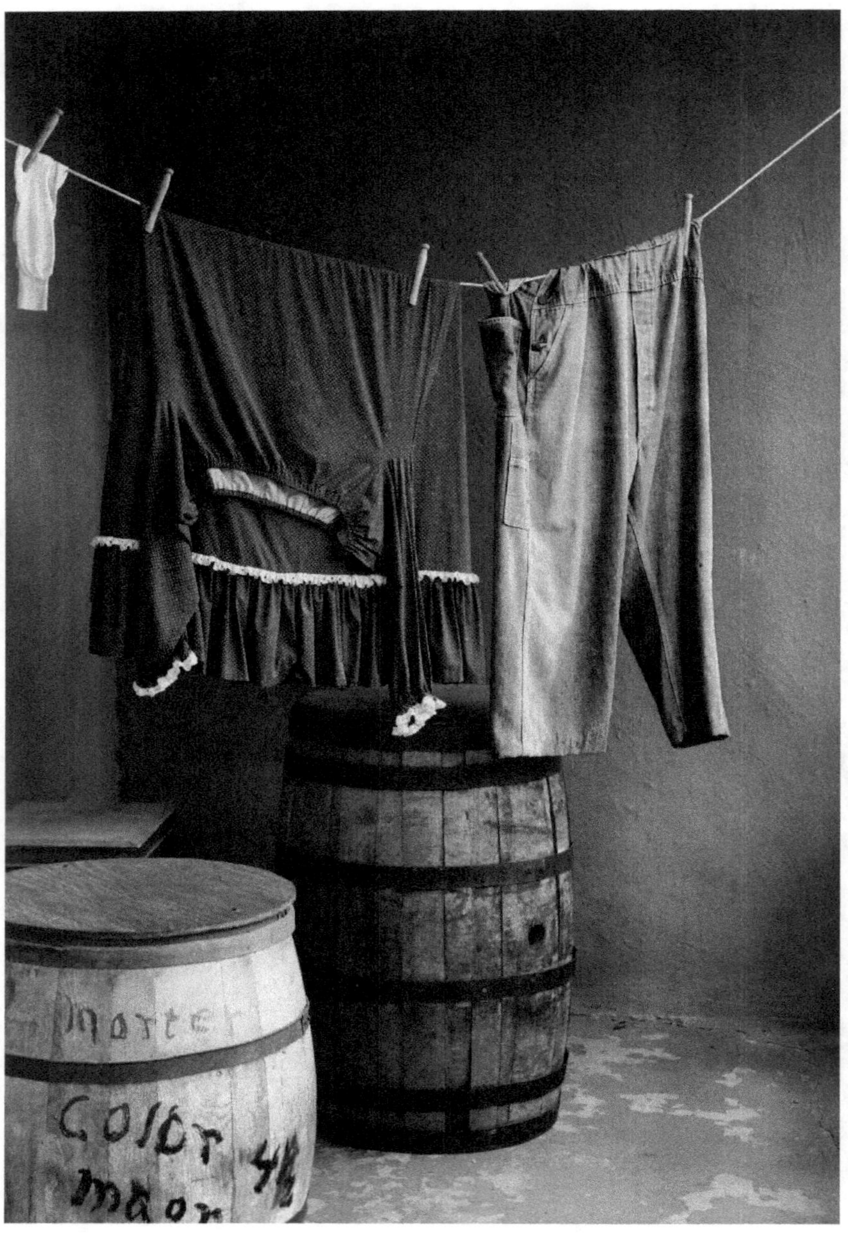

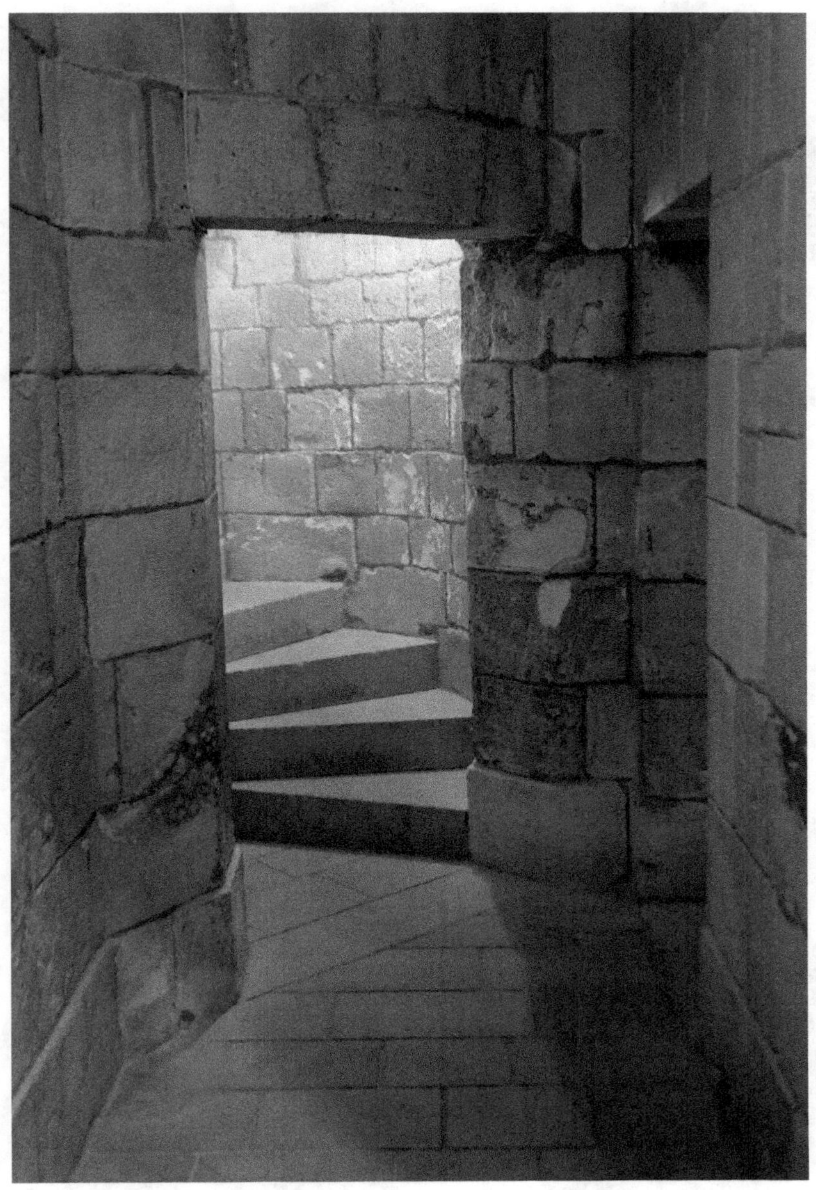

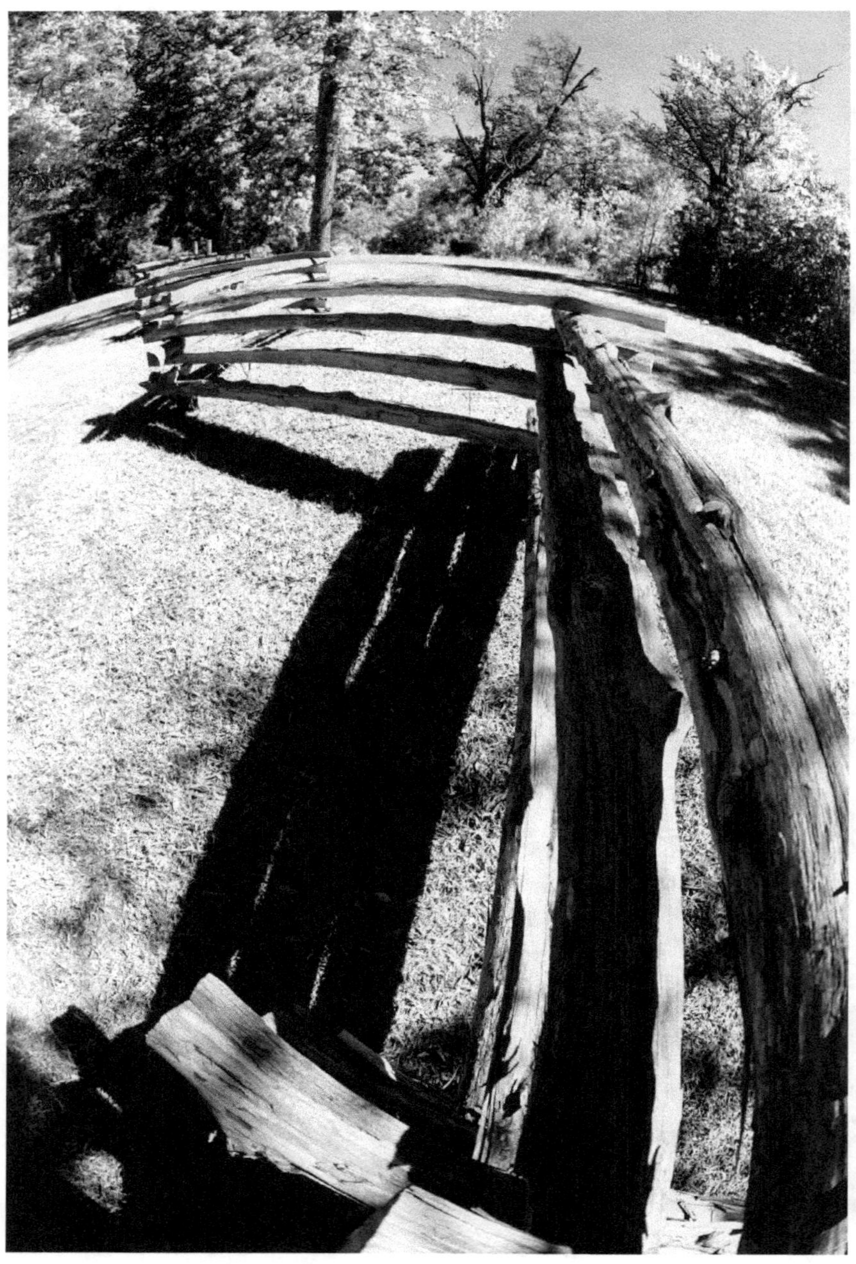

75

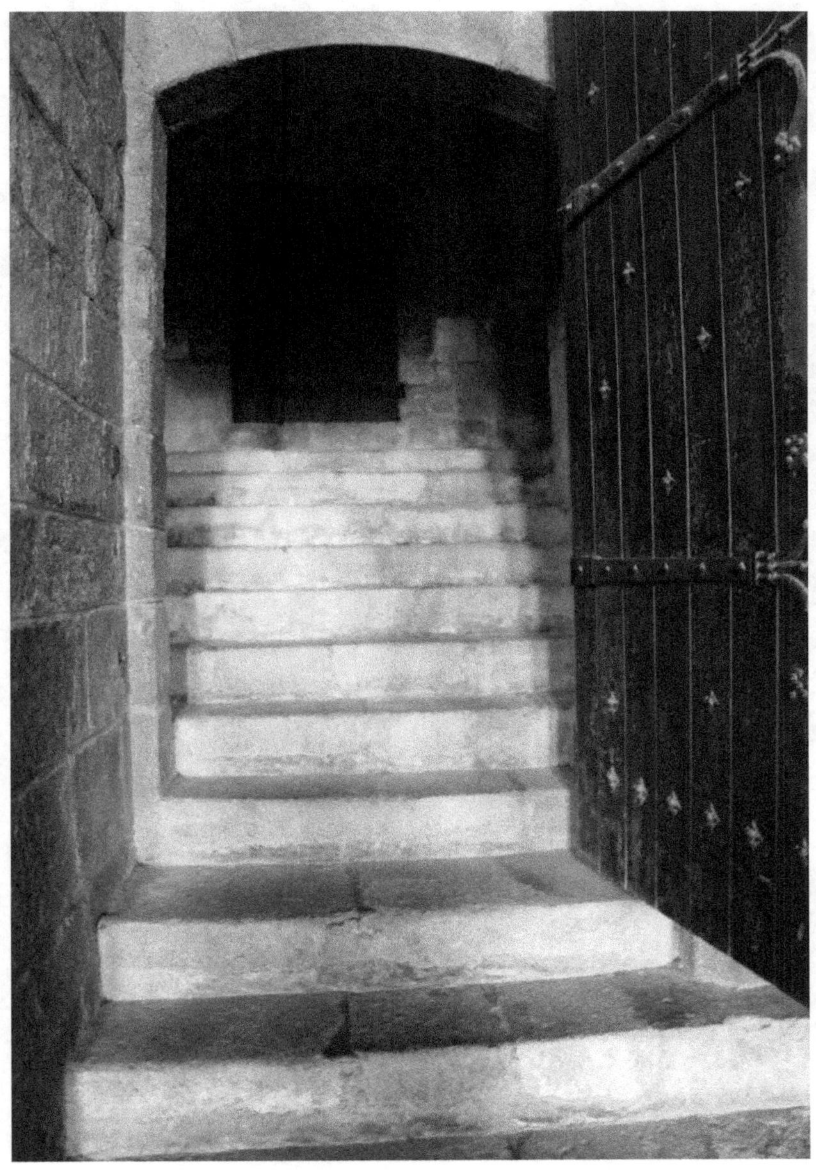

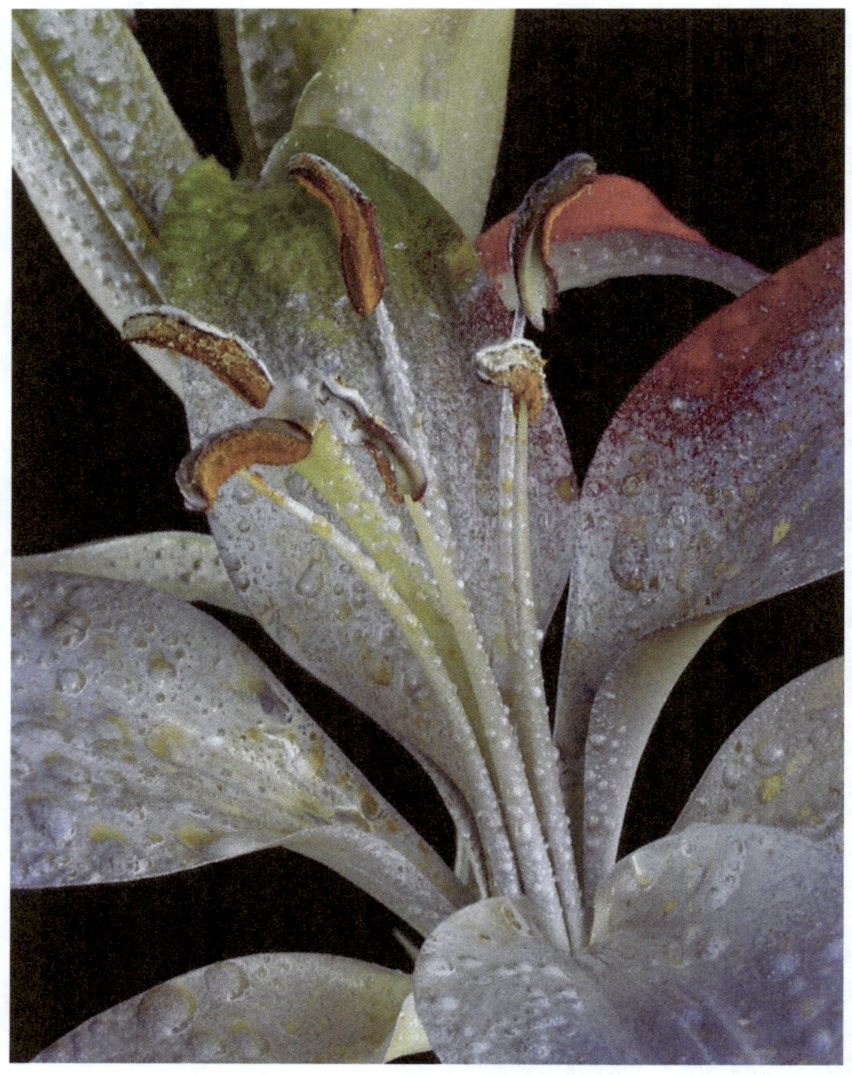

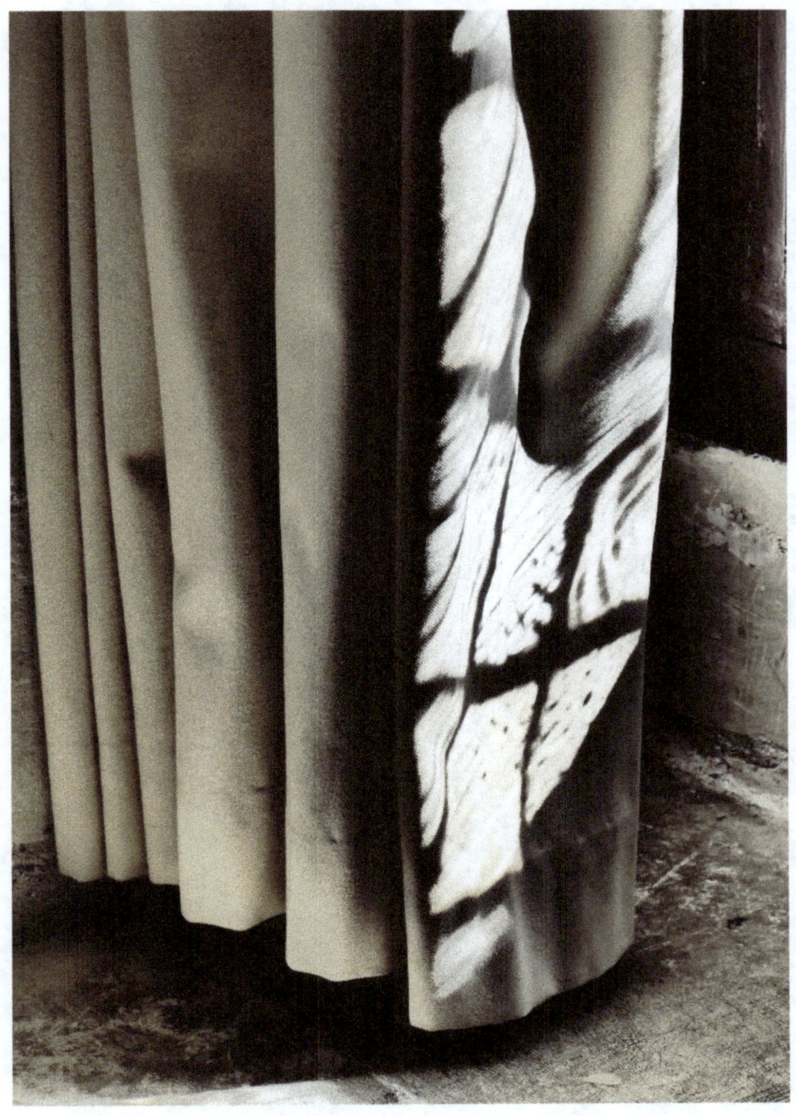

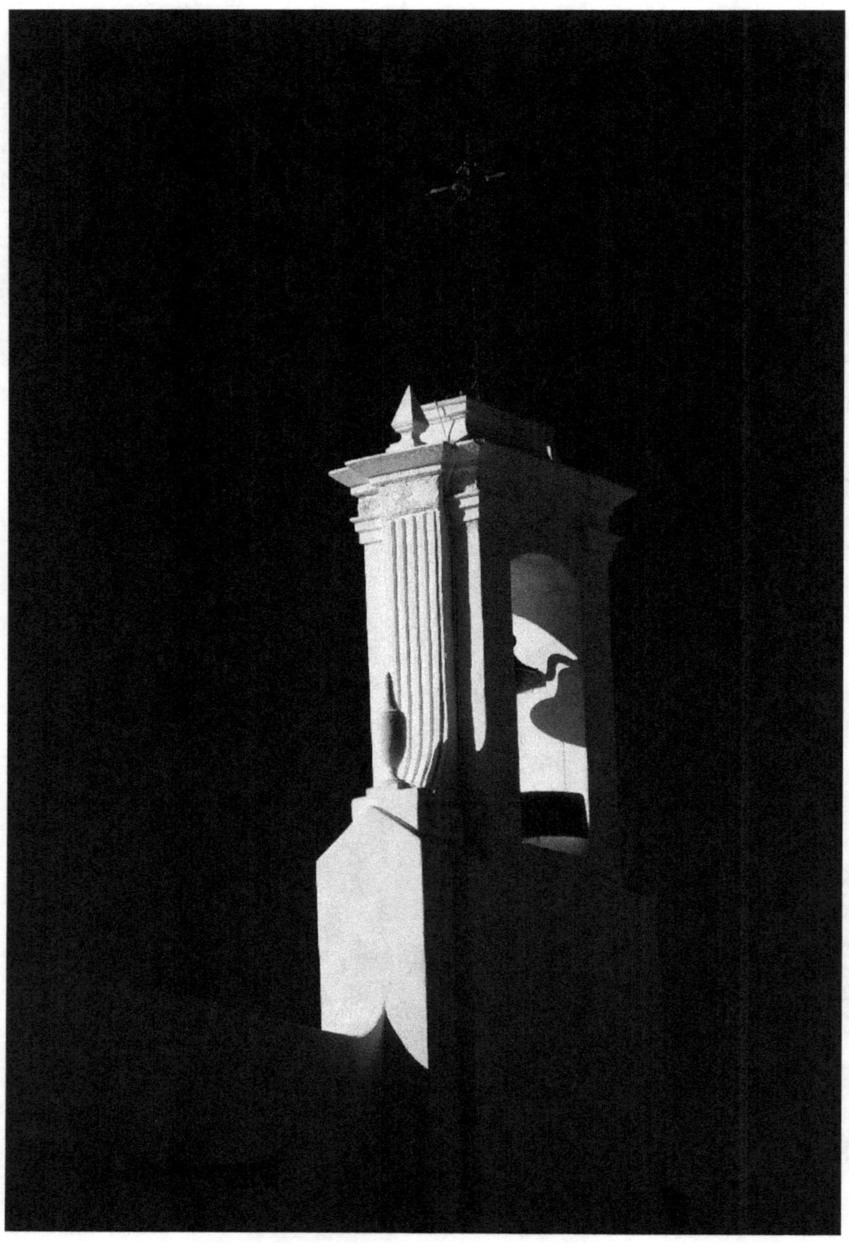

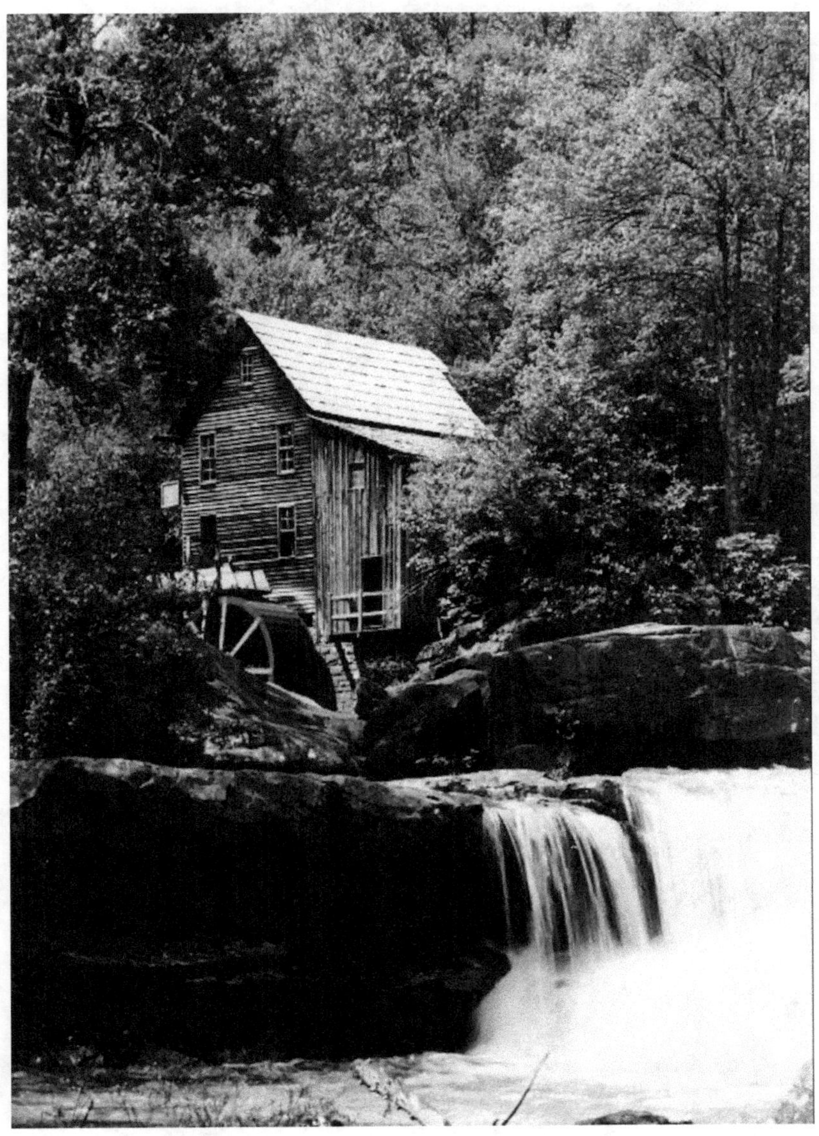

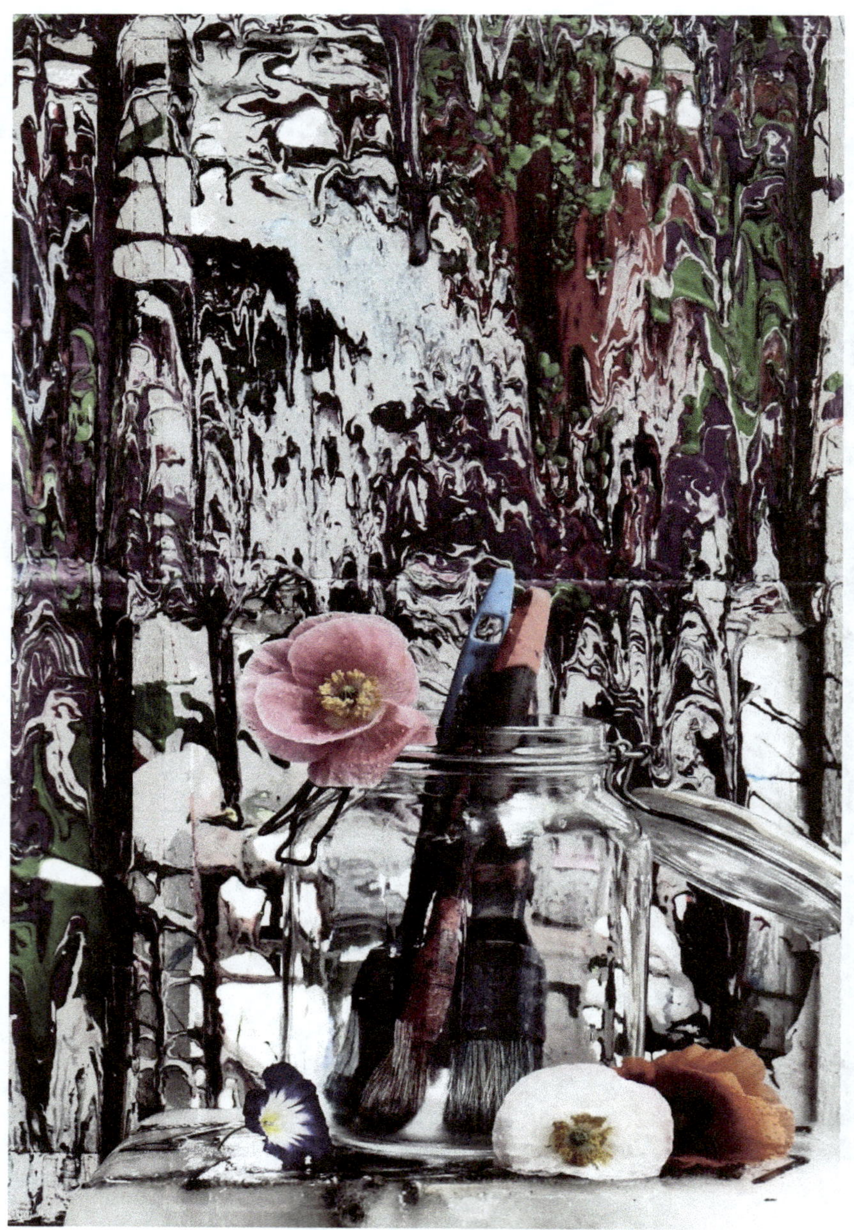

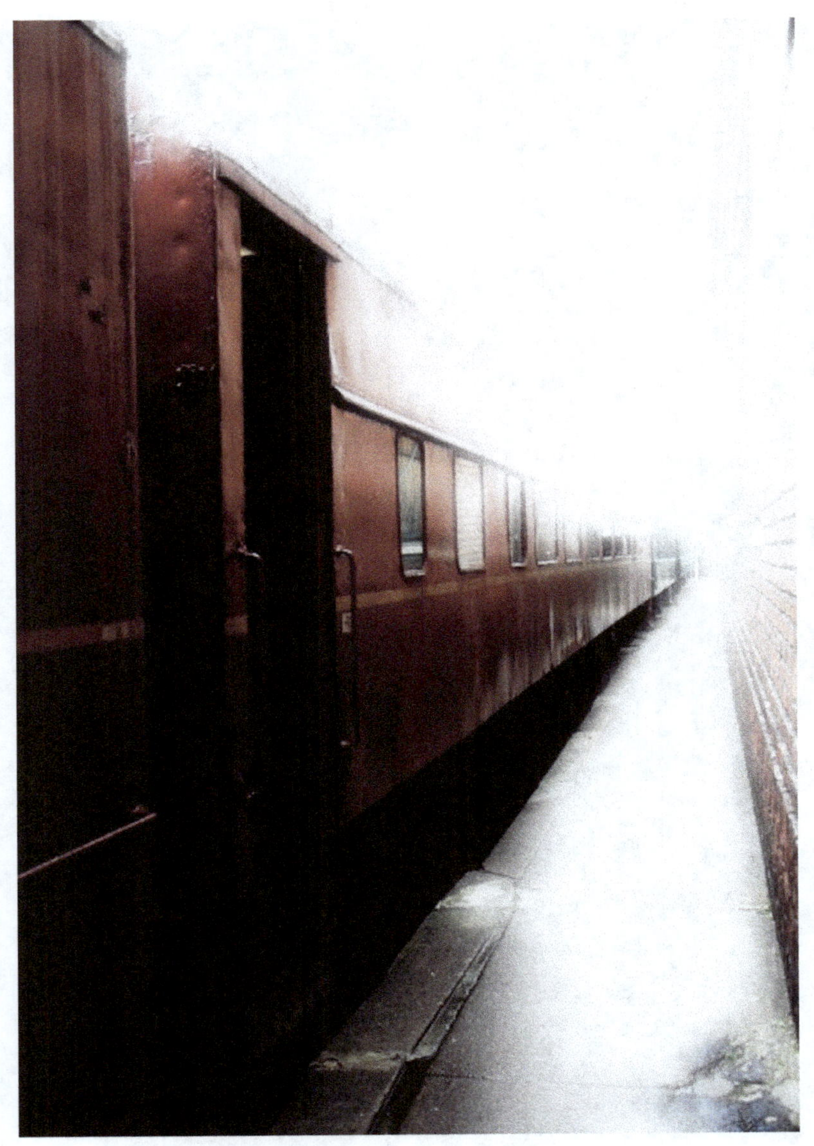

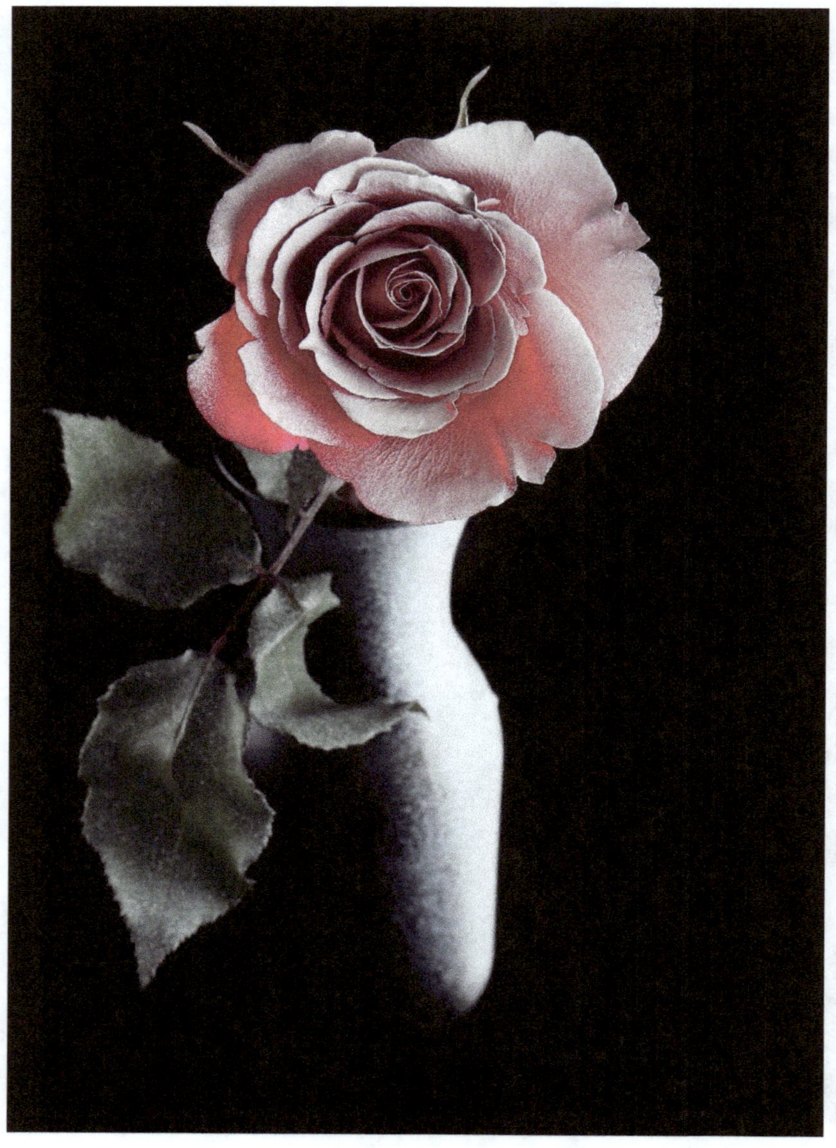

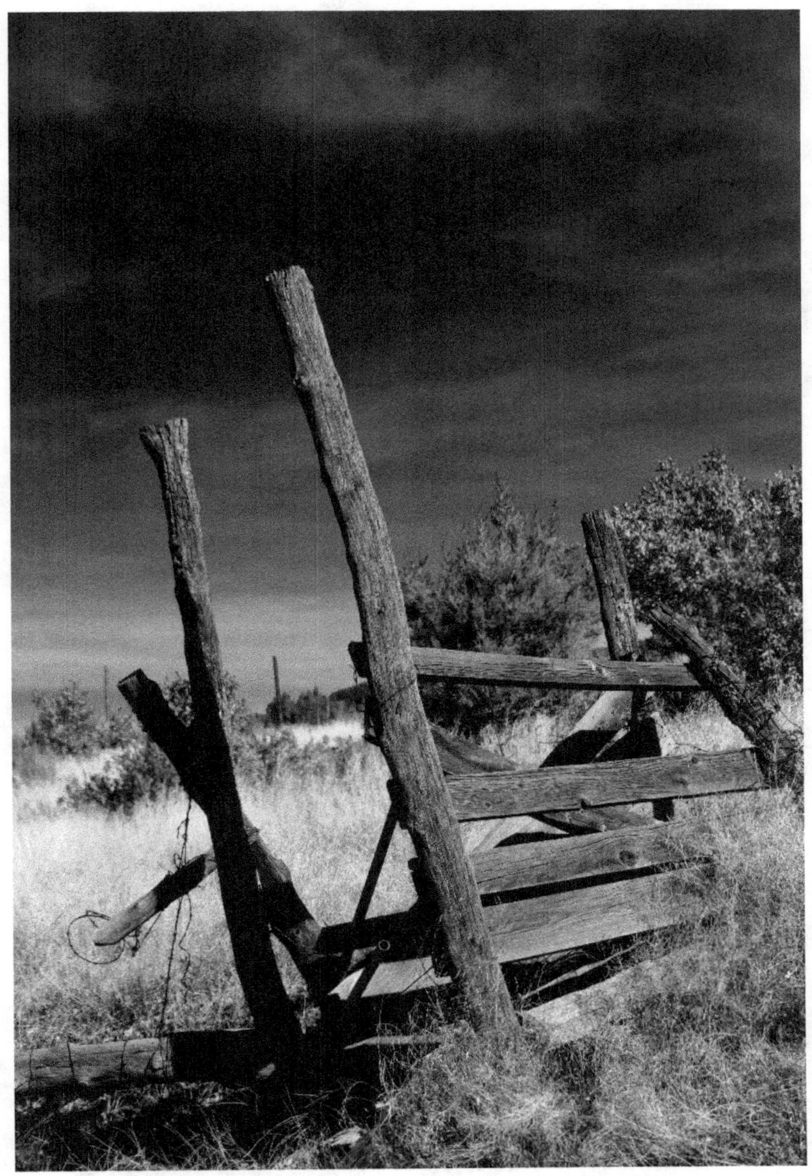

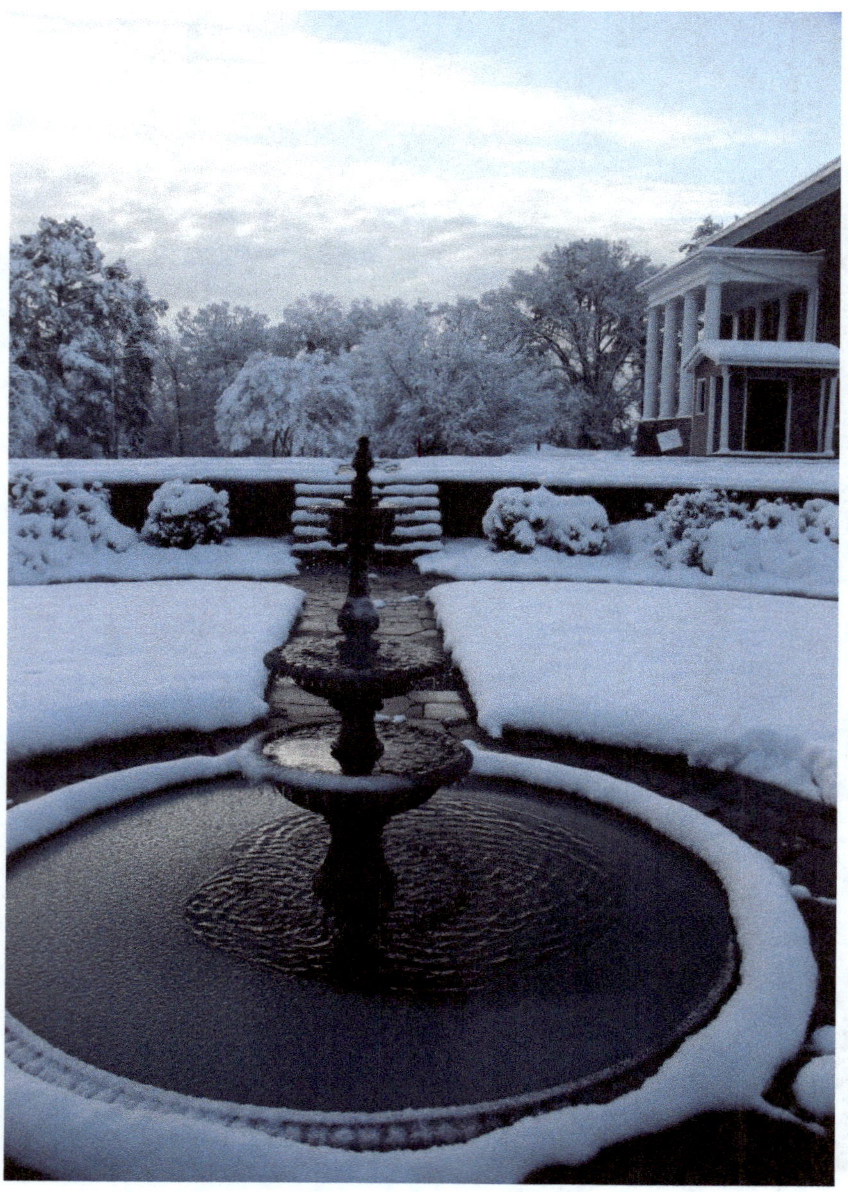

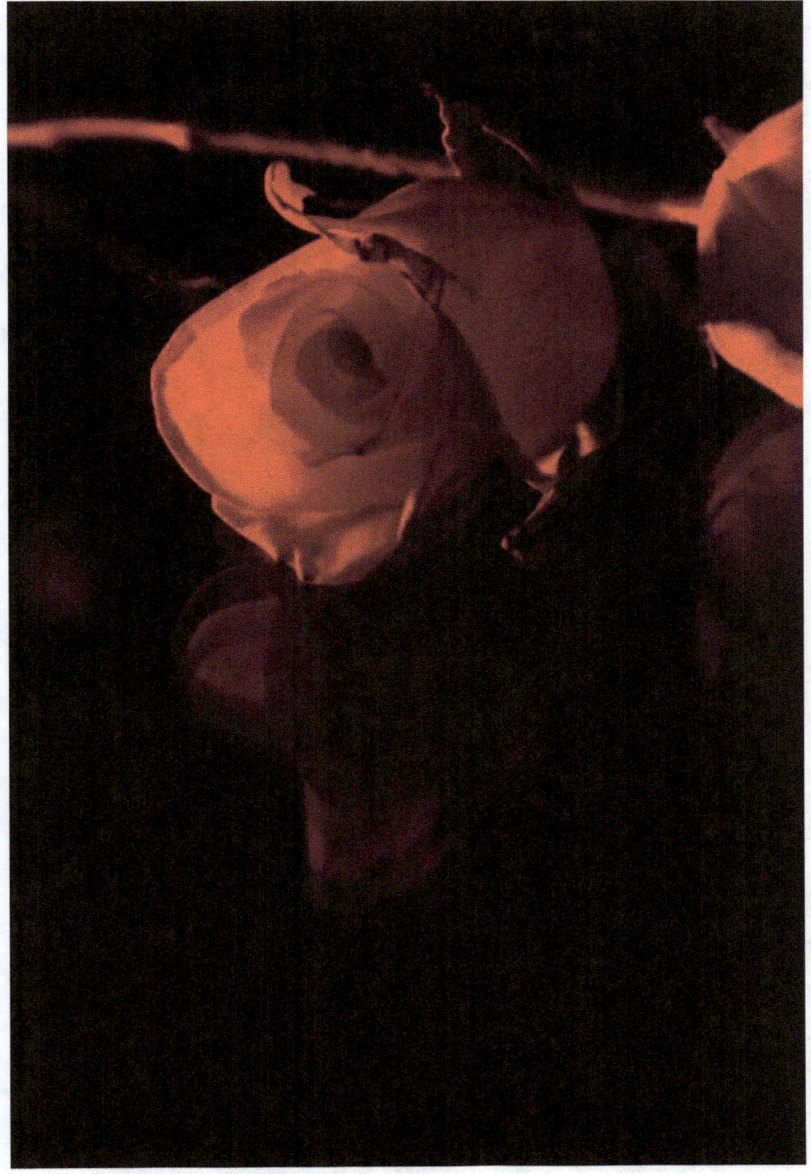

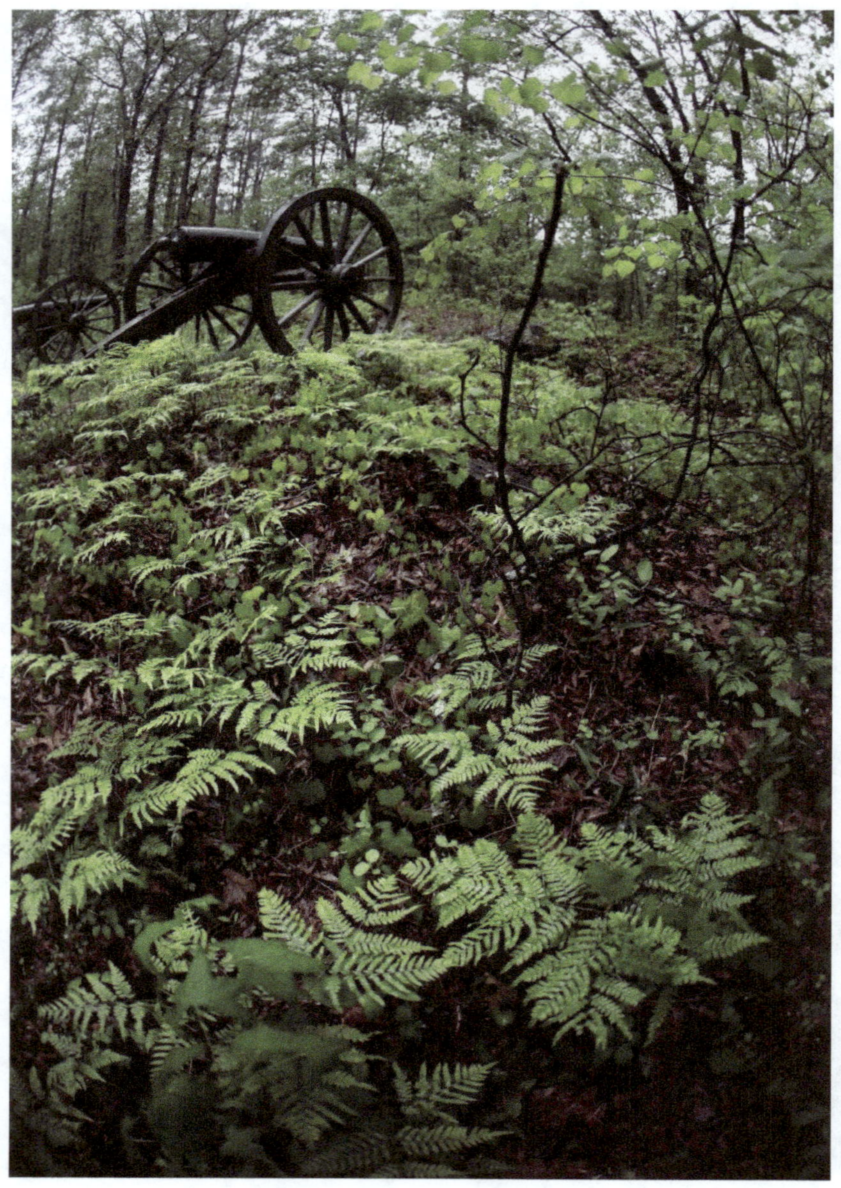

Through the Eye of Solitude - Fabrice Poussin

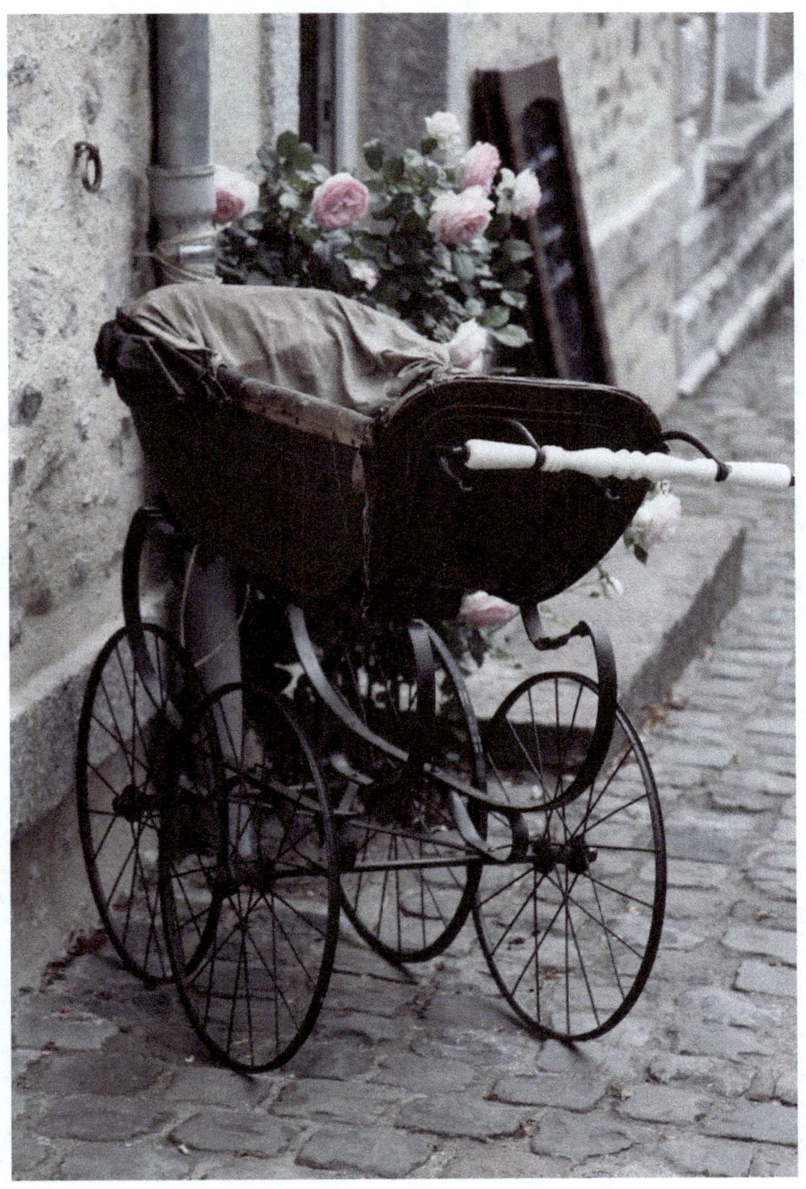

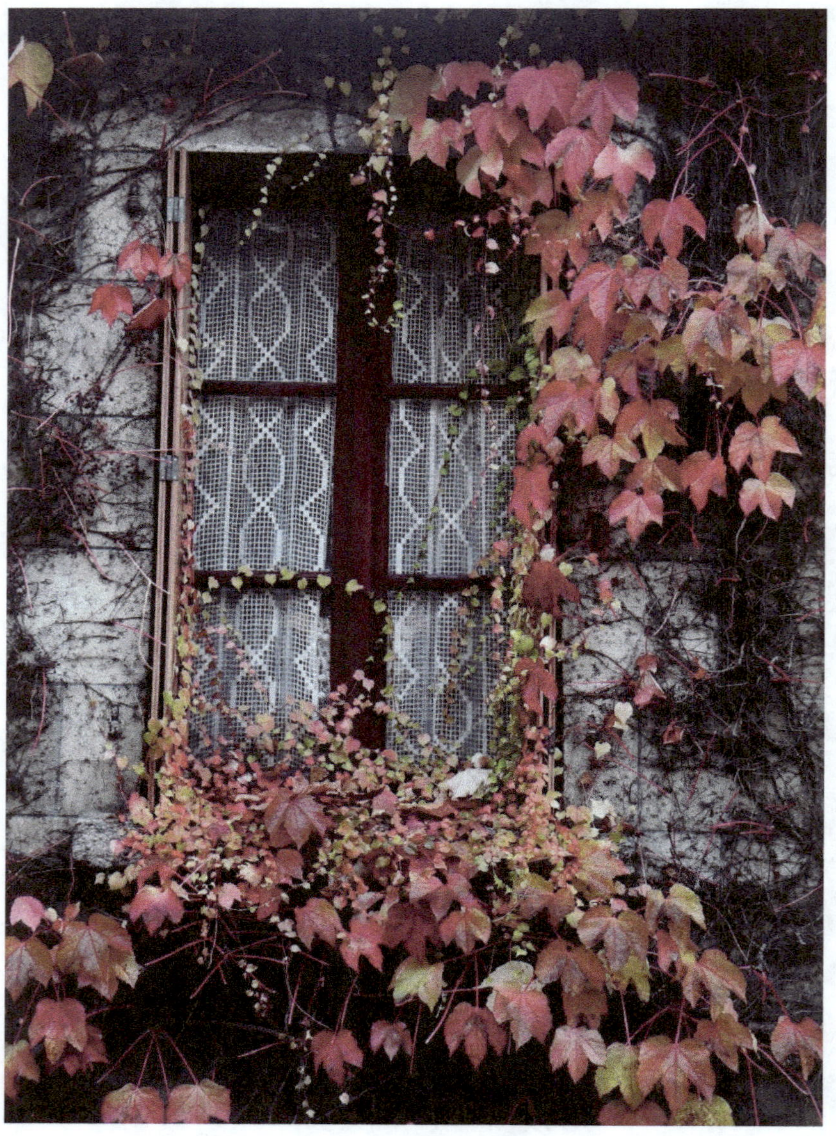

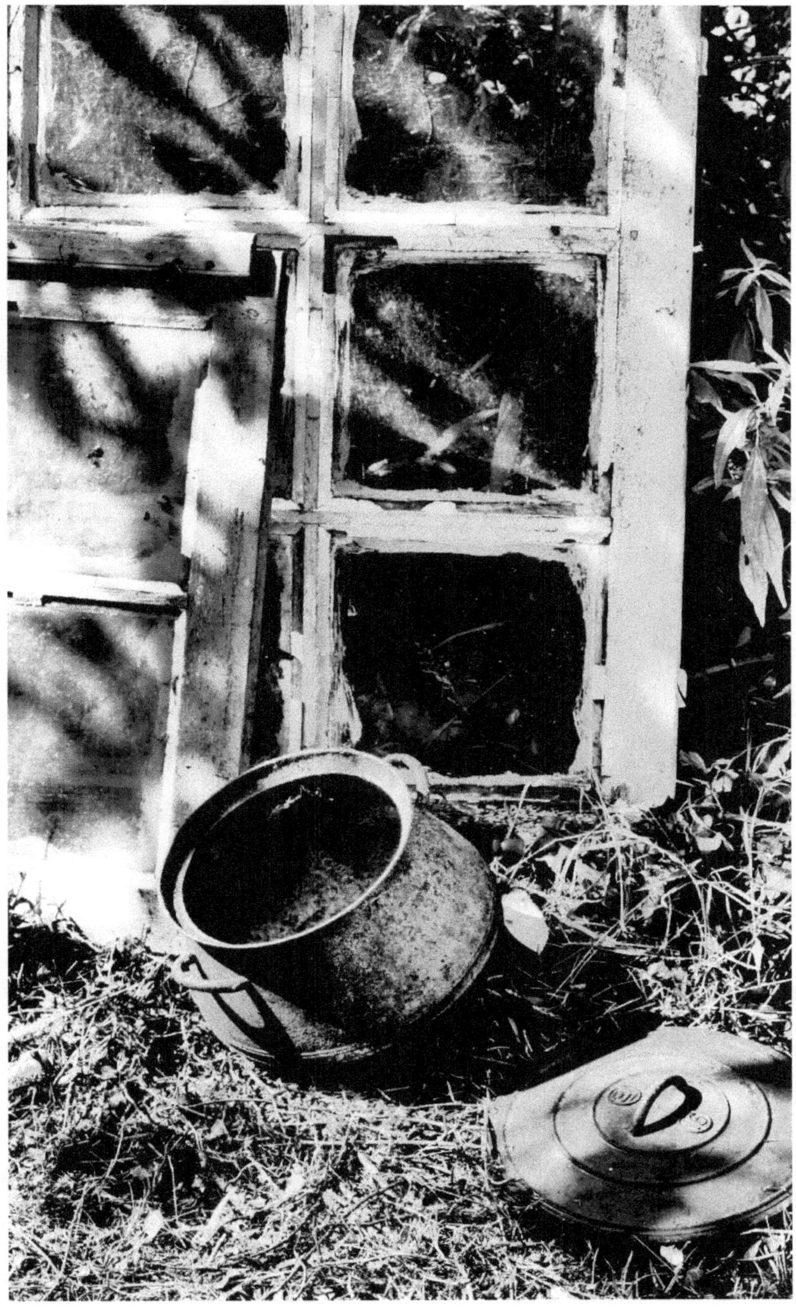

THE HORIZONTALS

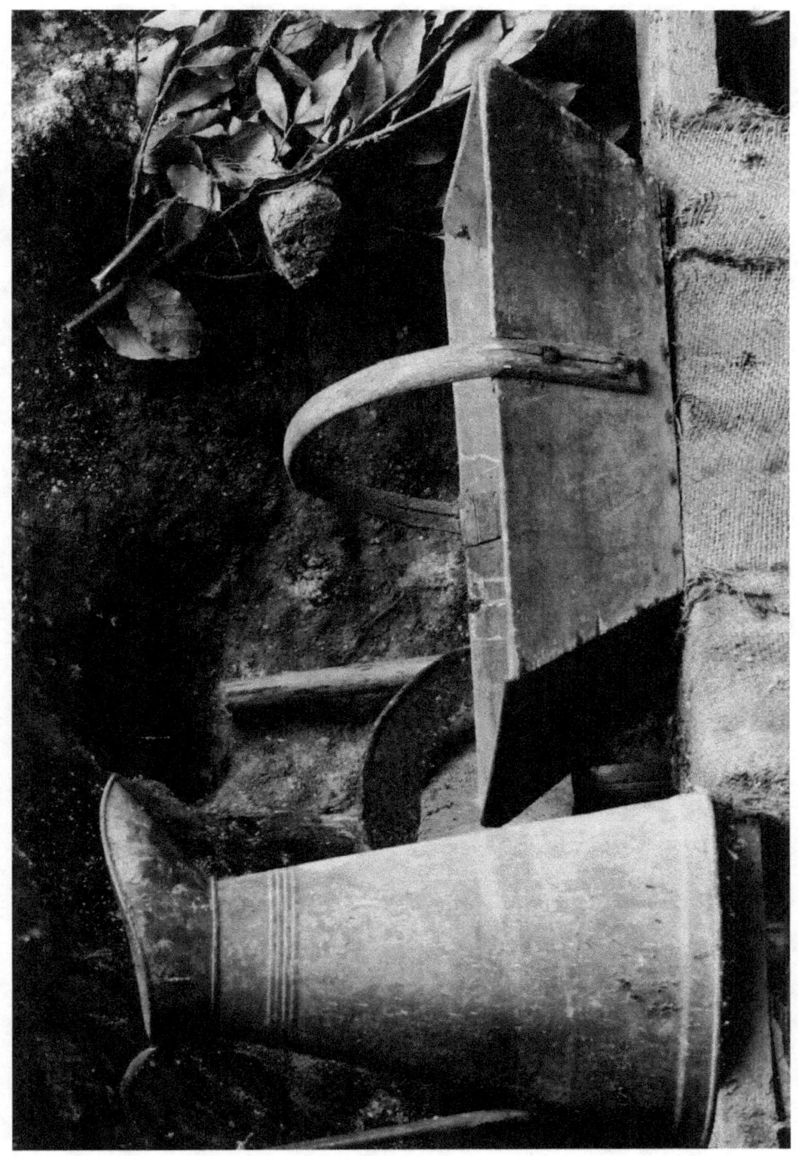

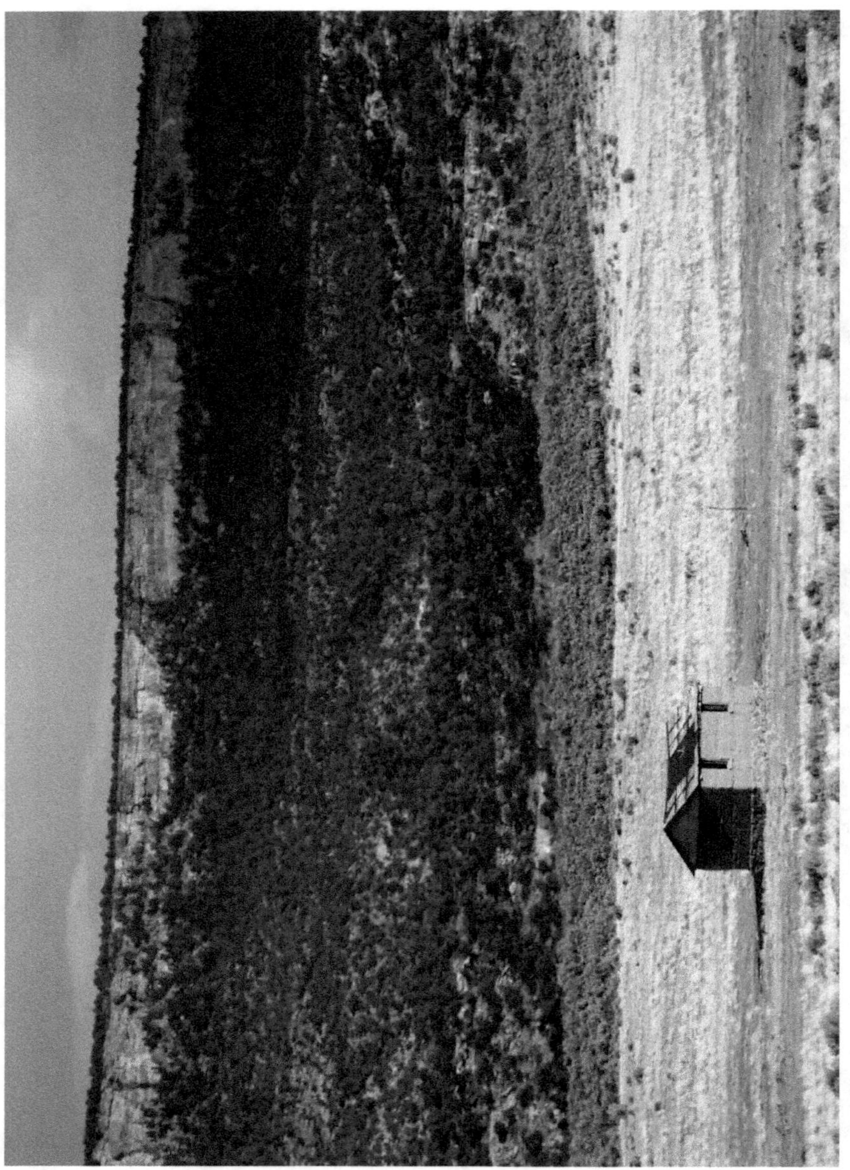

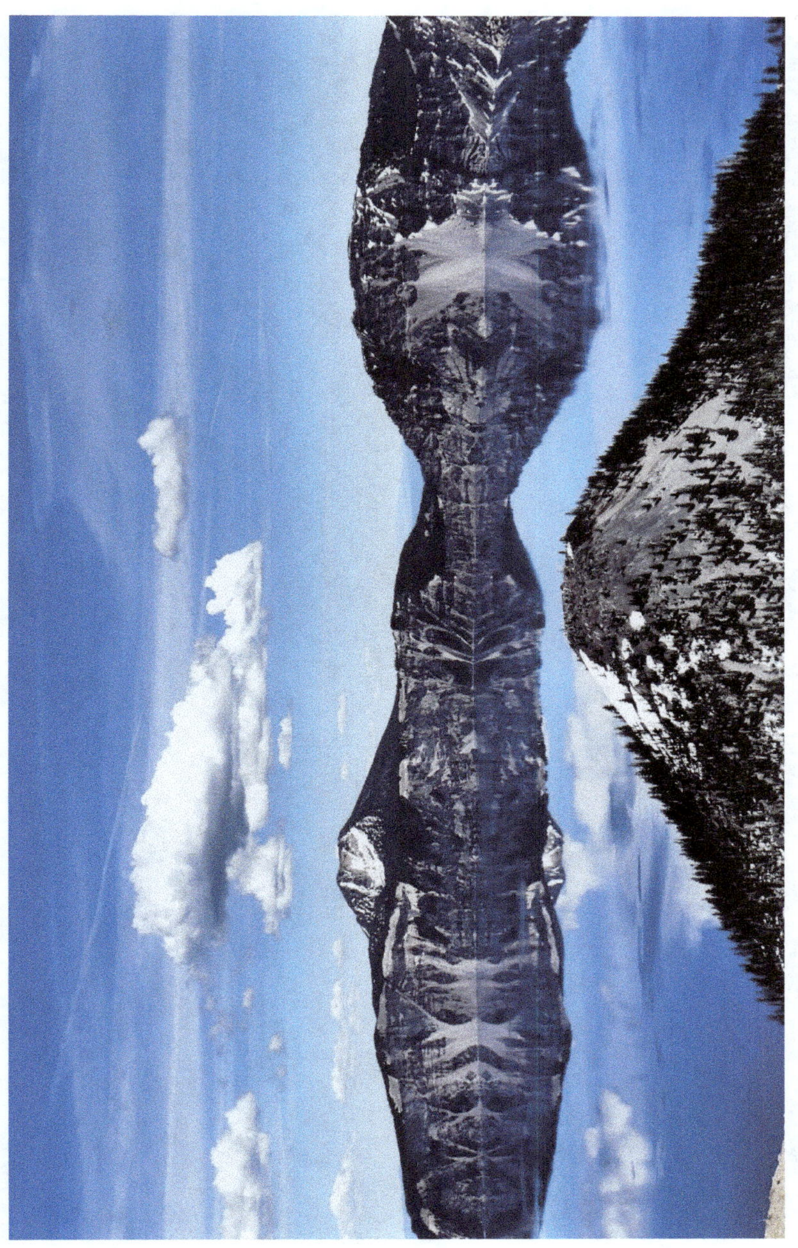

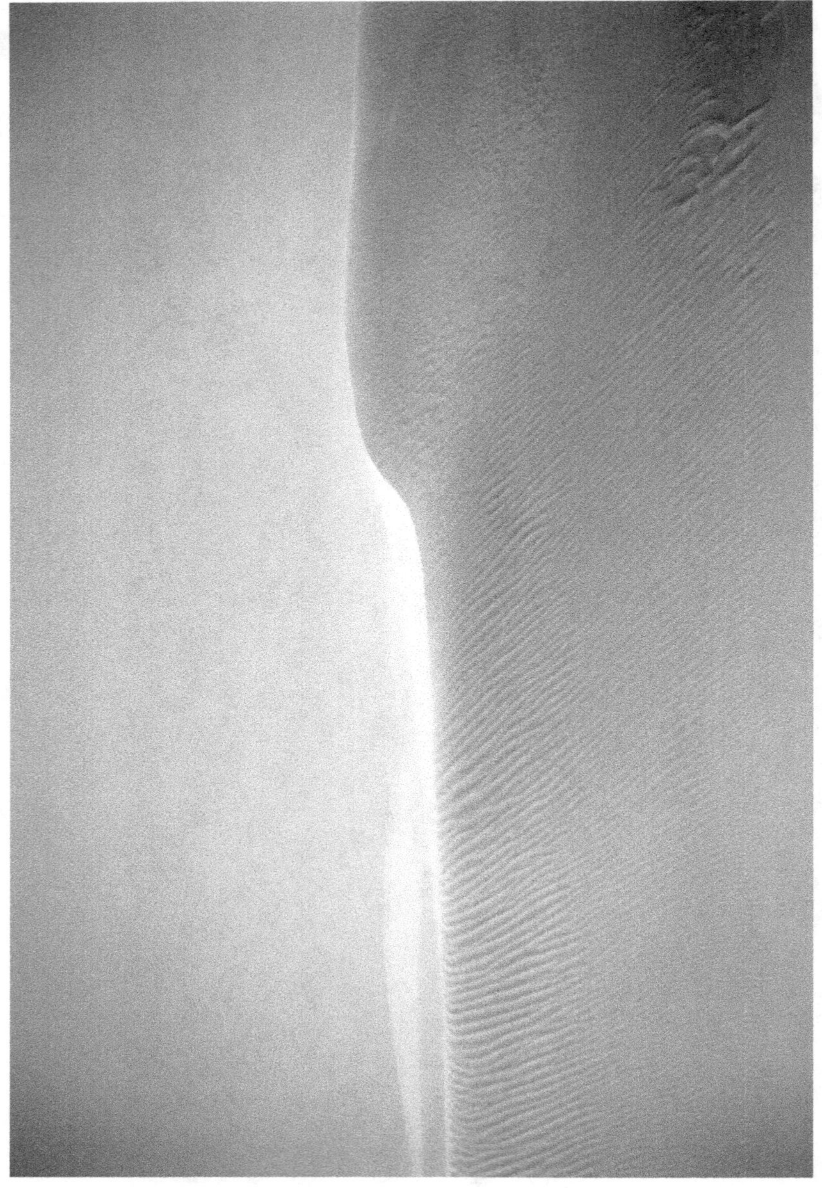

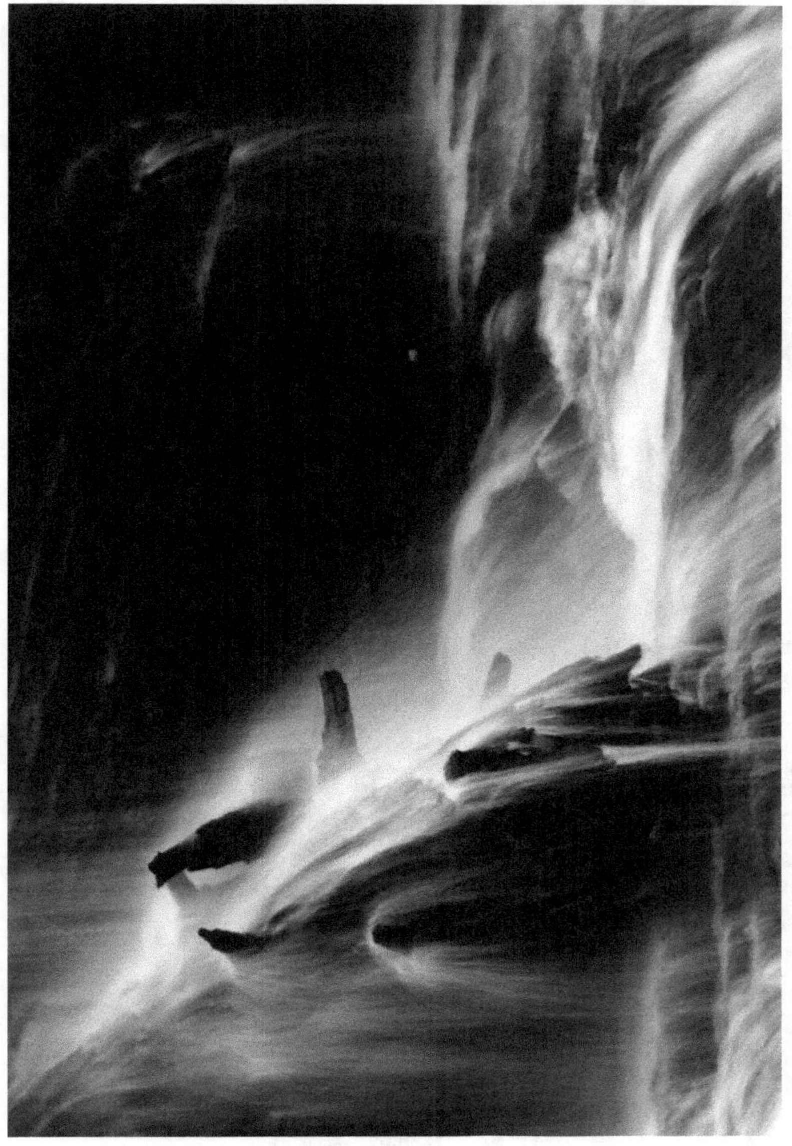

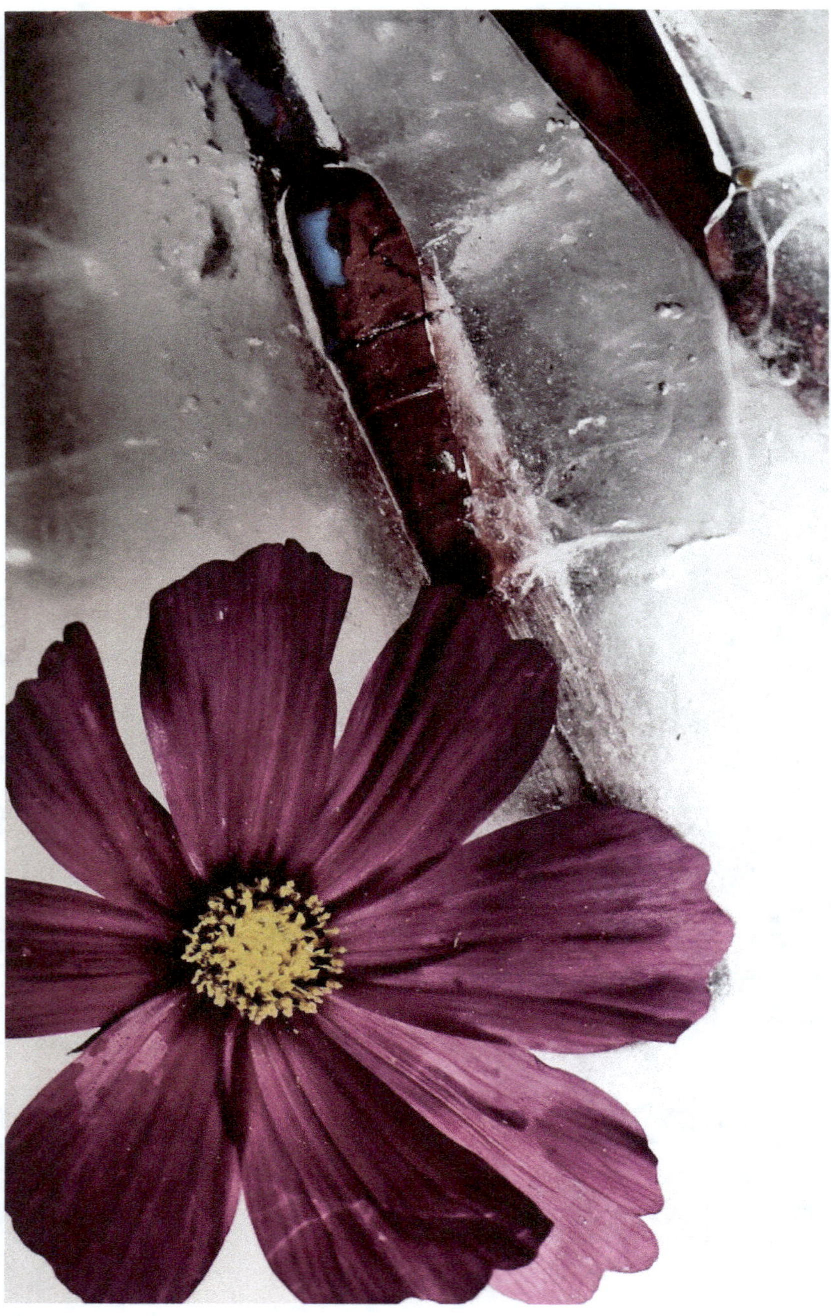

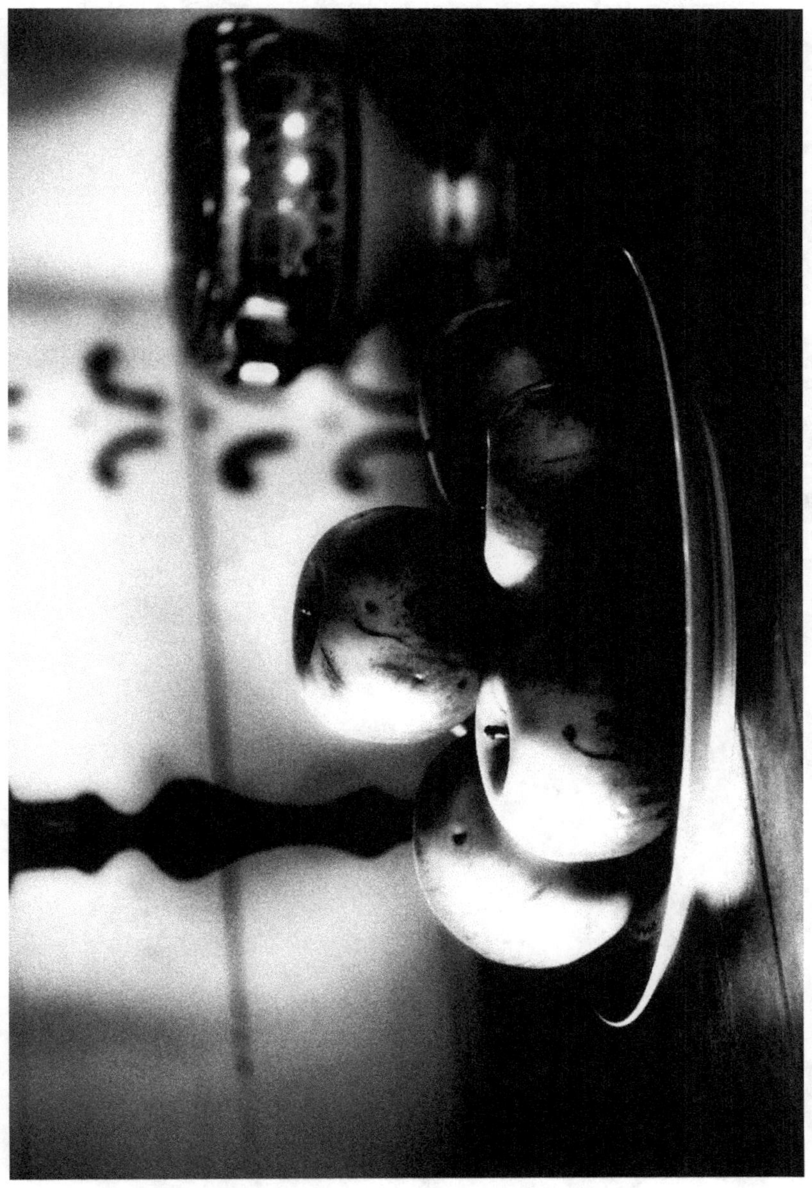

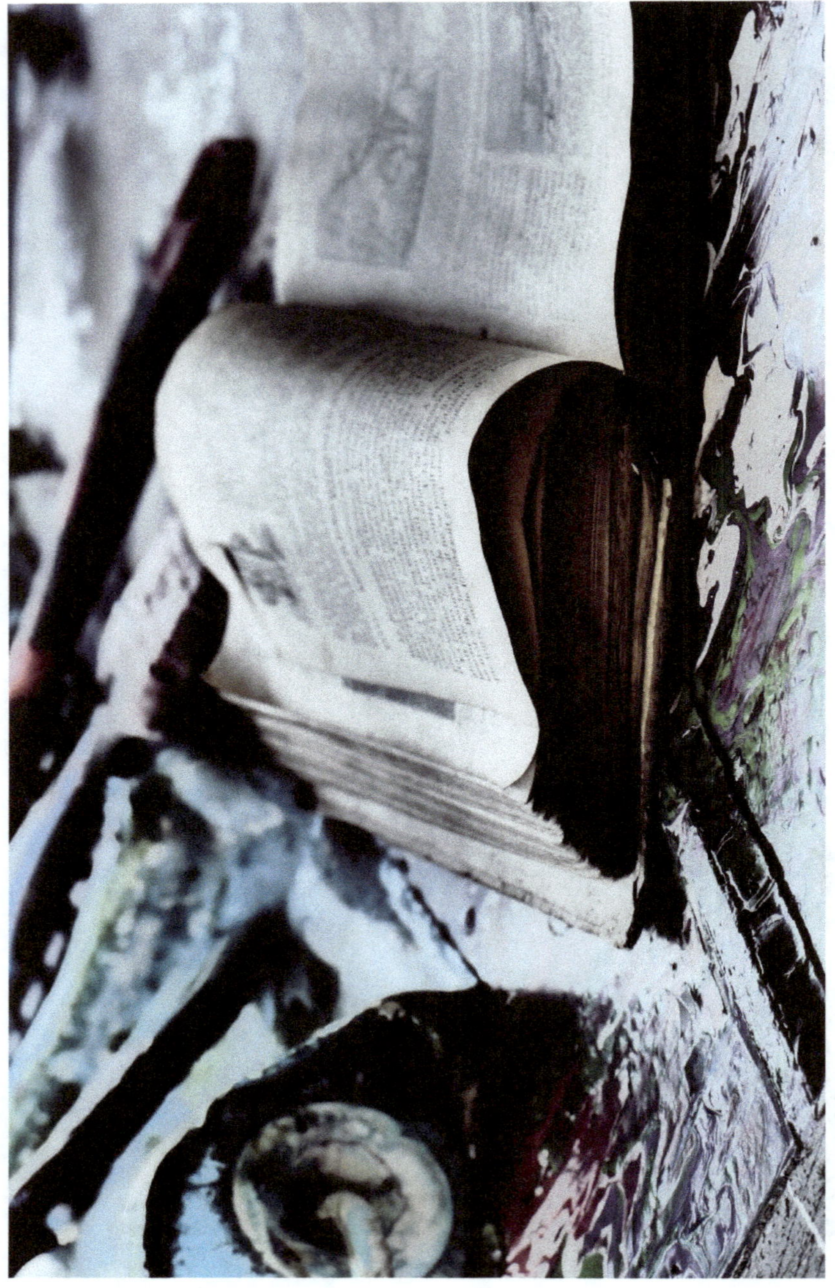

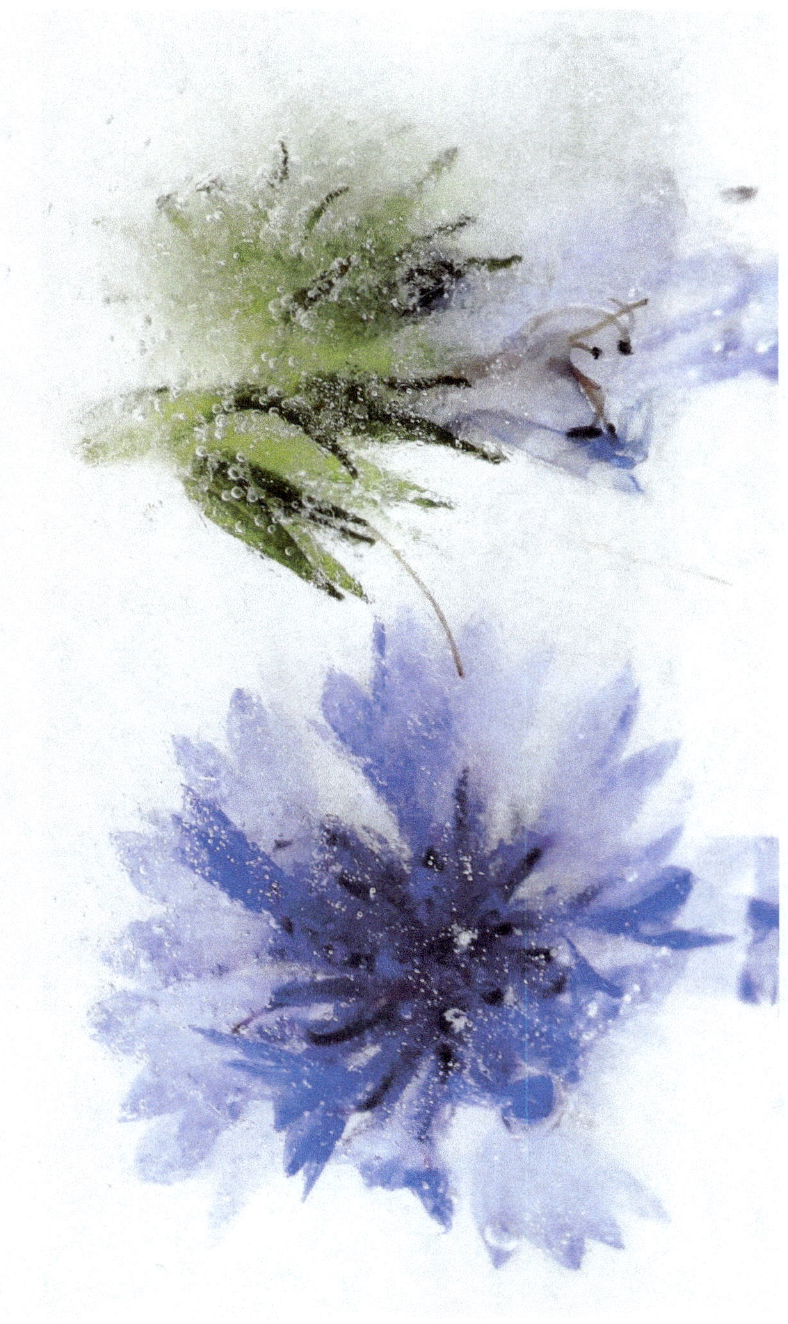

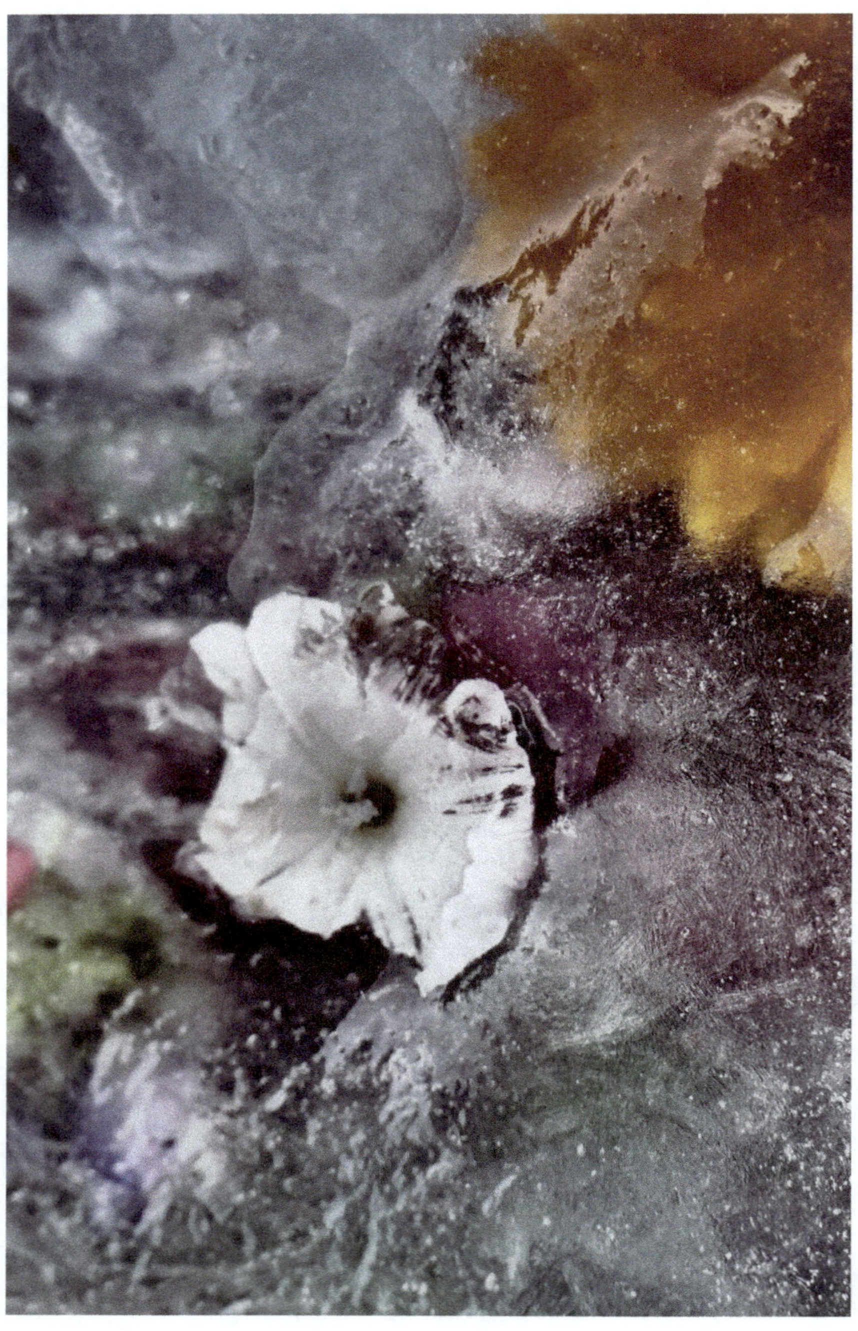

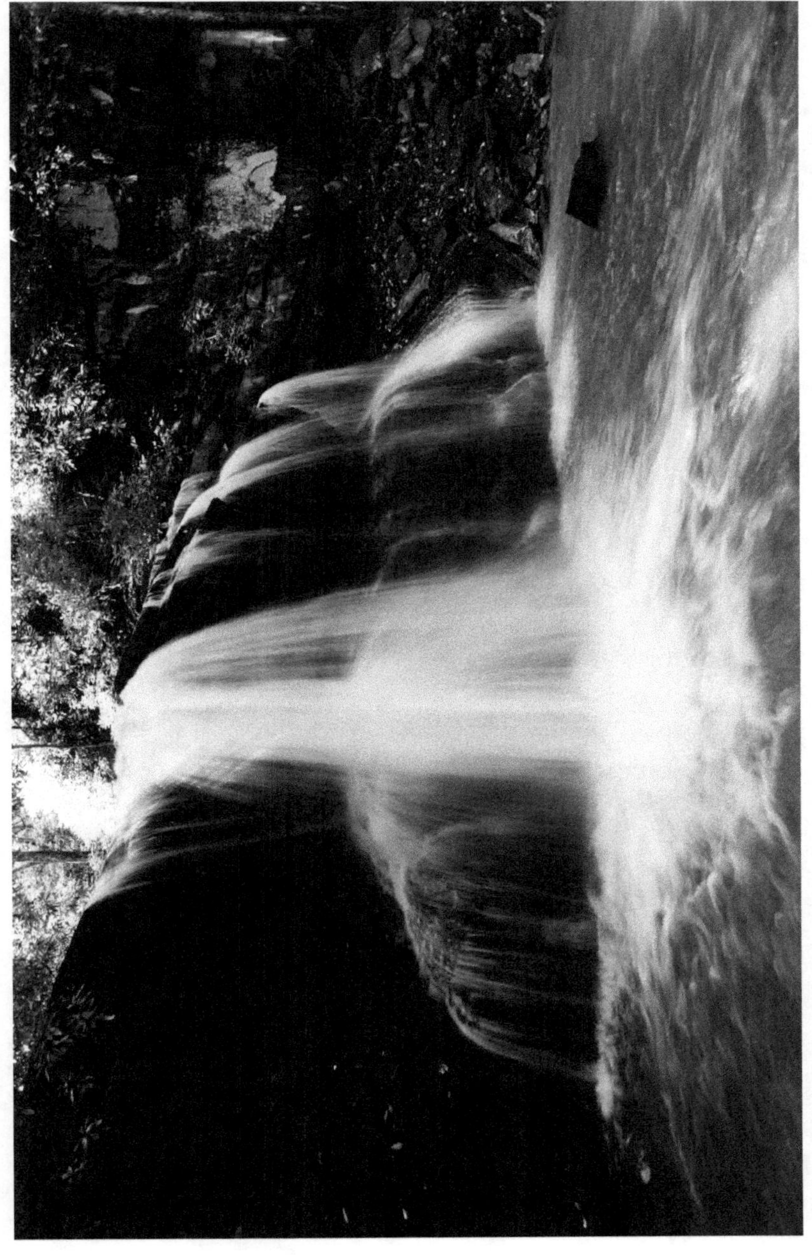

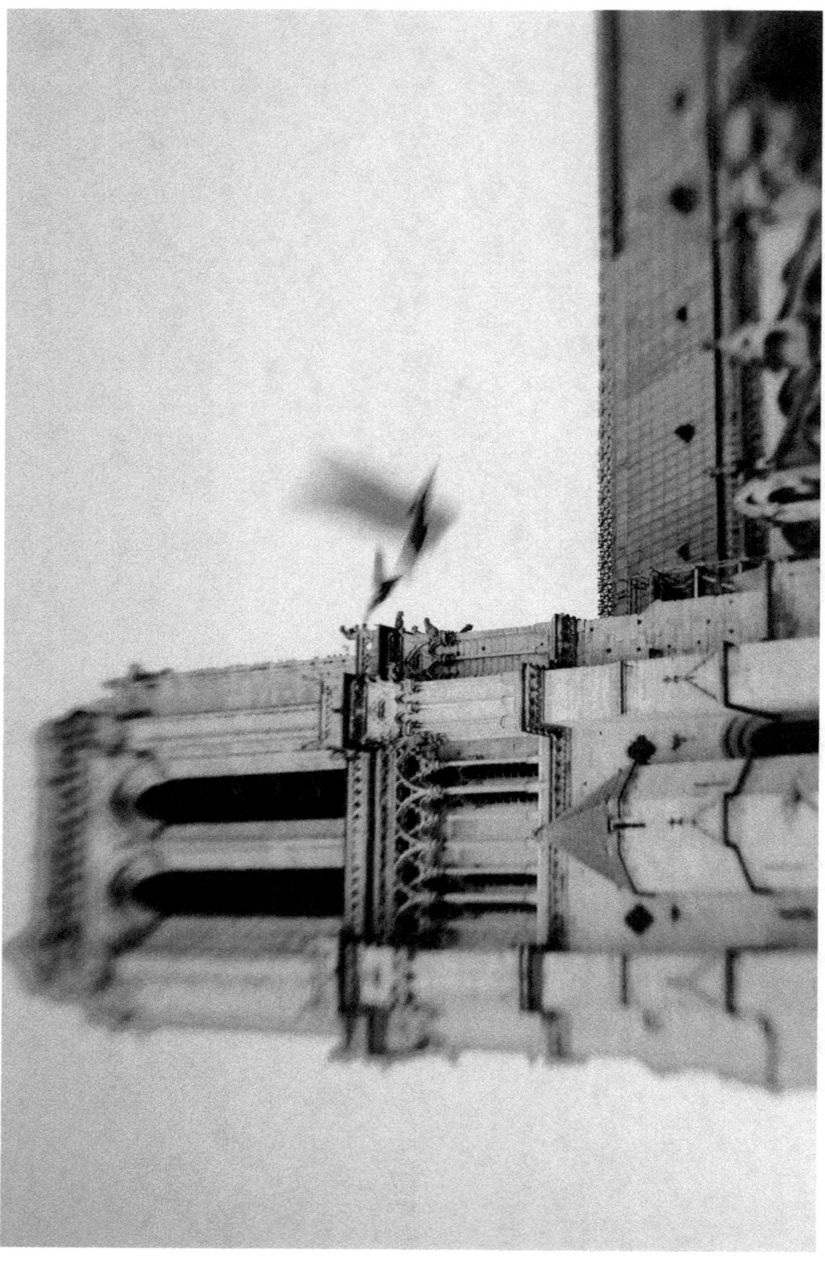

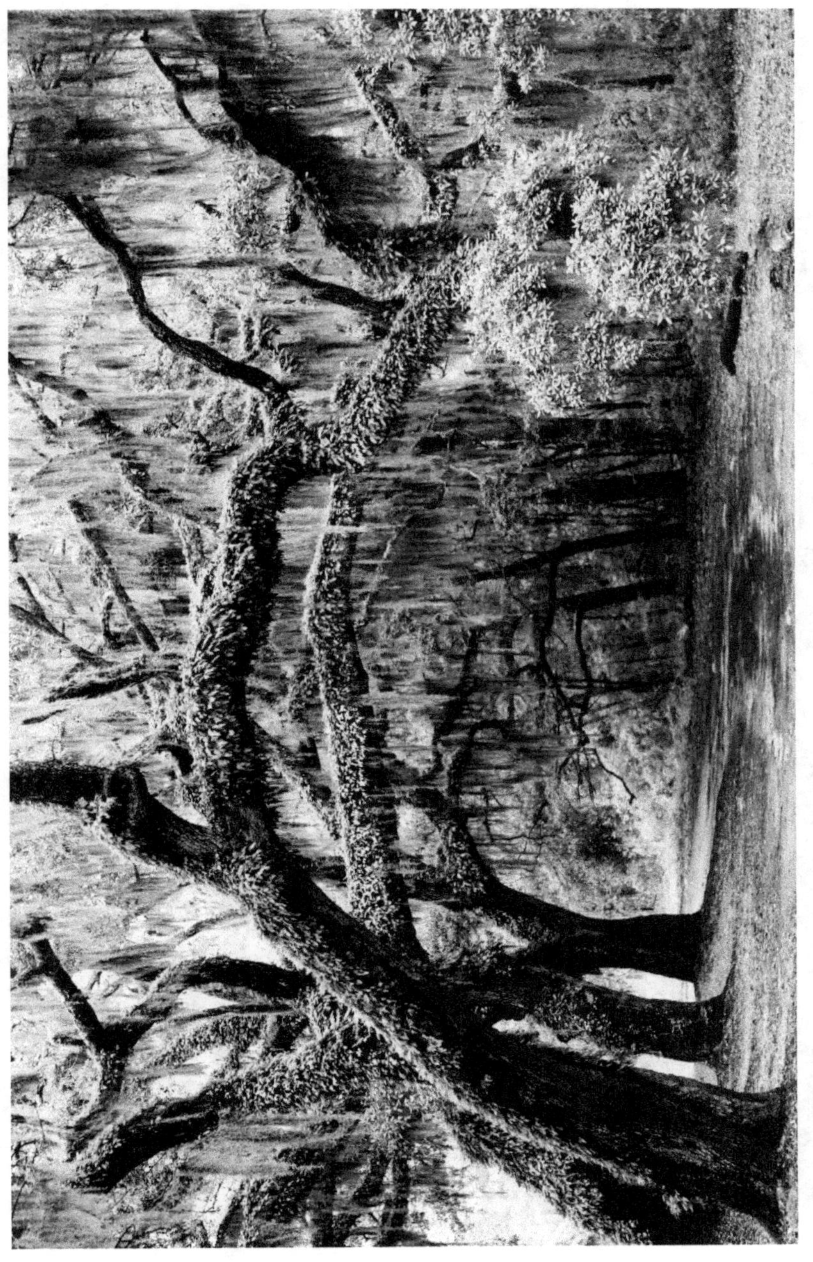

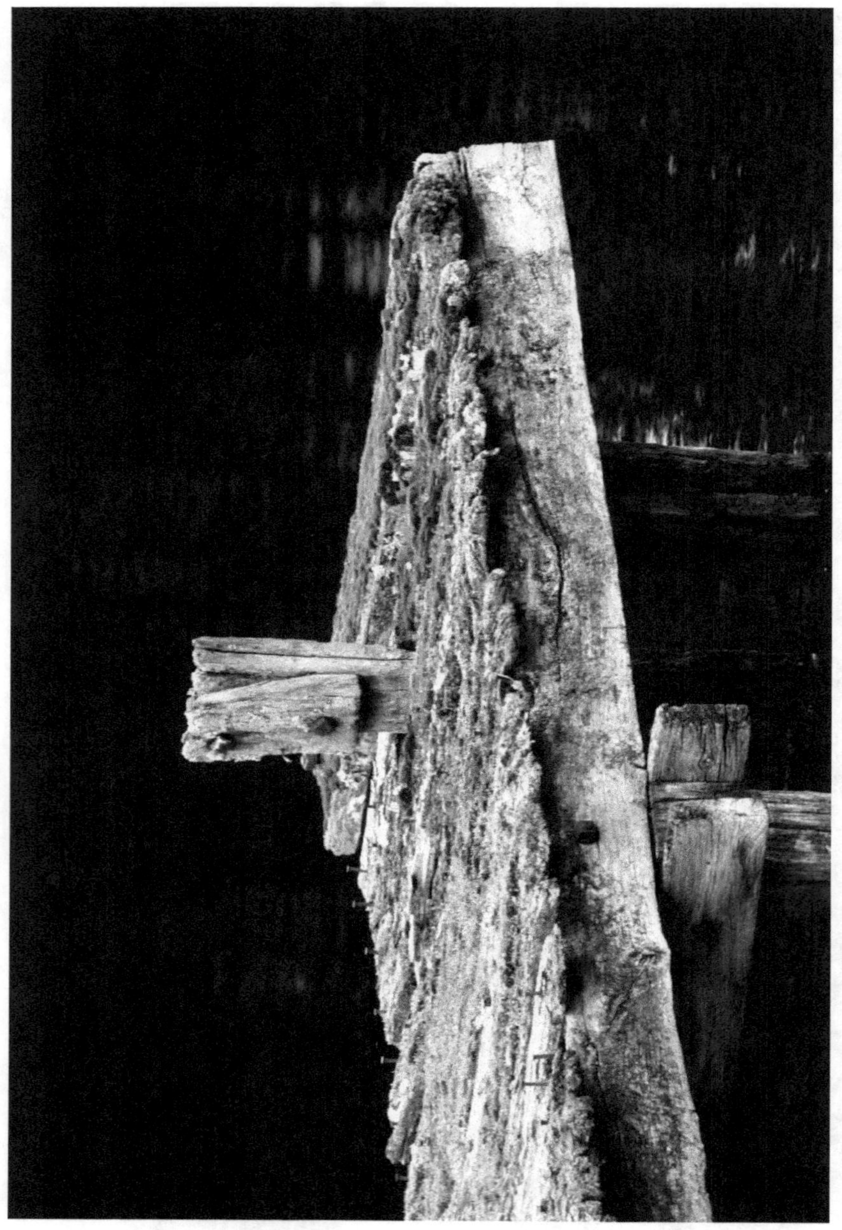

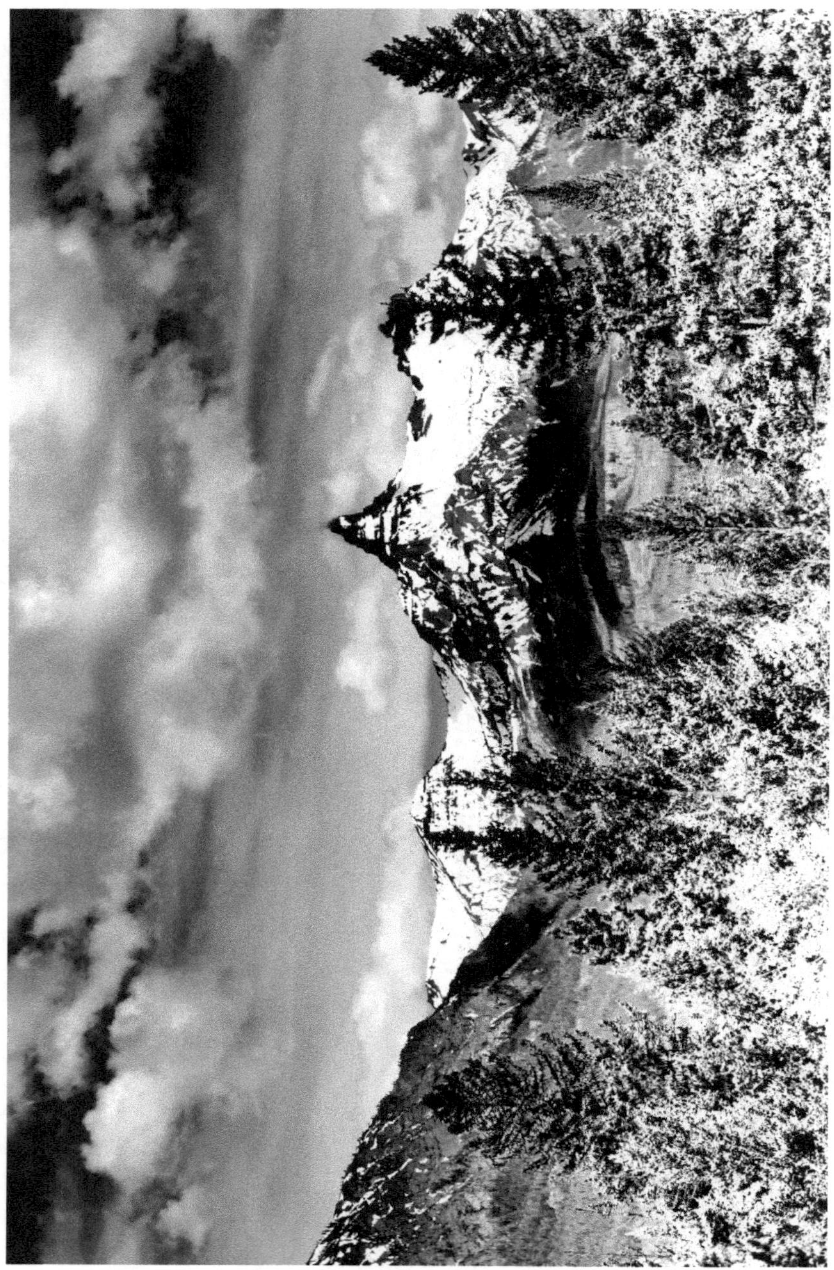

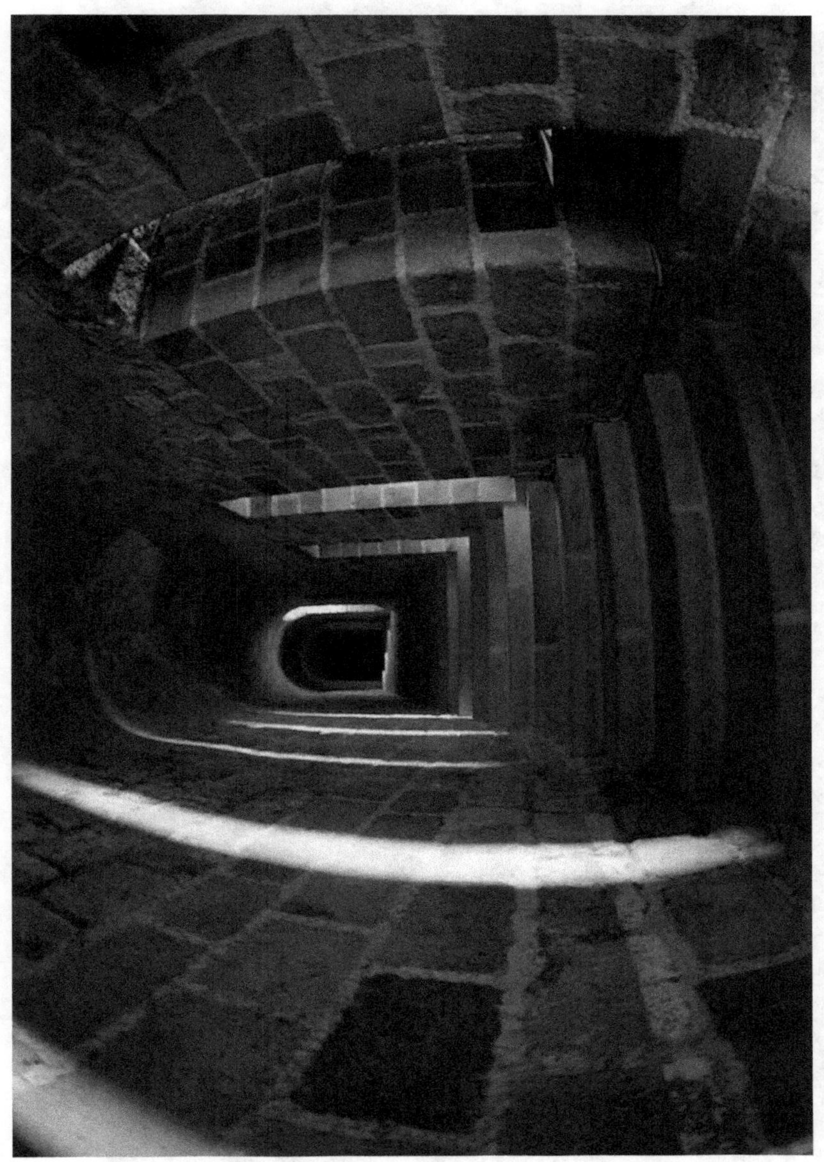

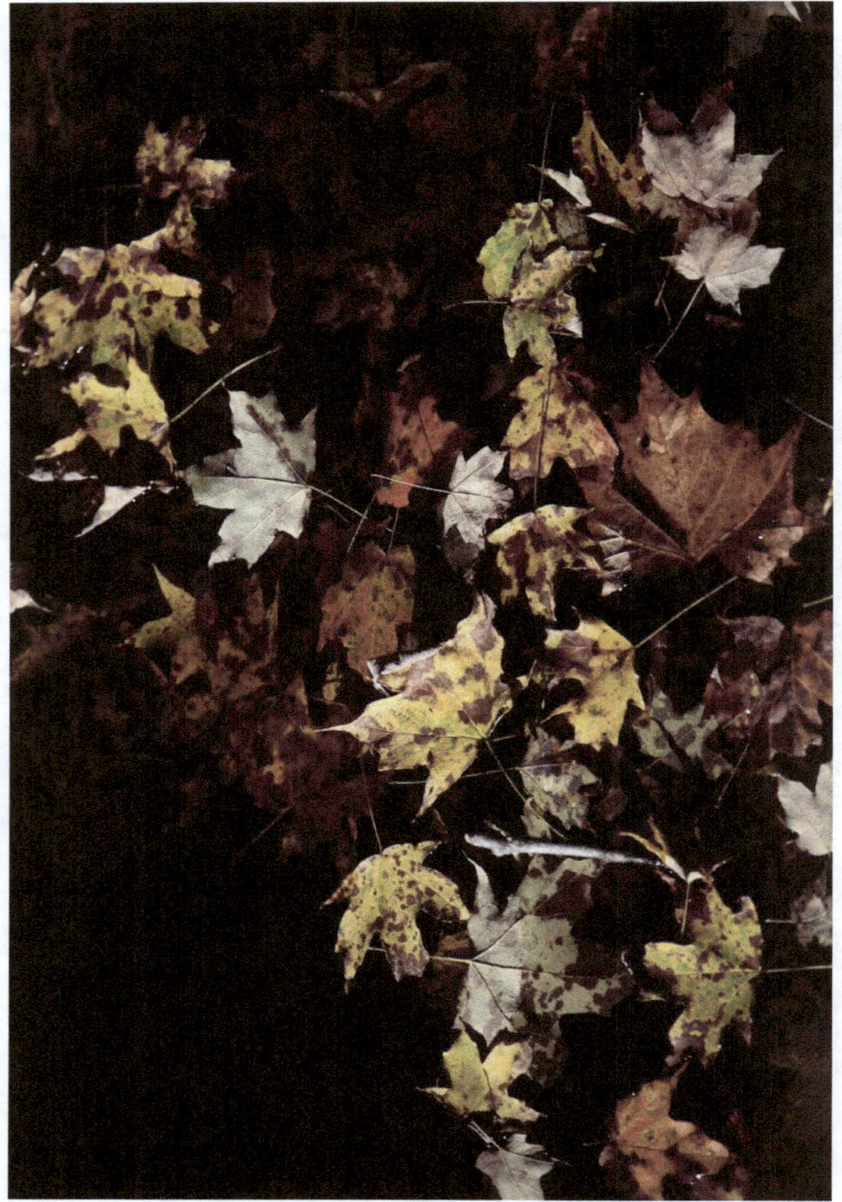

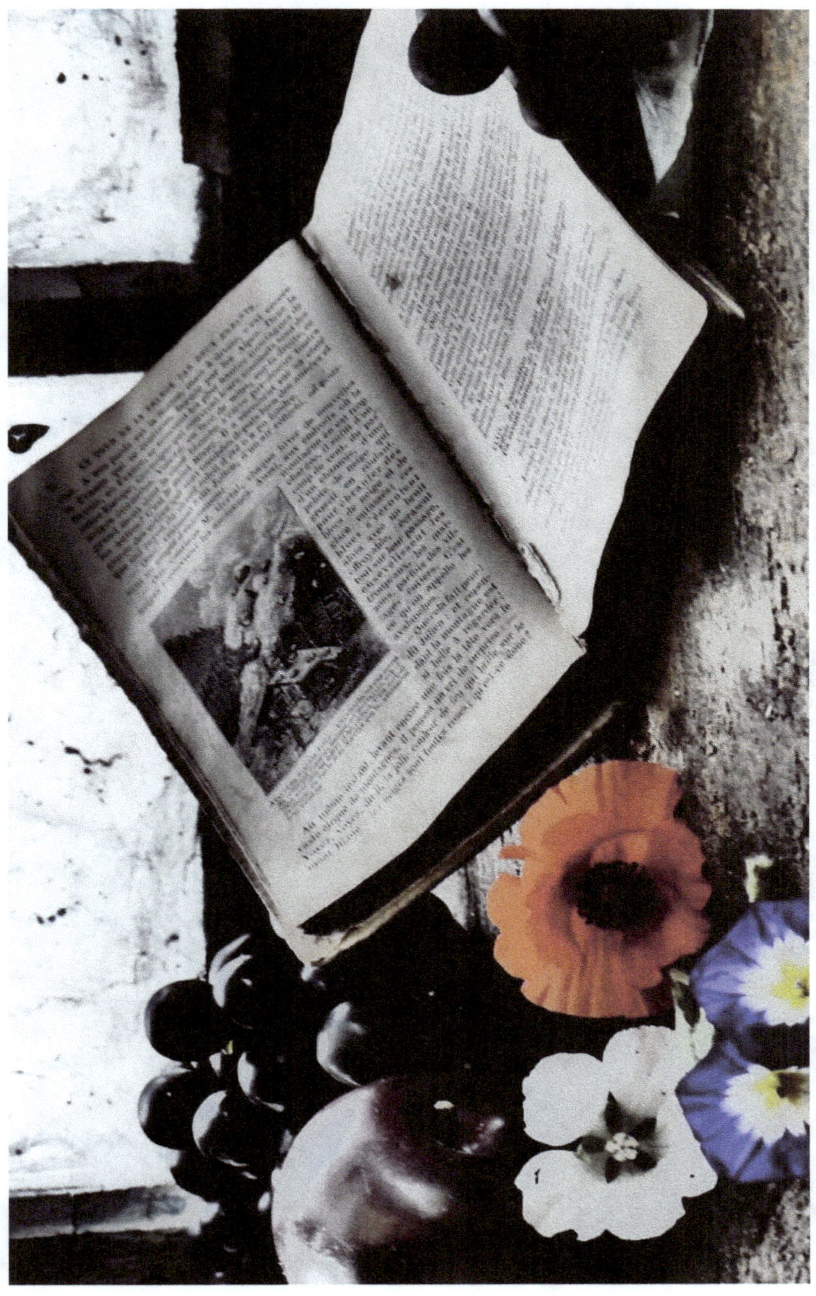

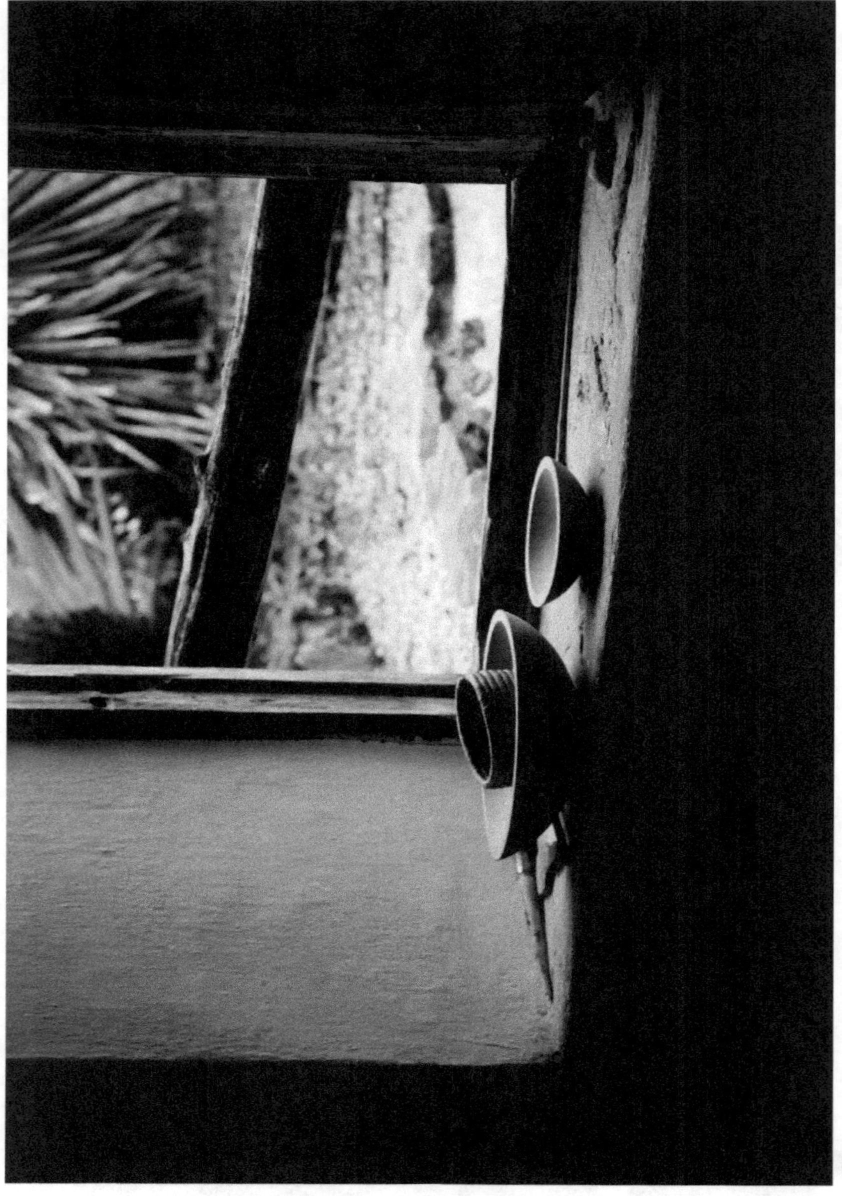

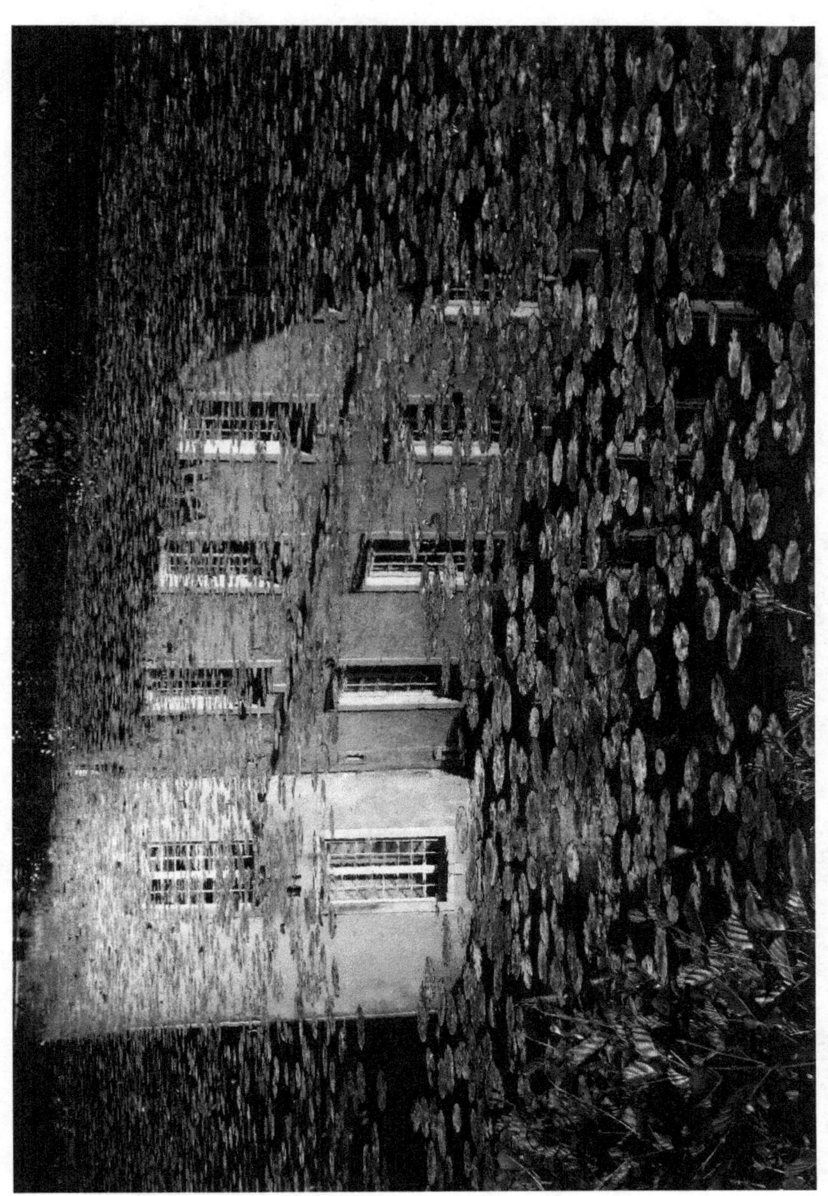

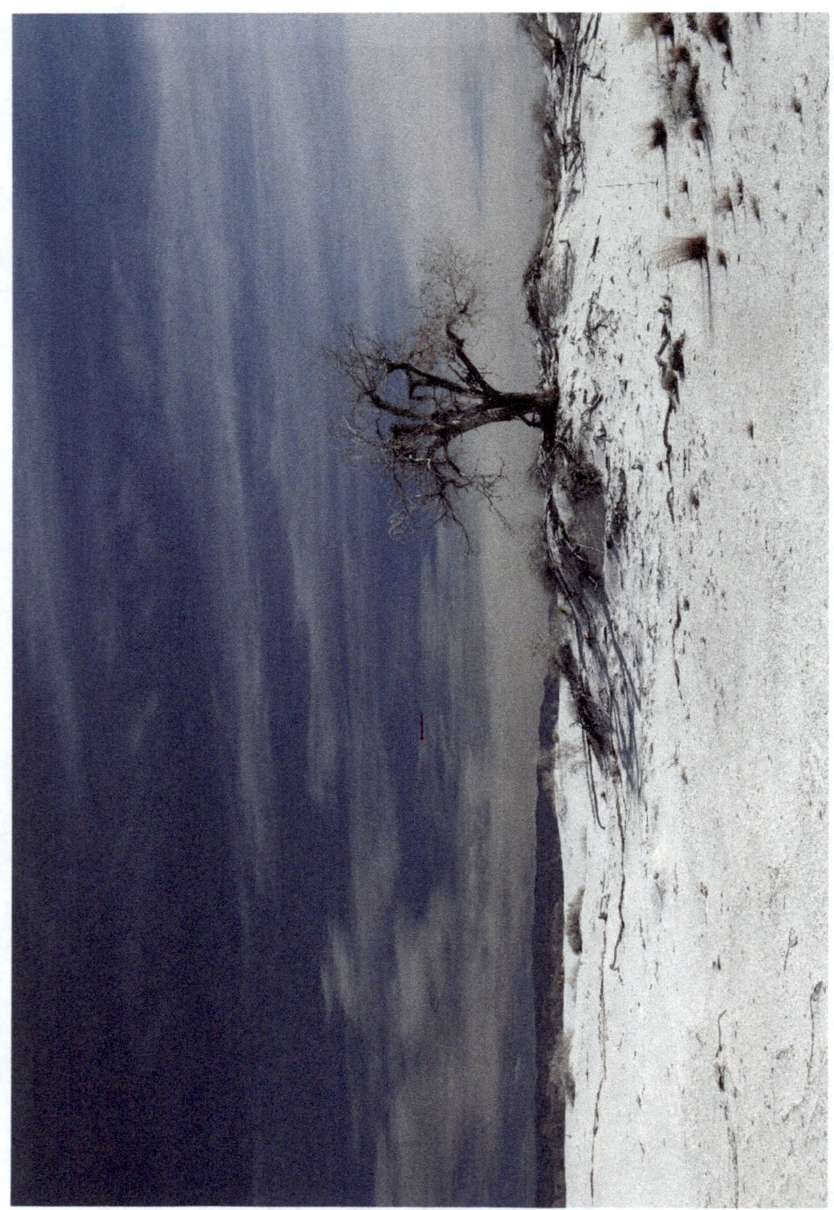

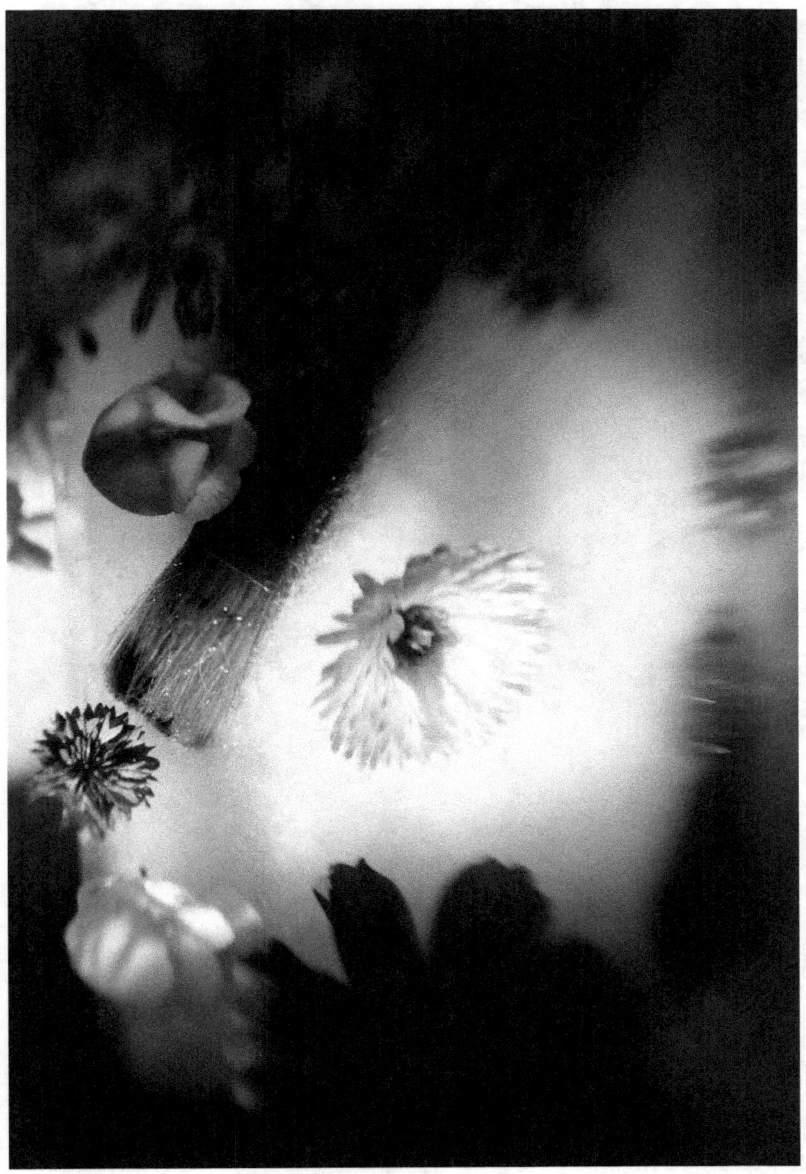

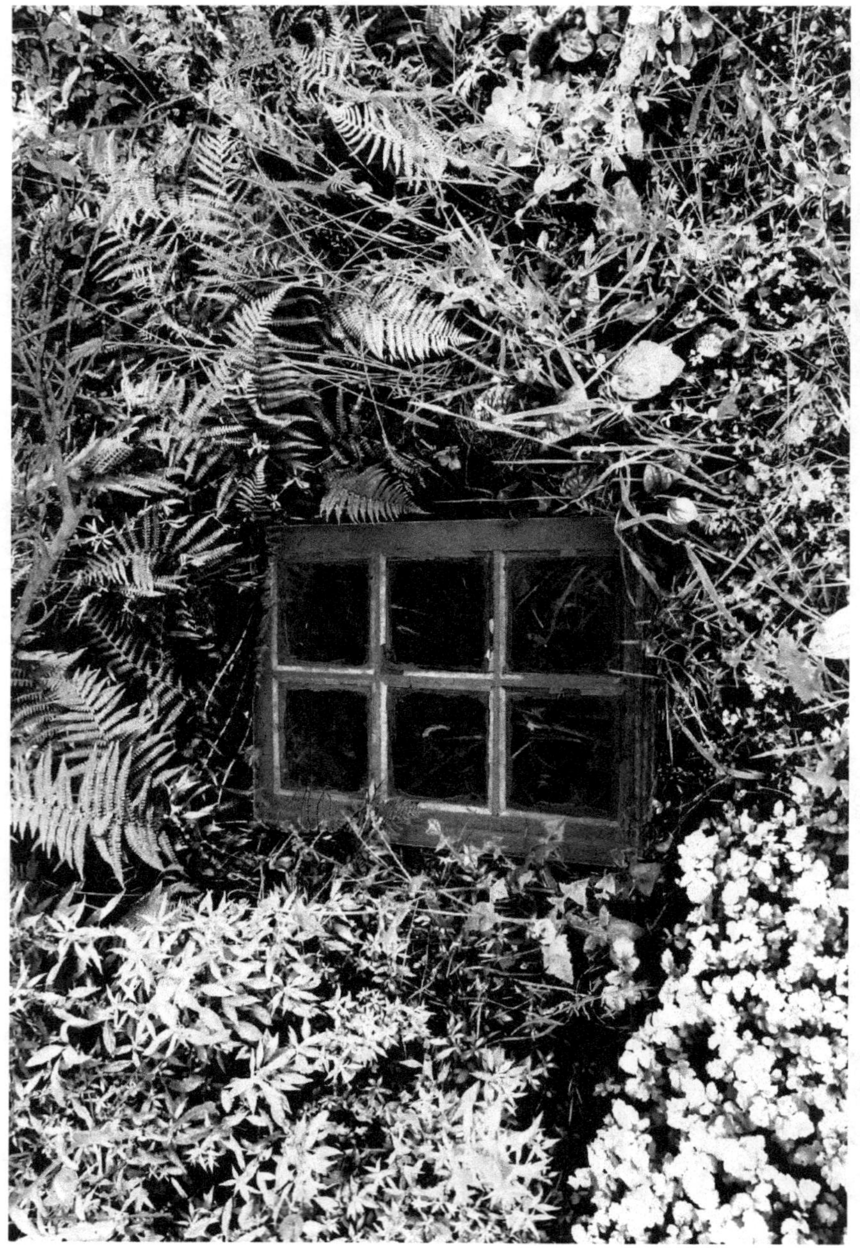

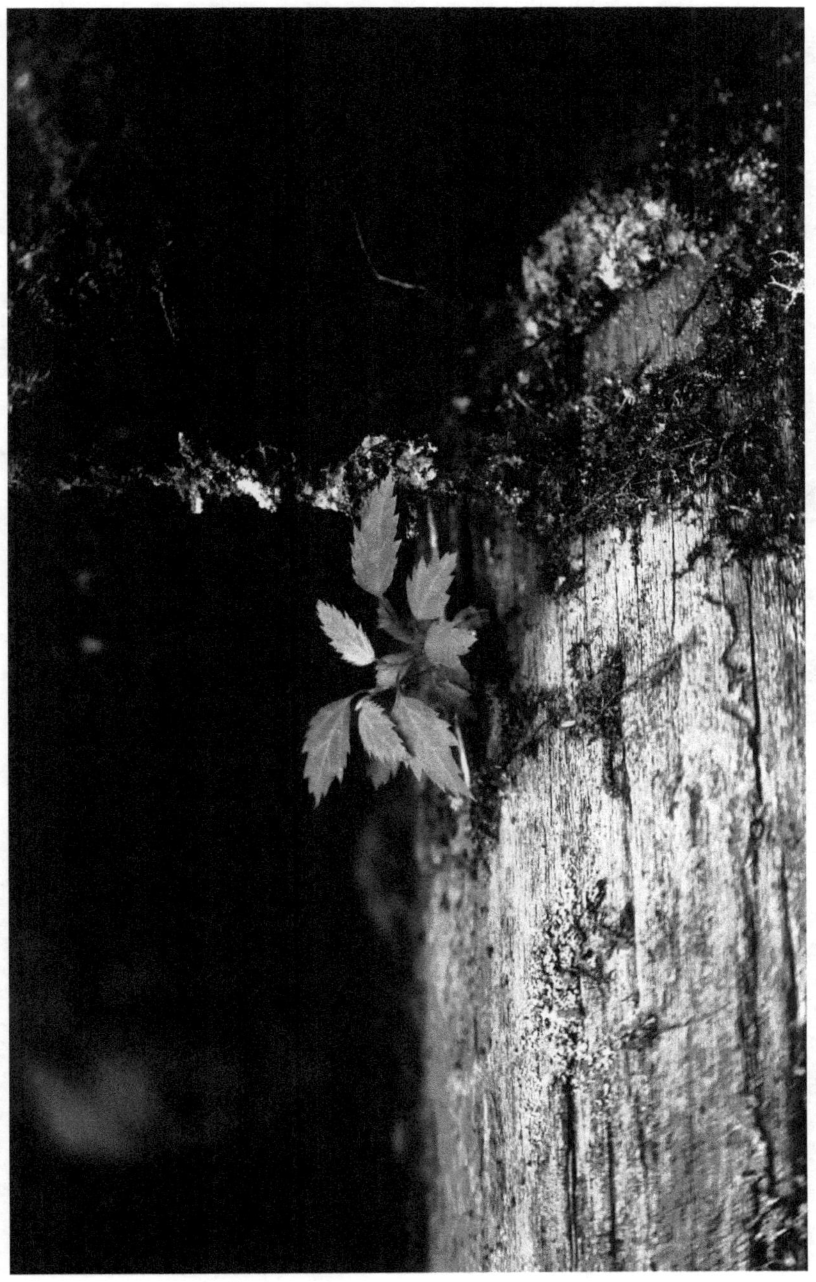

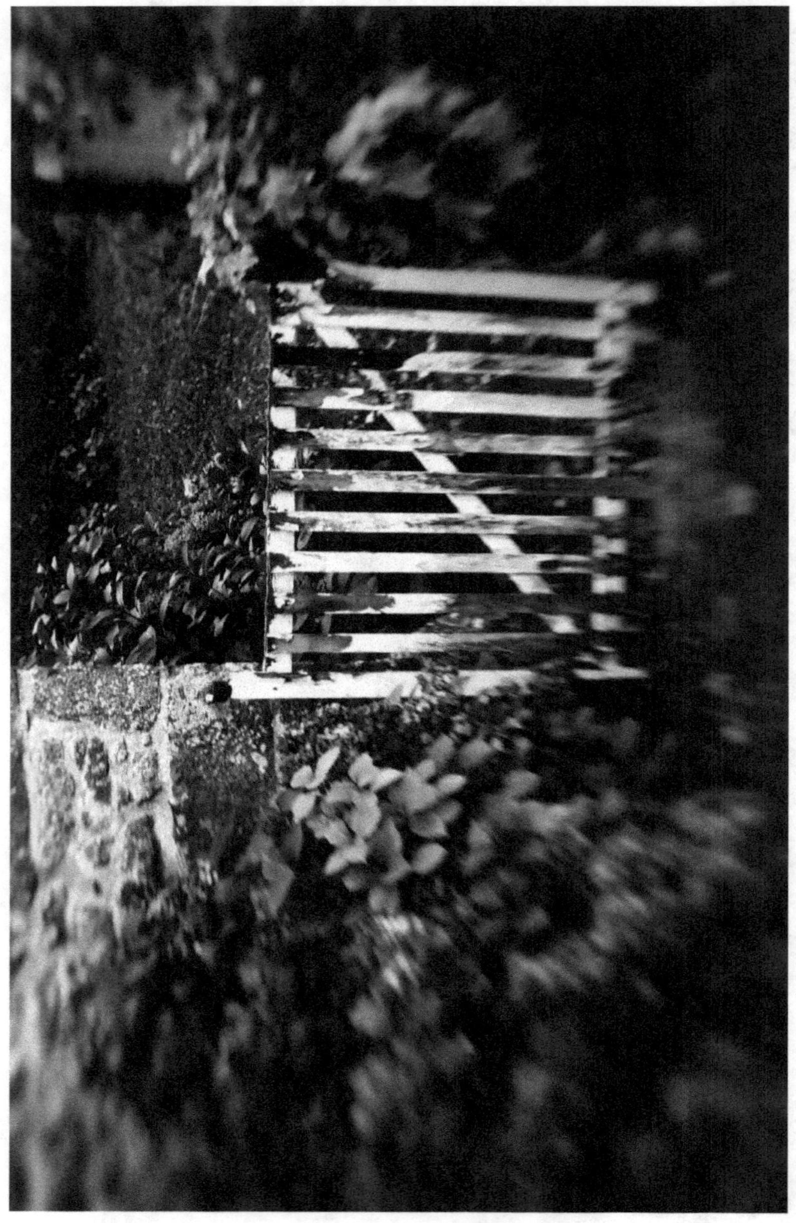

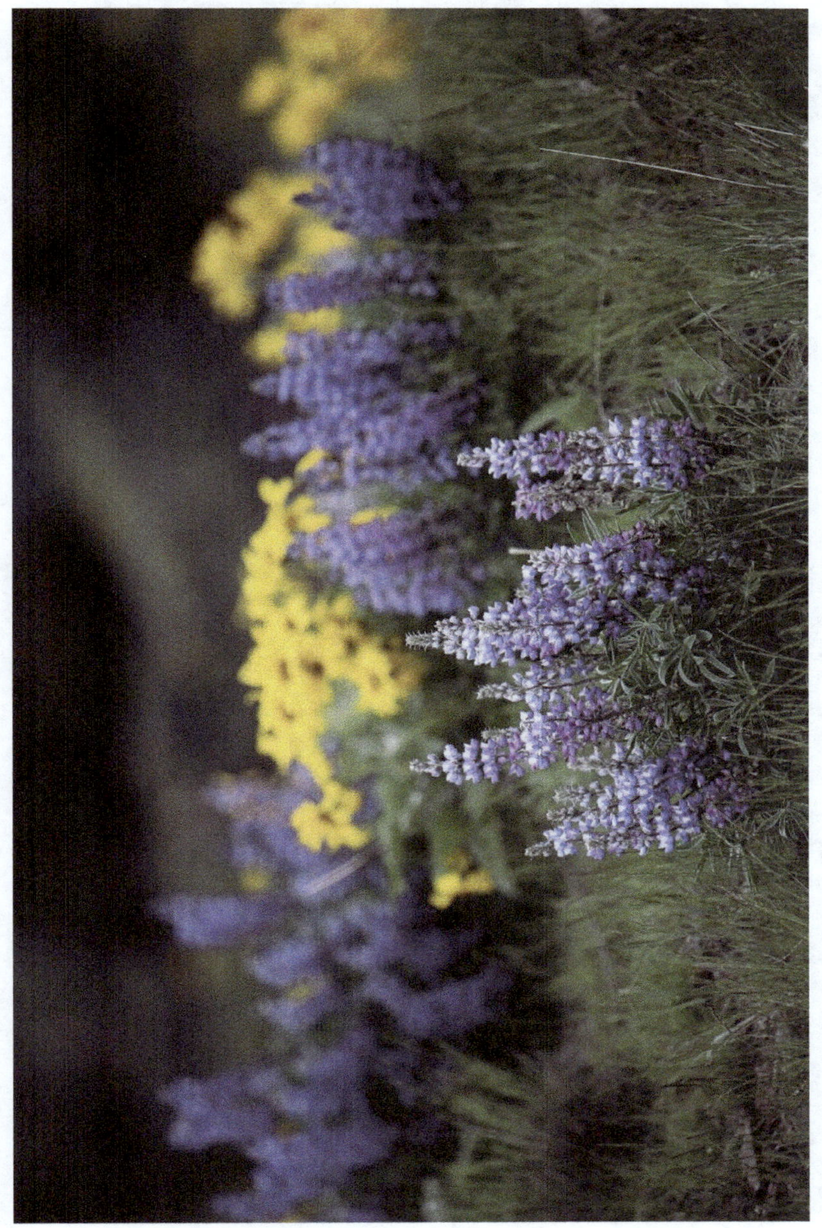

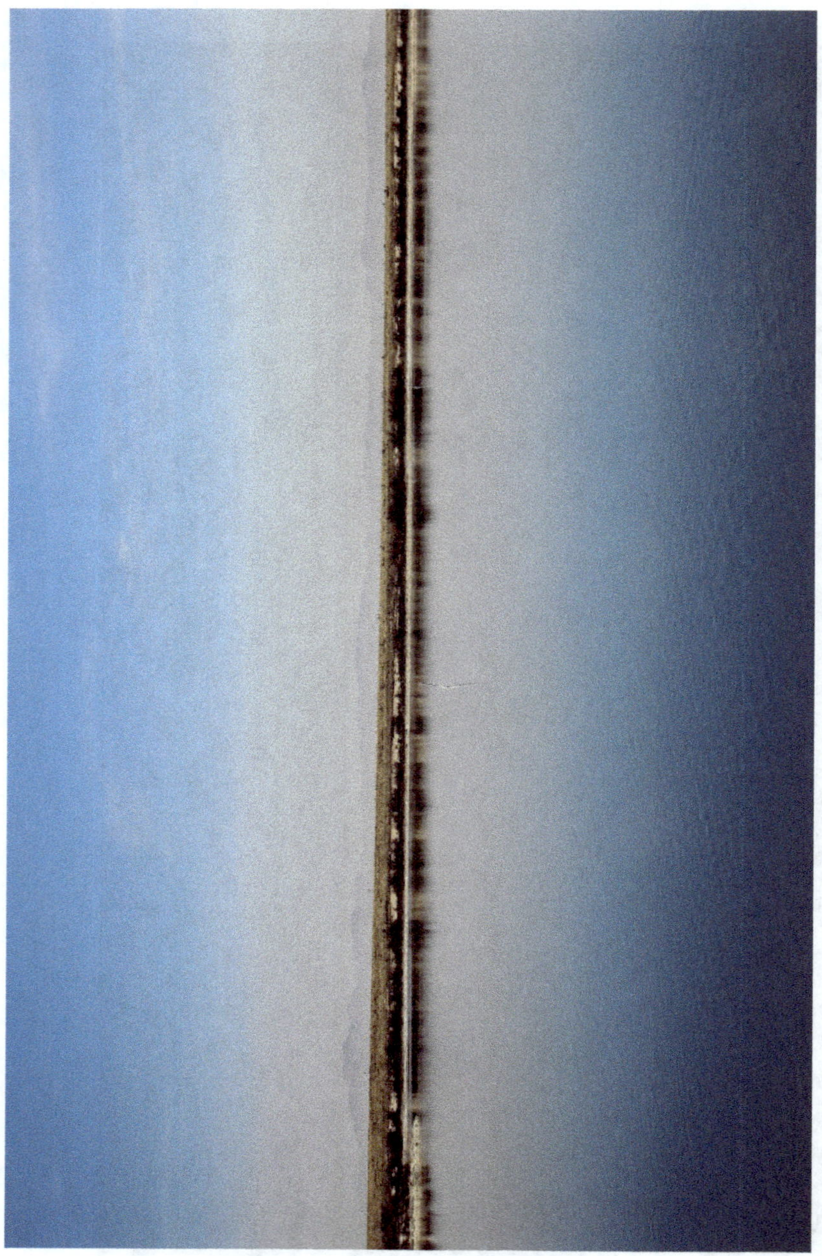

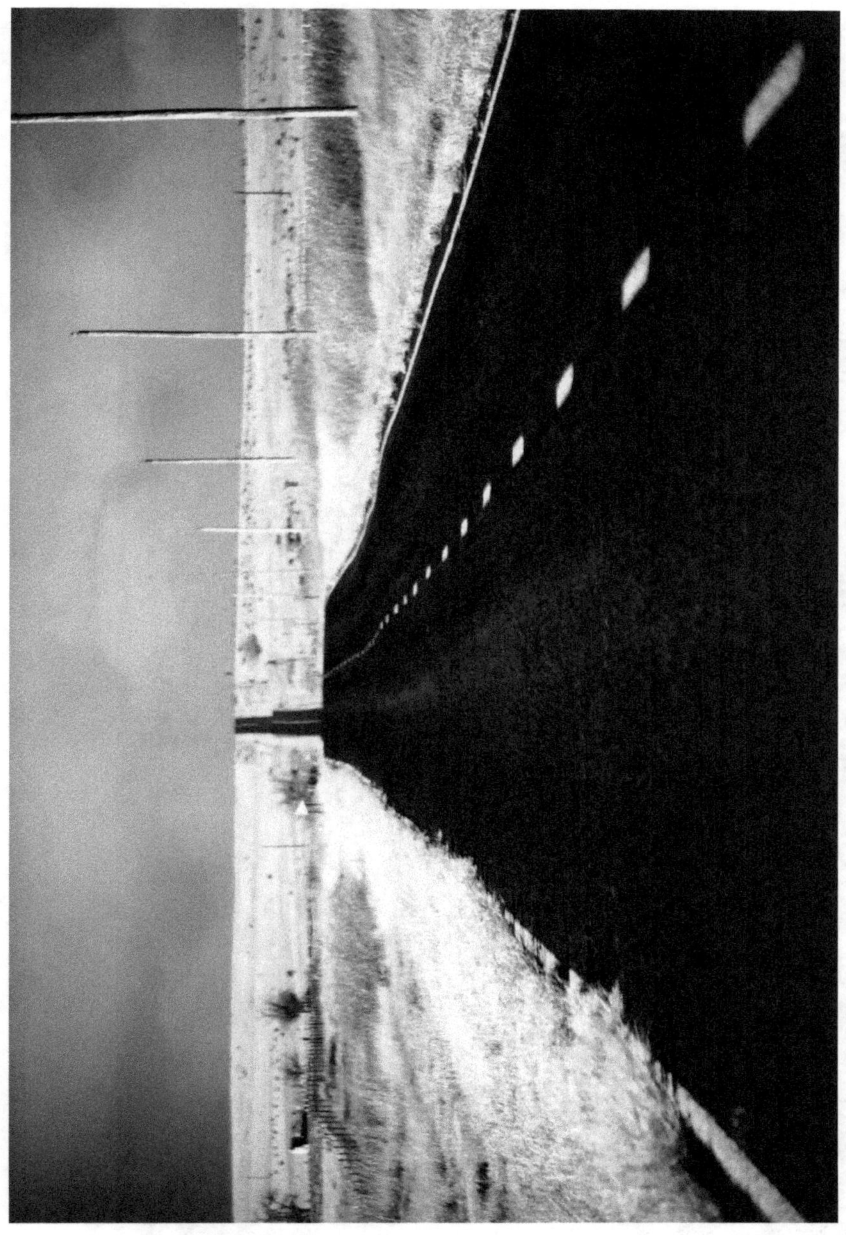

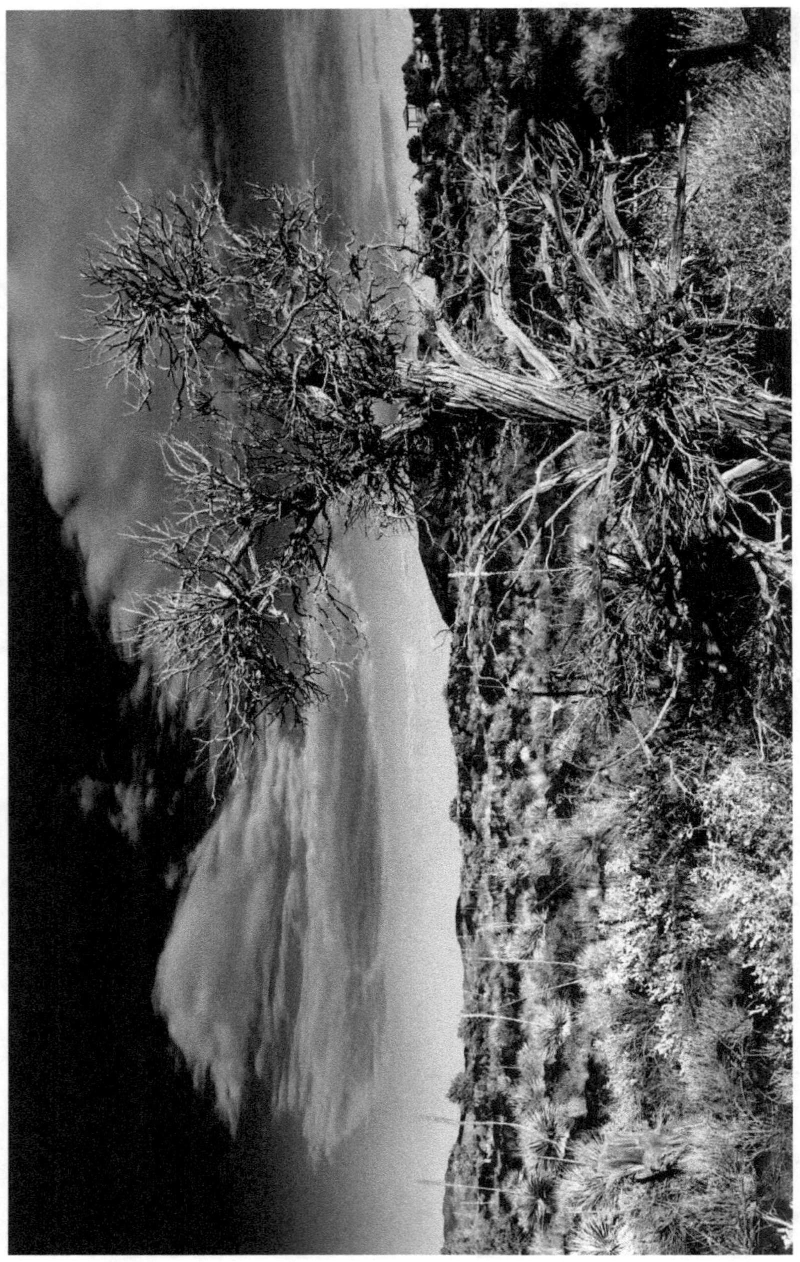

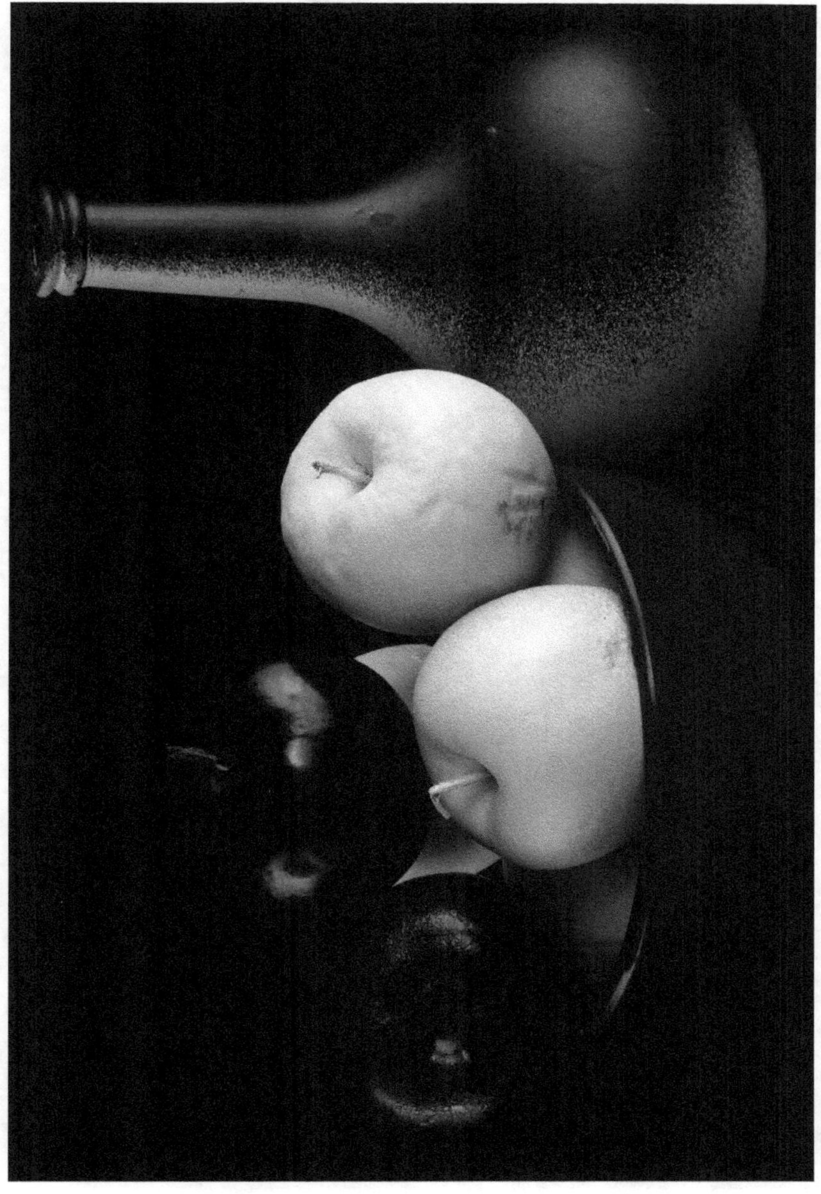

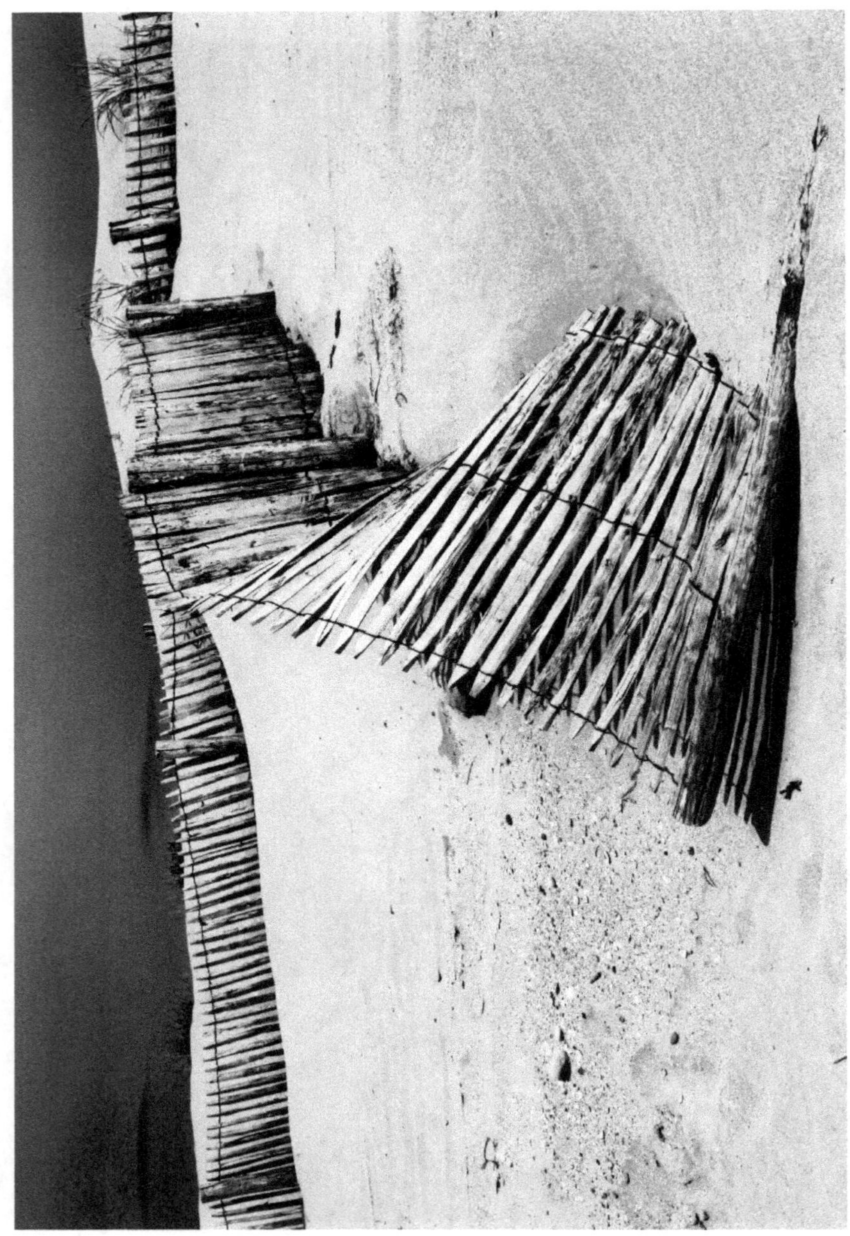

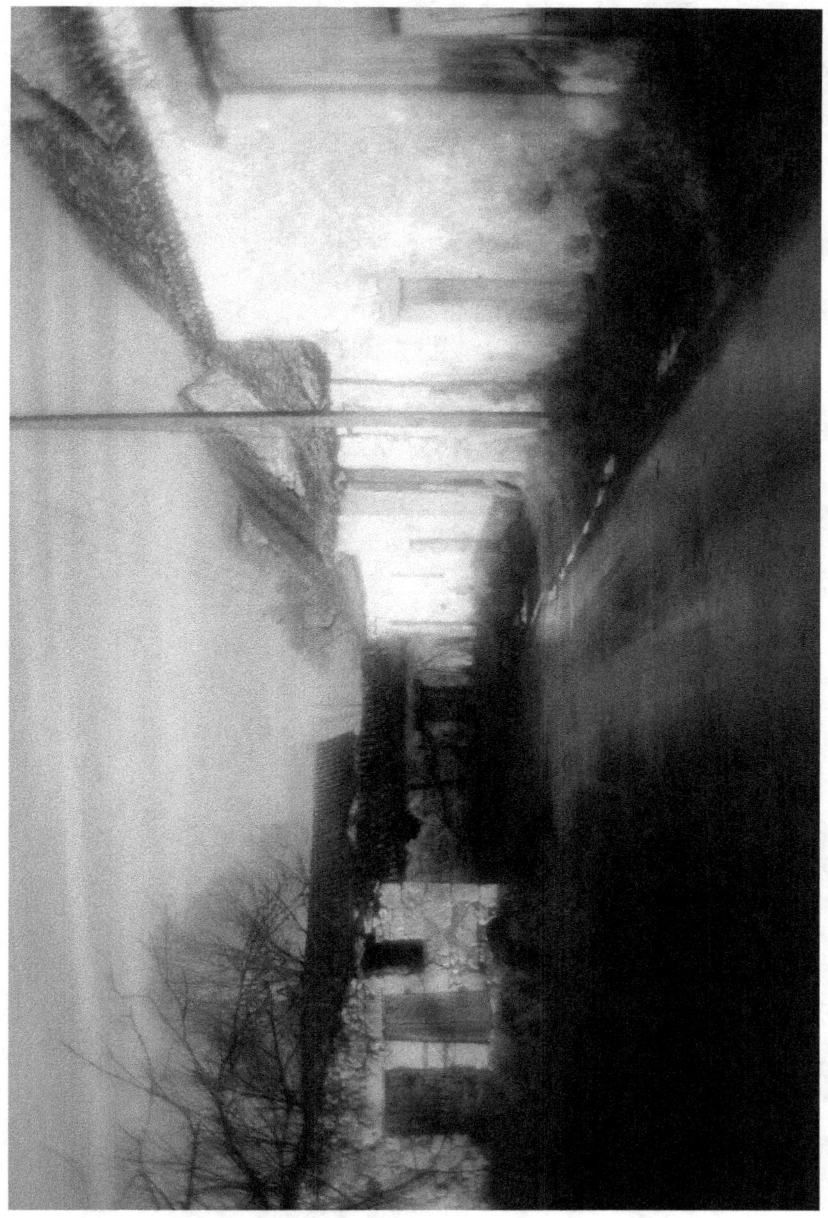

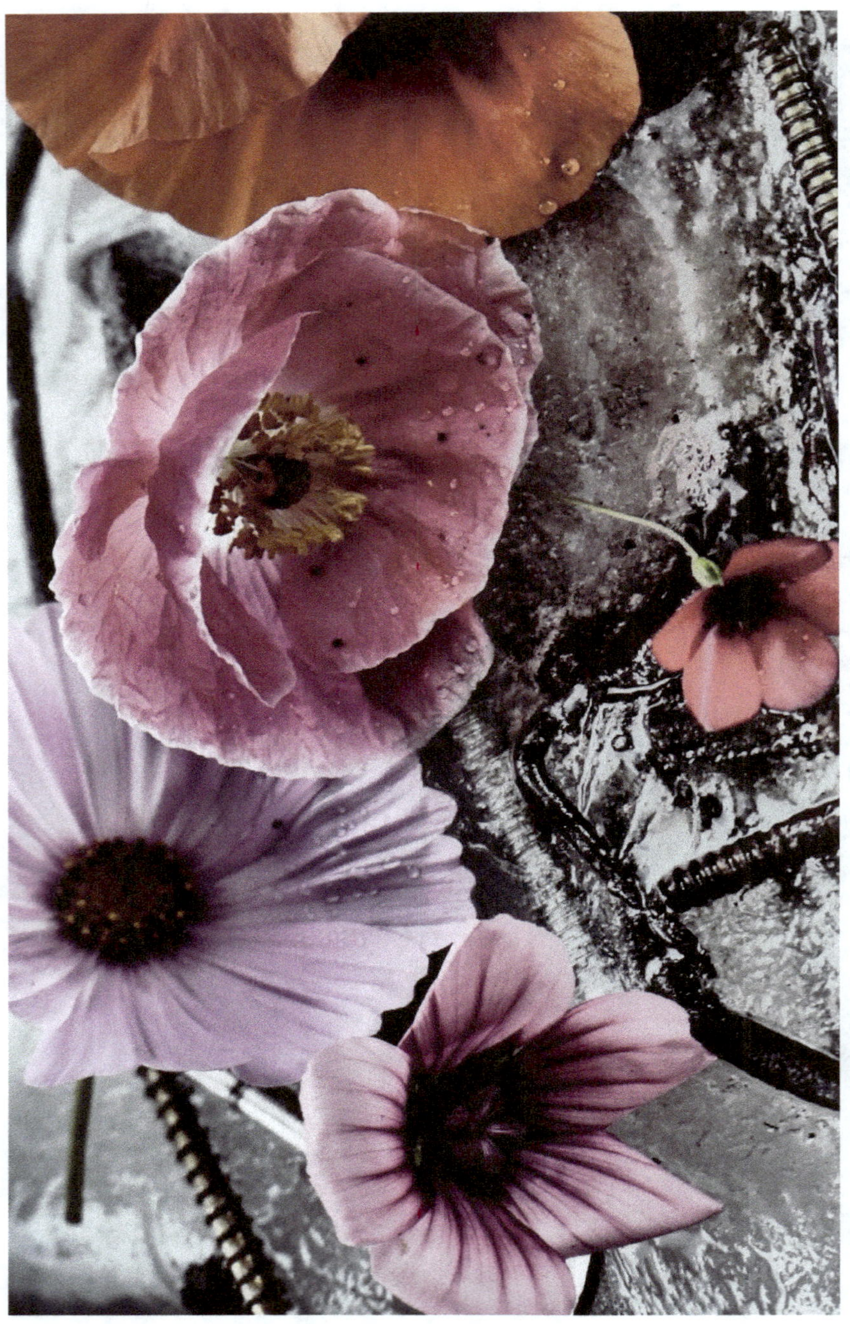

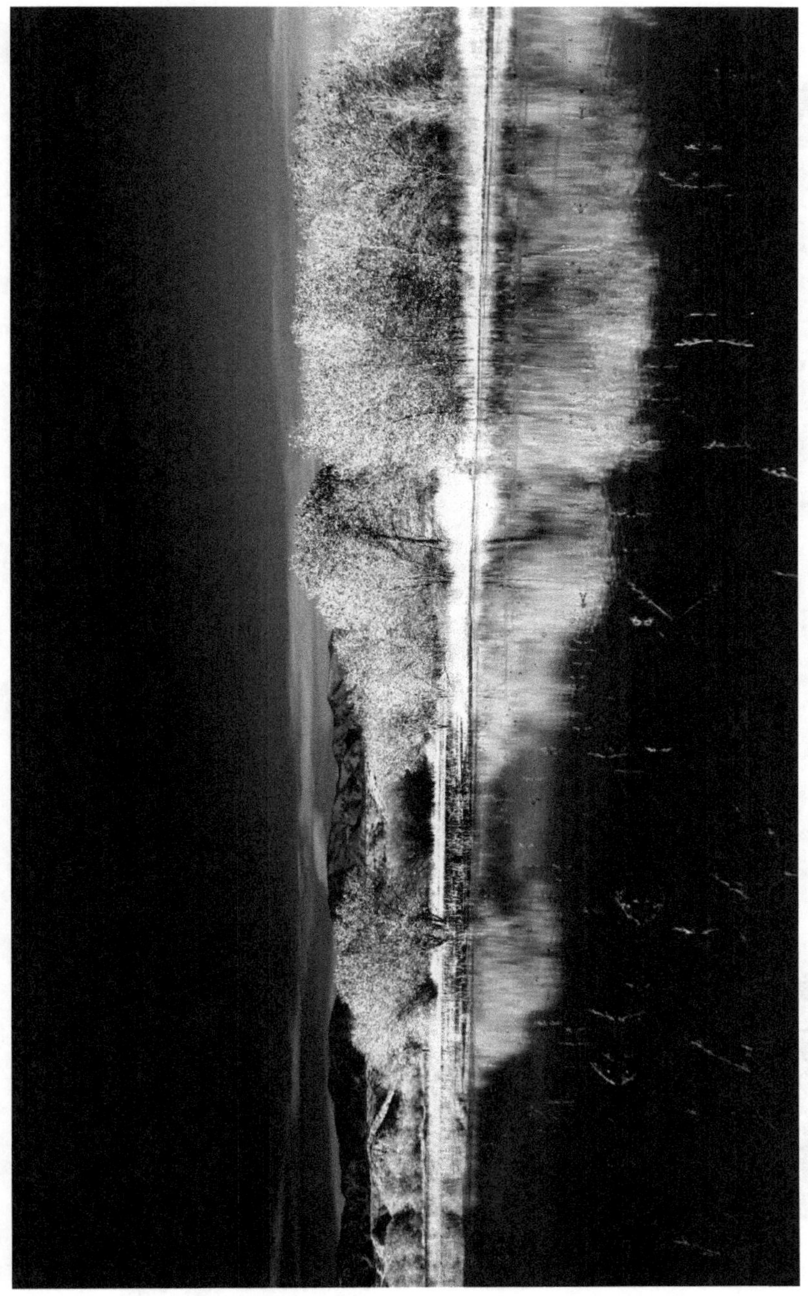

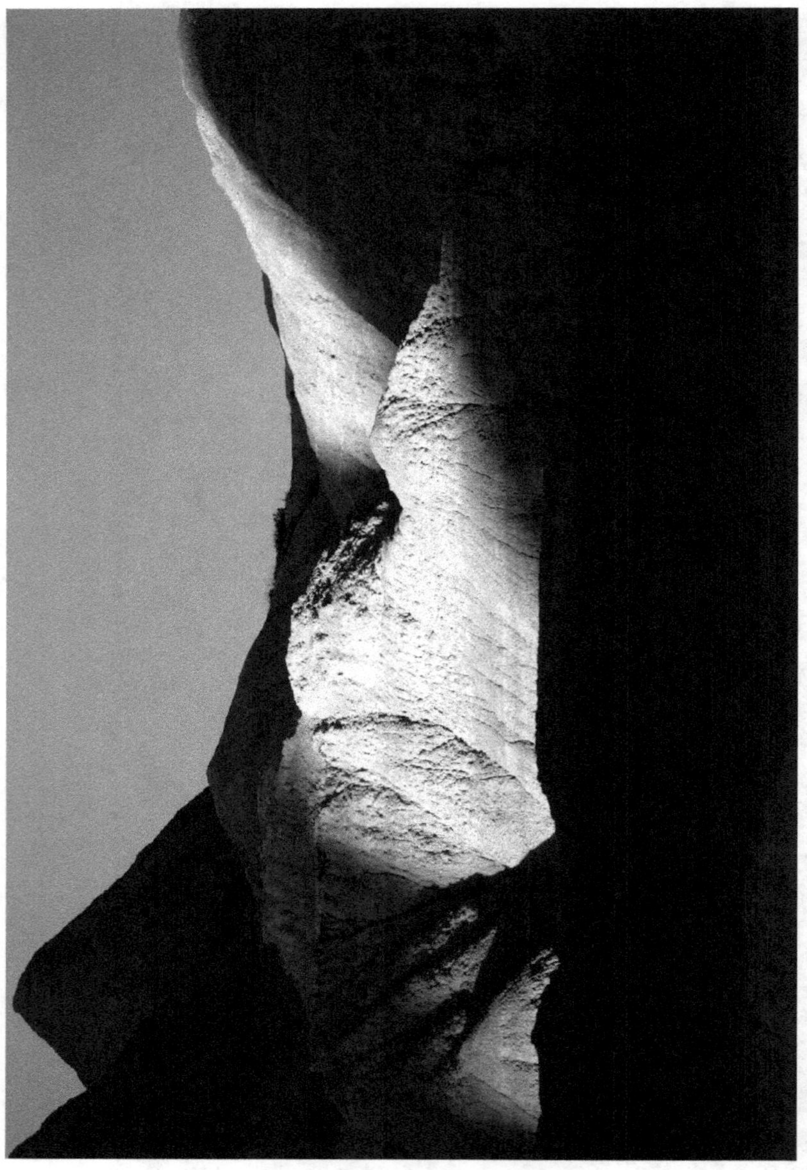

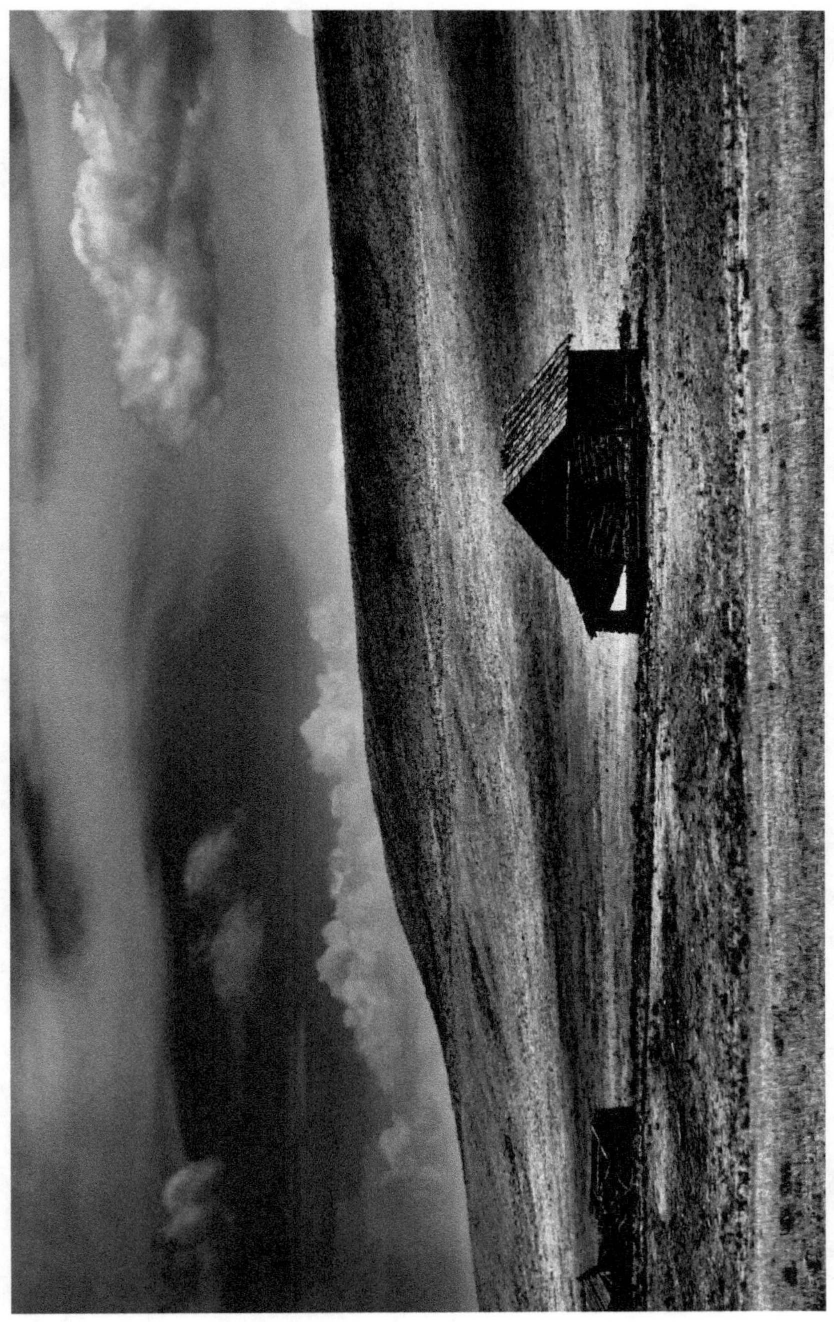

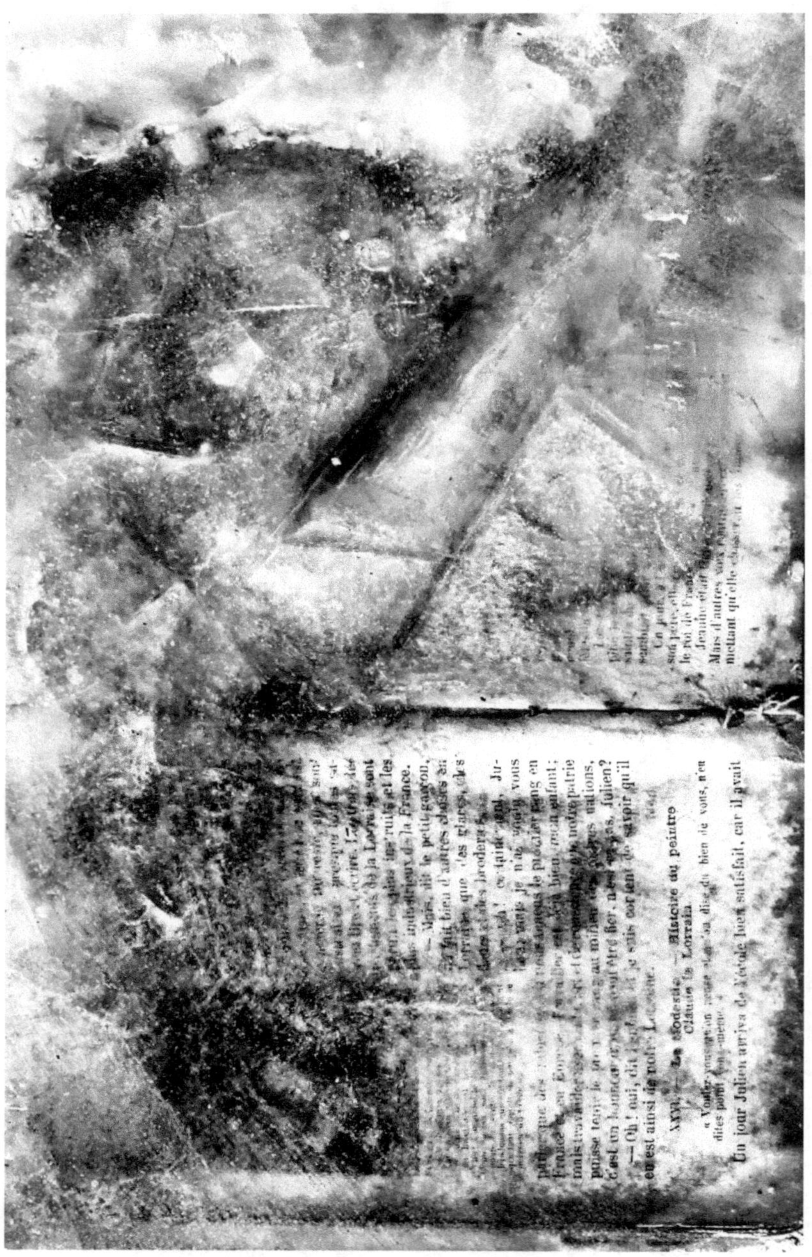

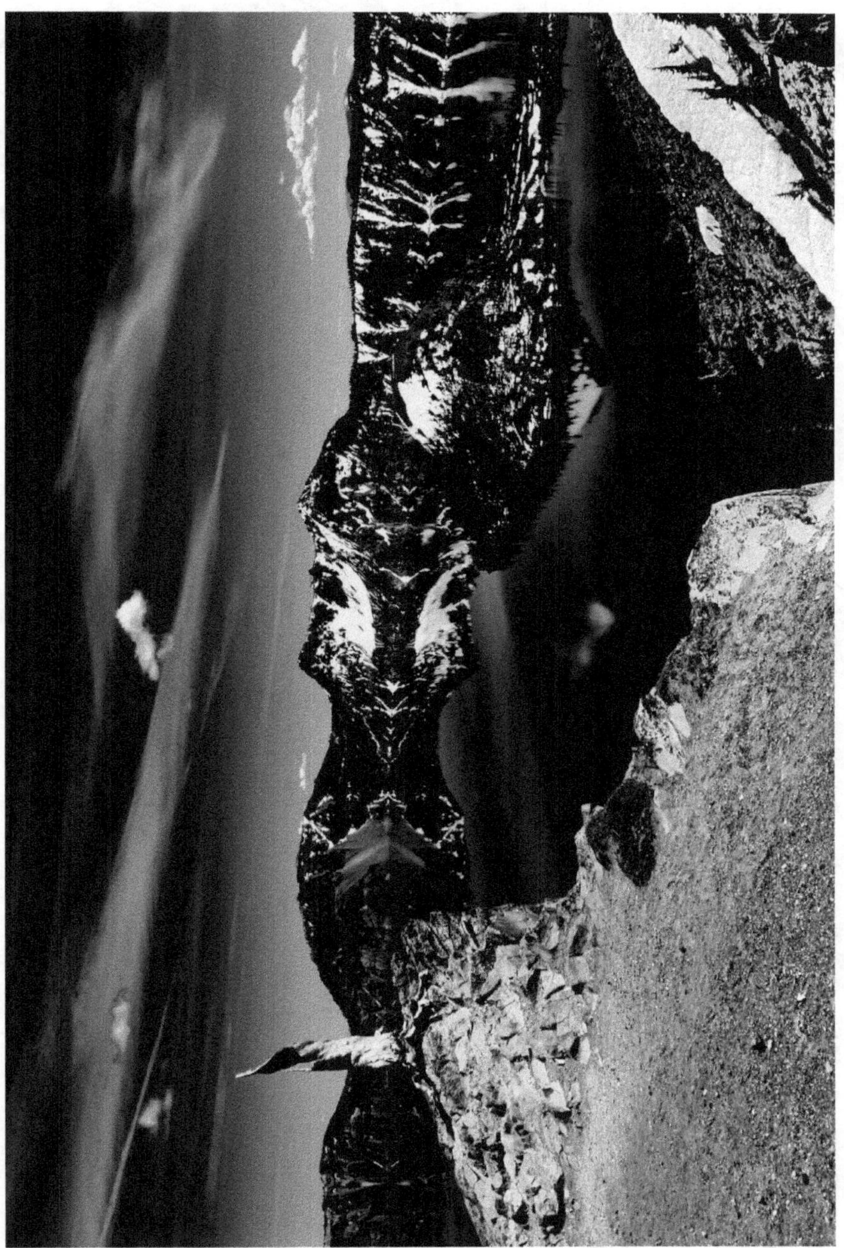

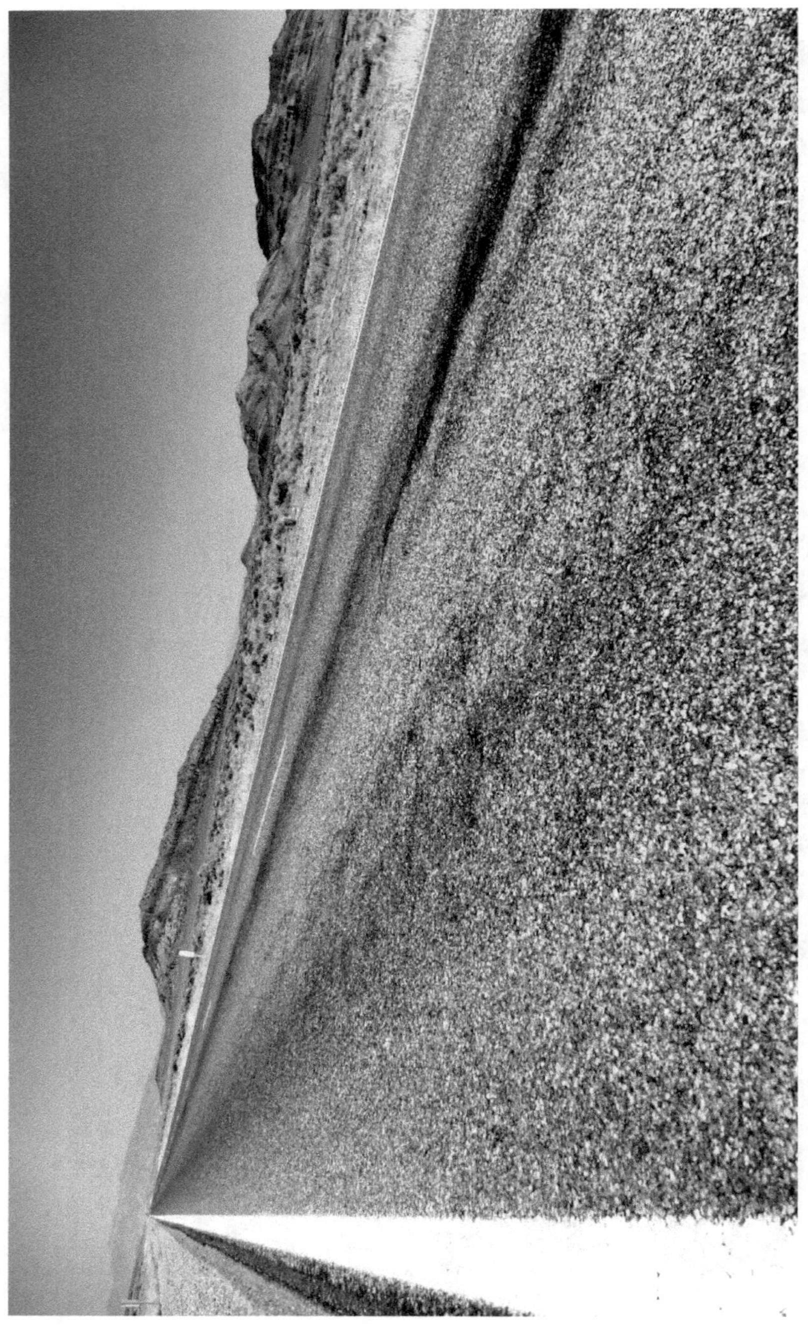

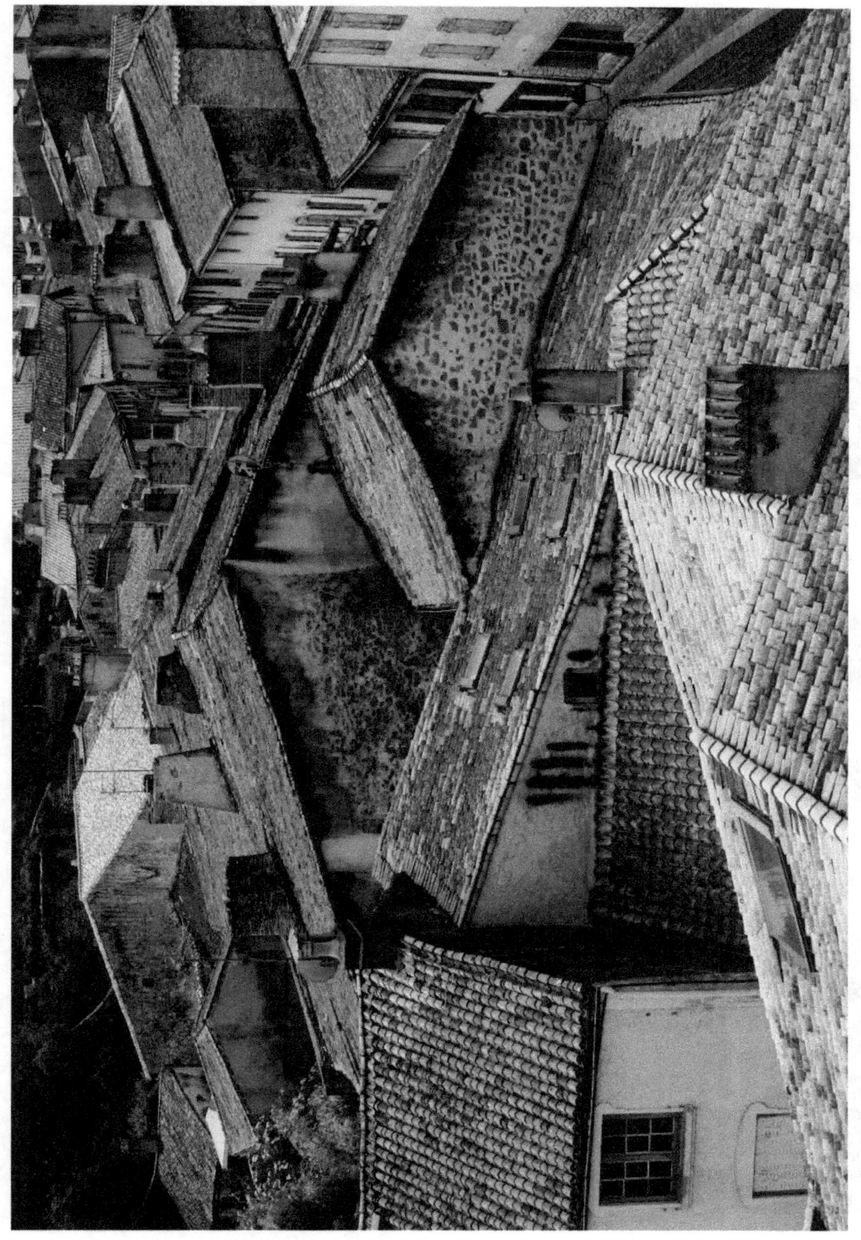

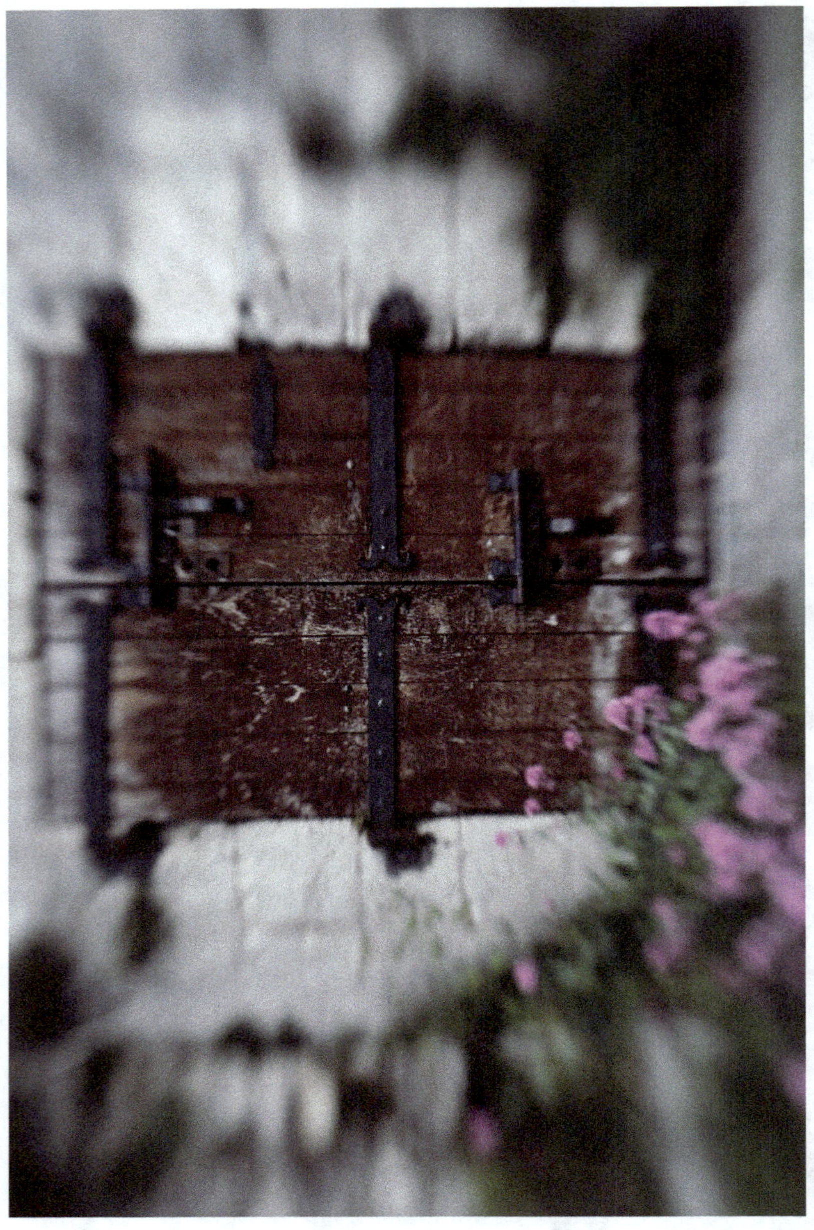

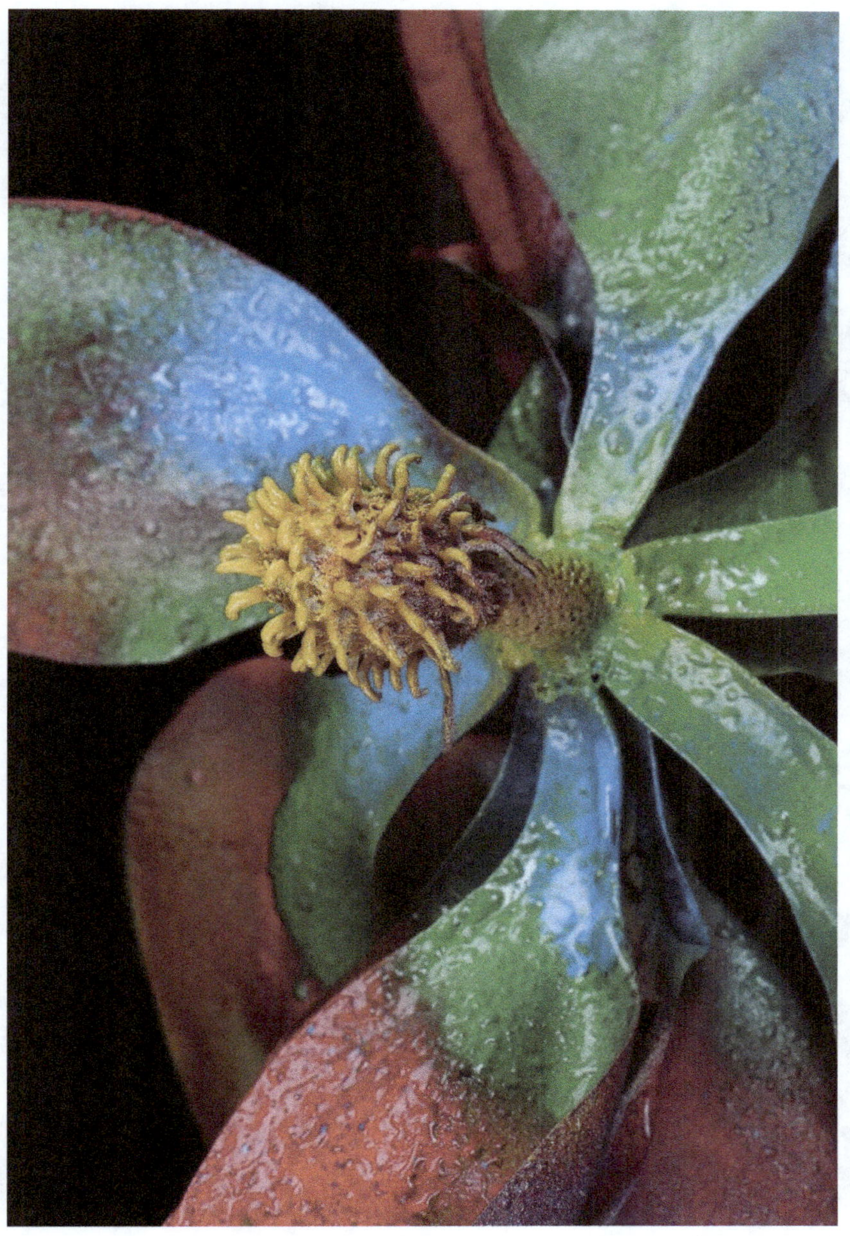

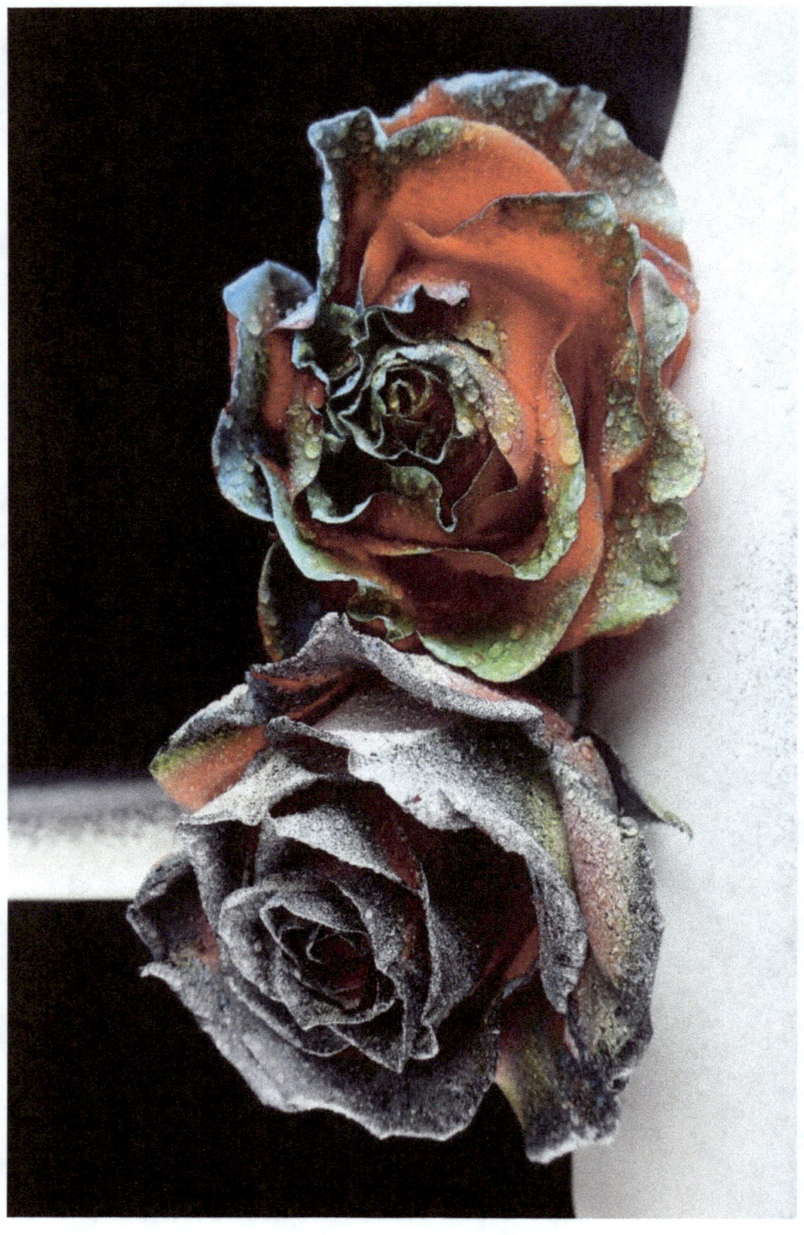

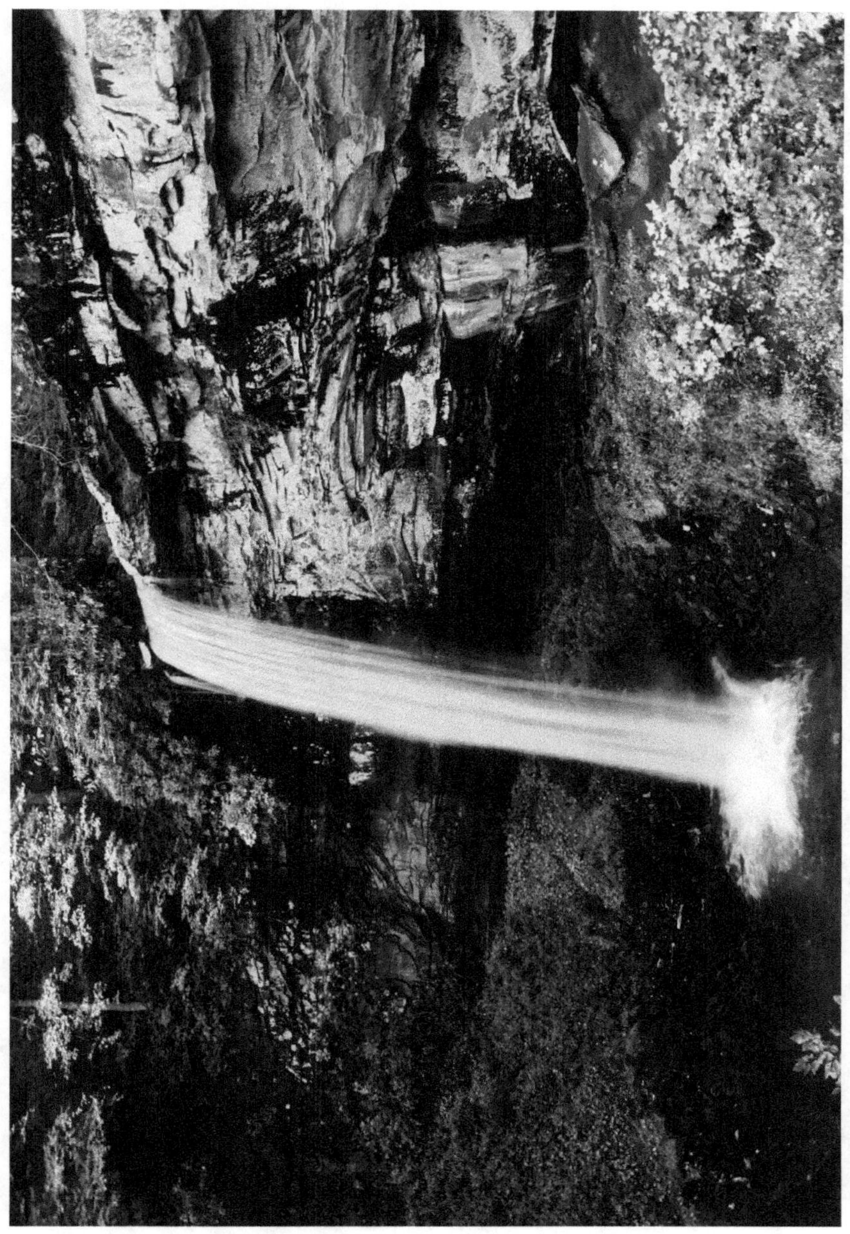

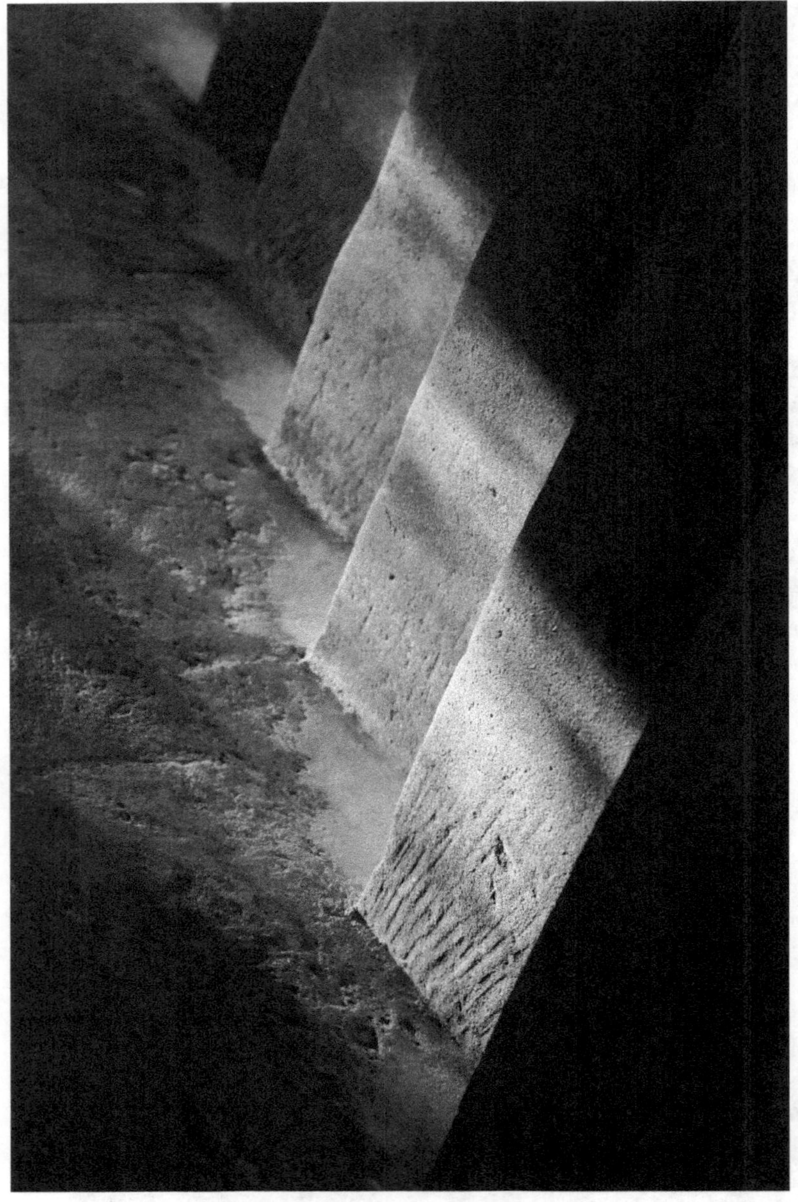

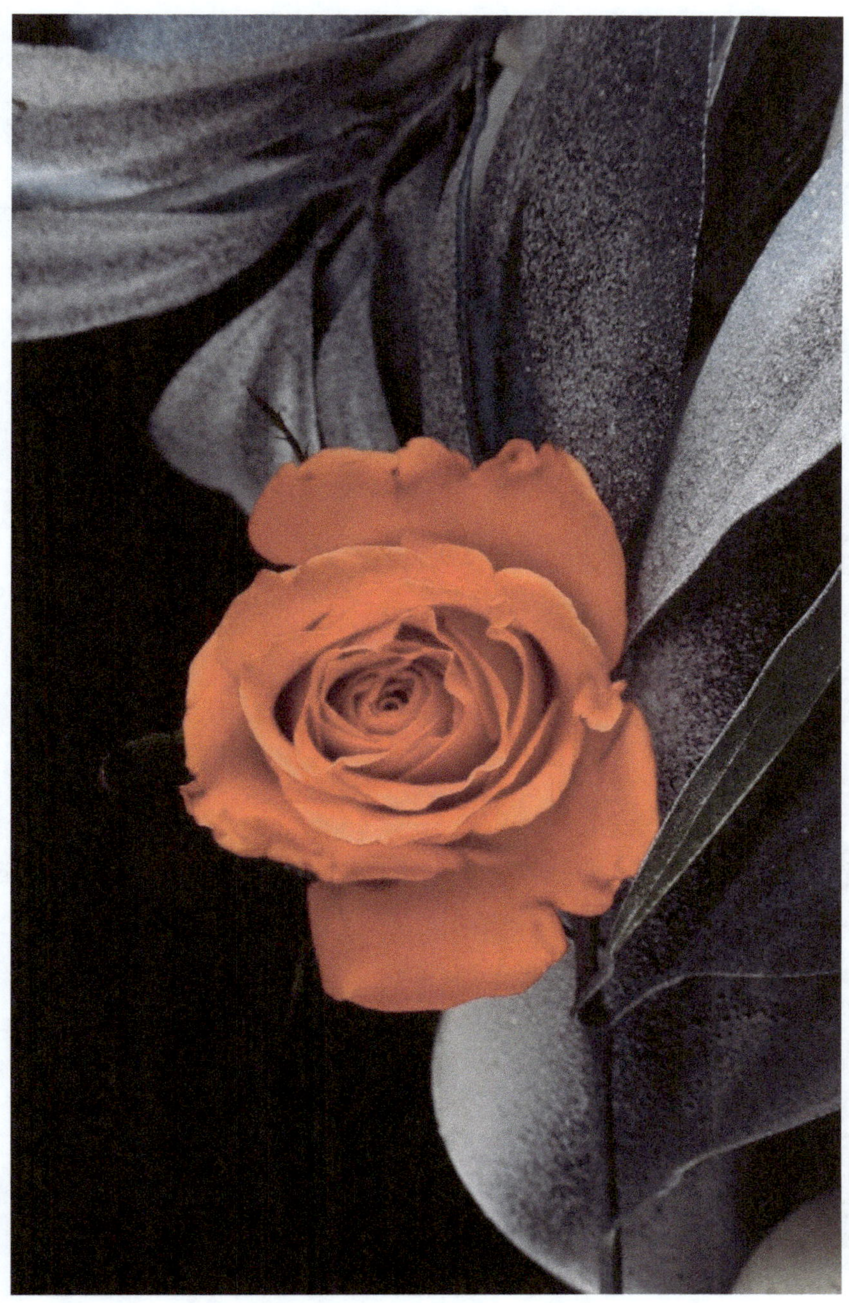

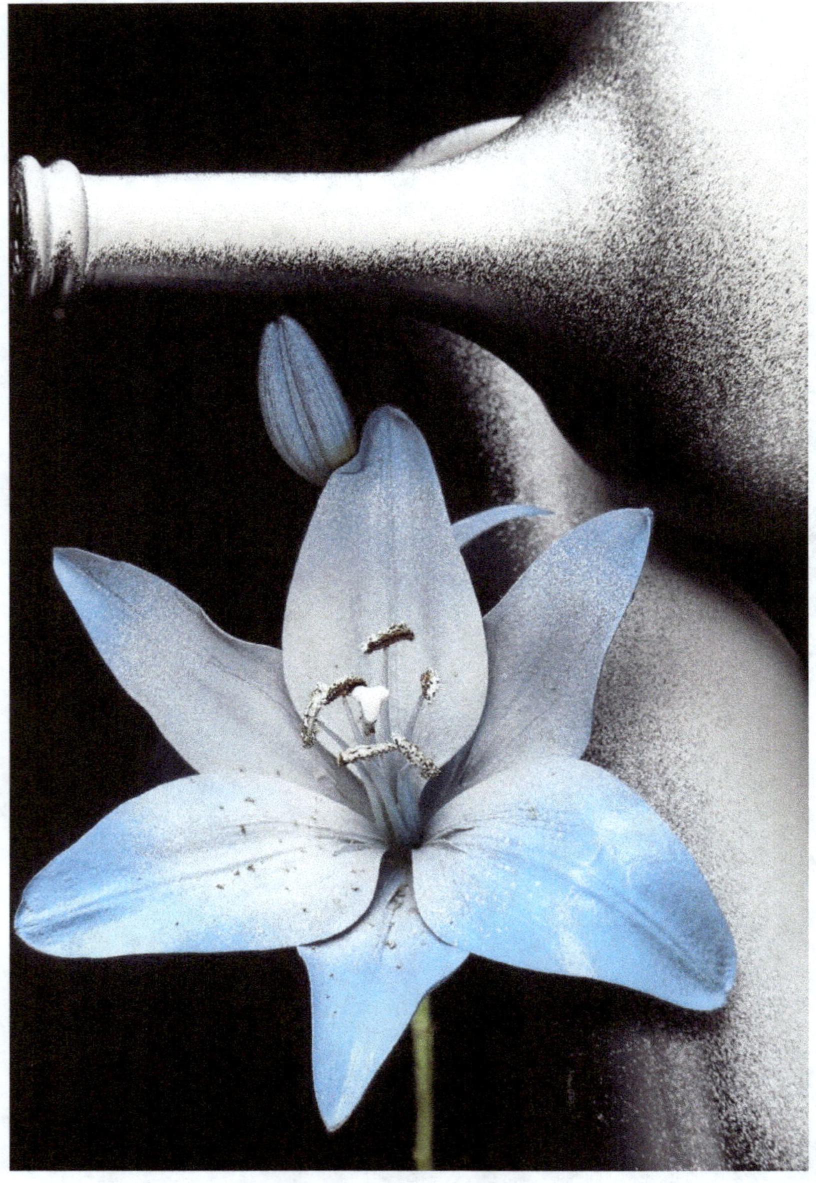

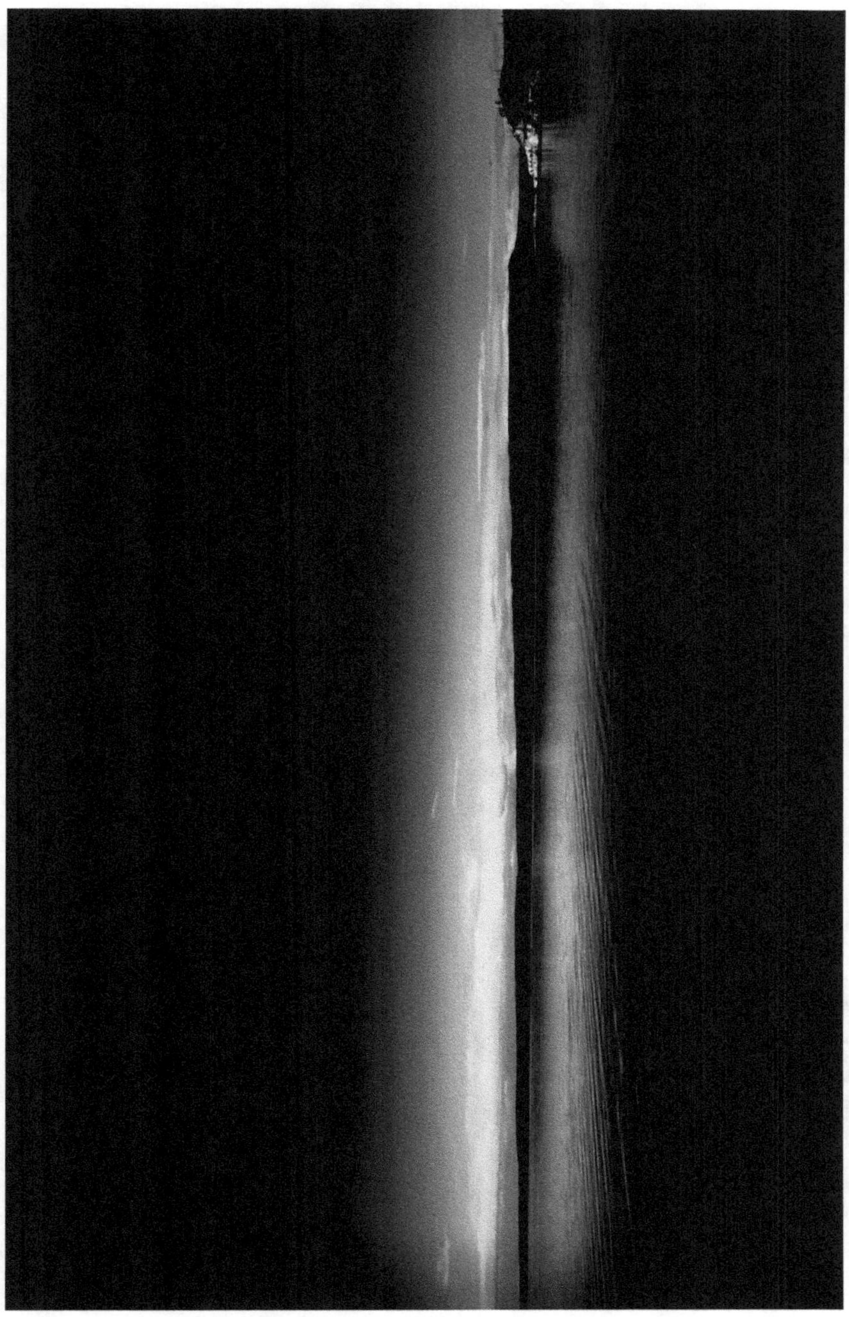

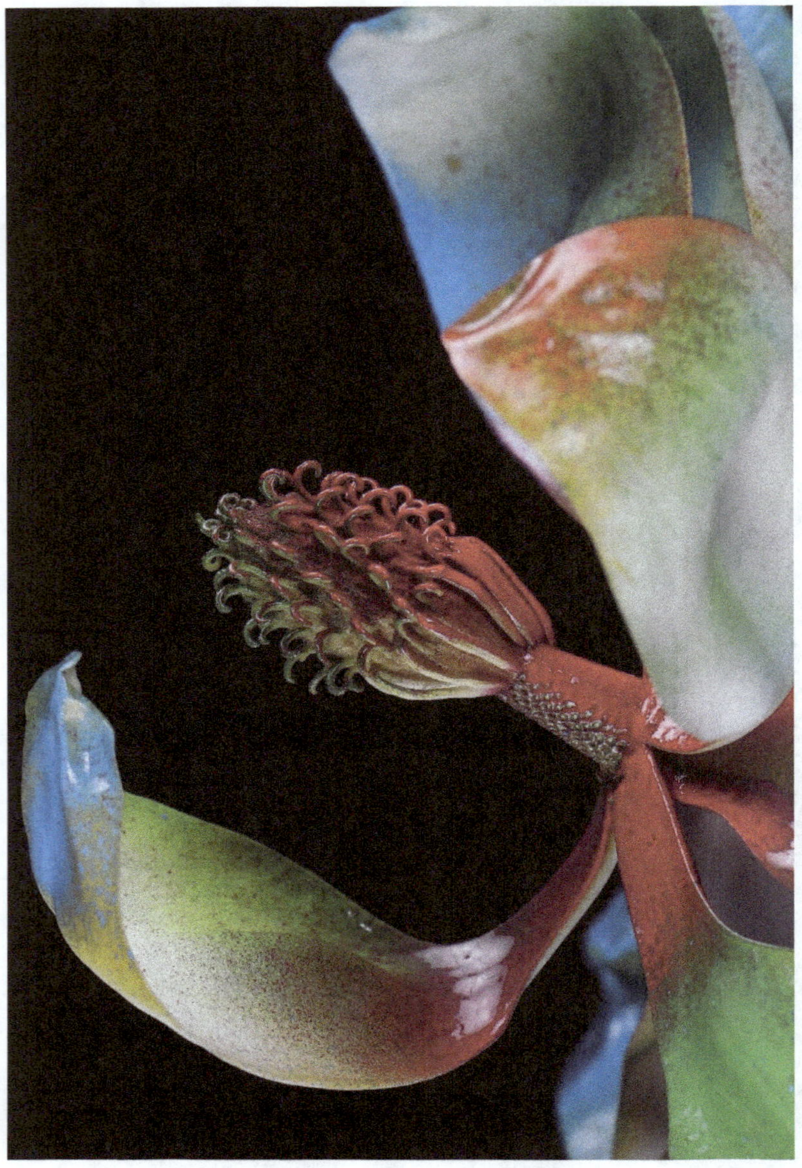

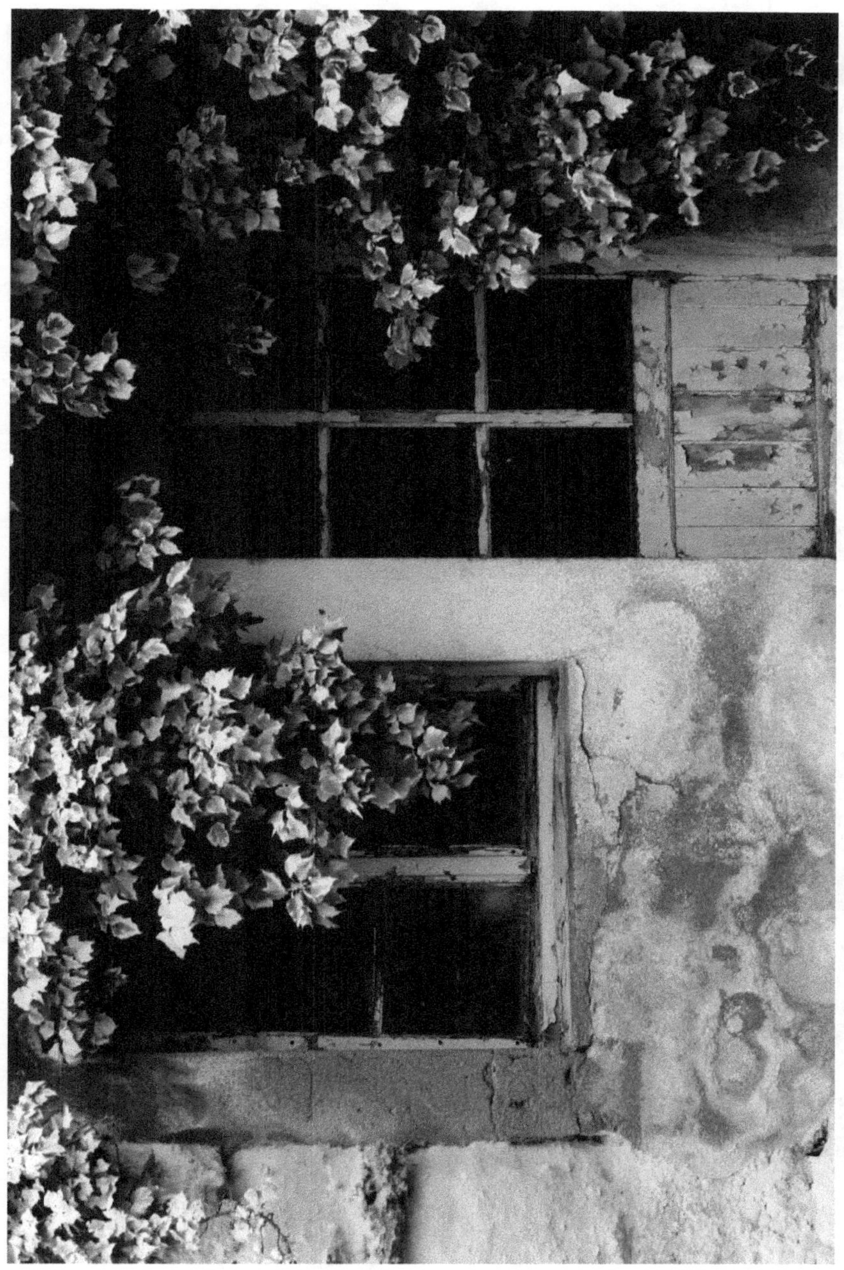

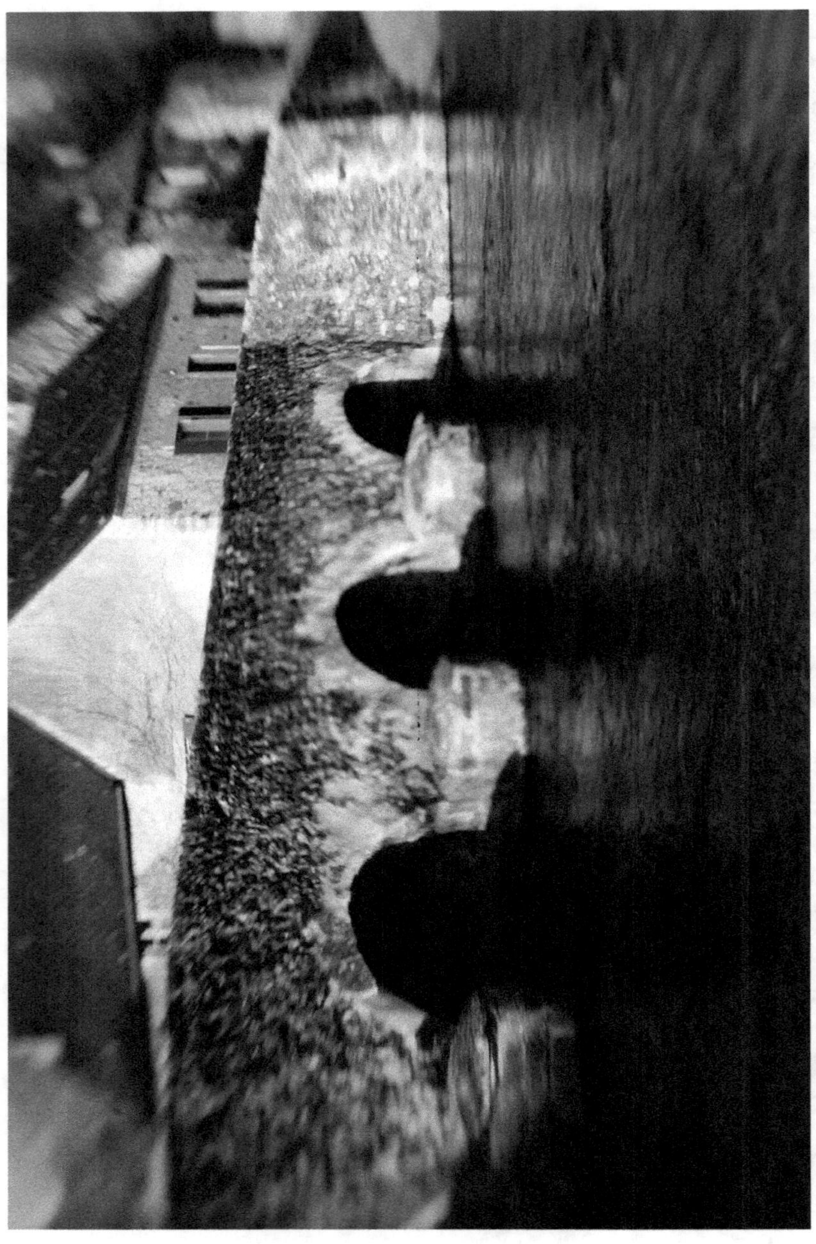

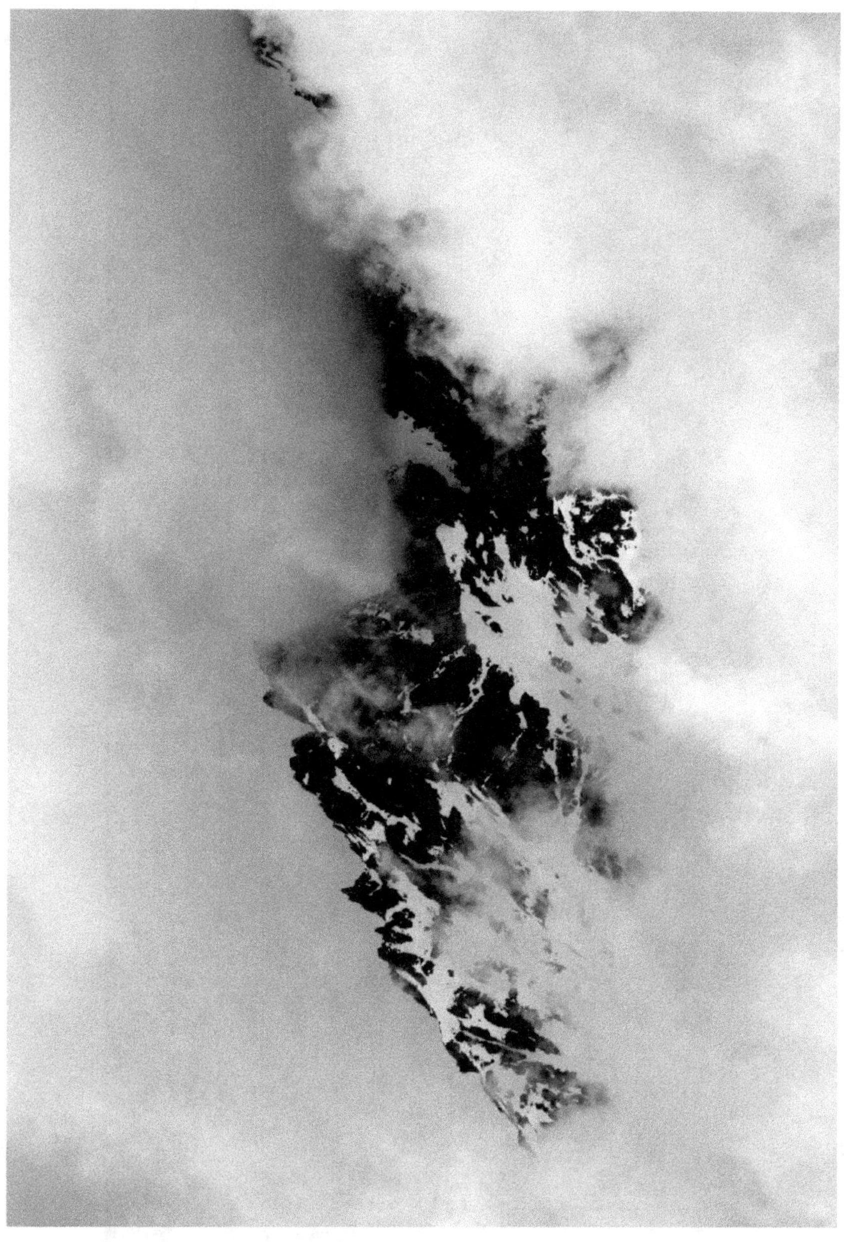

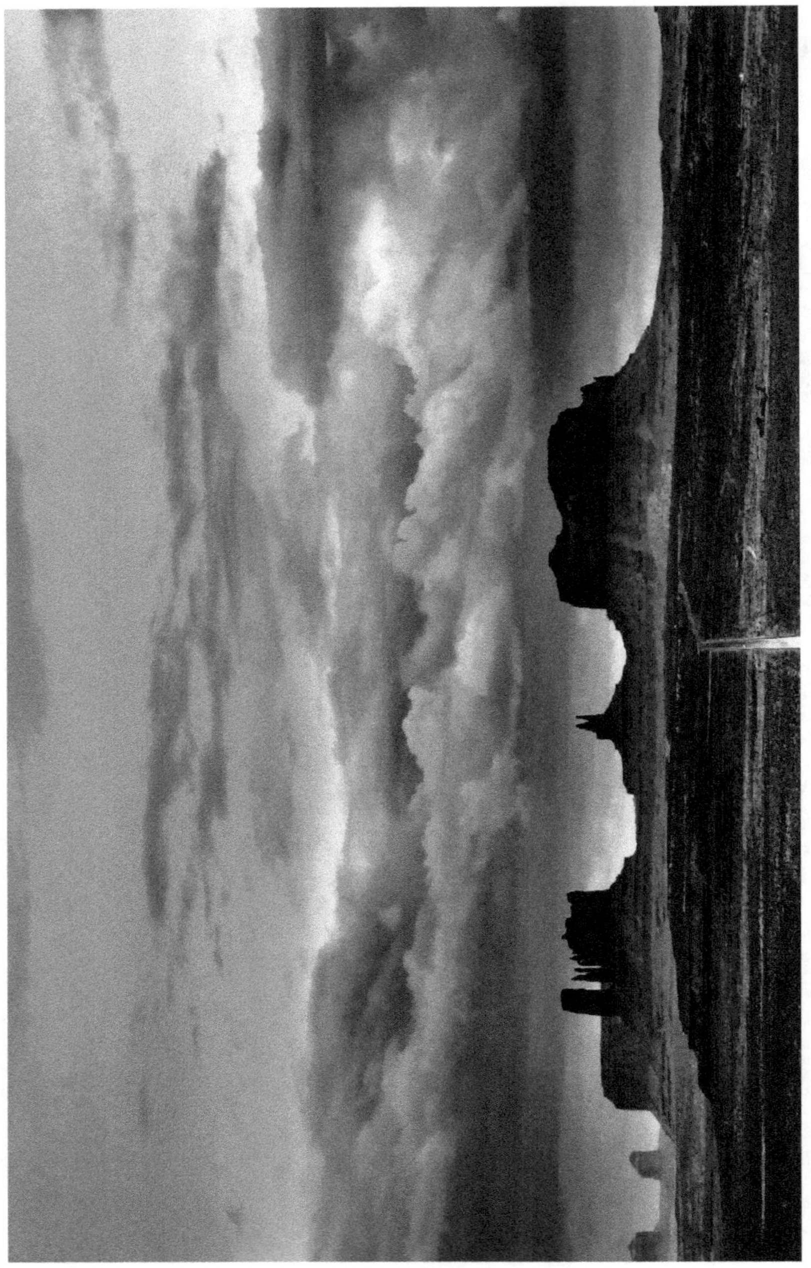

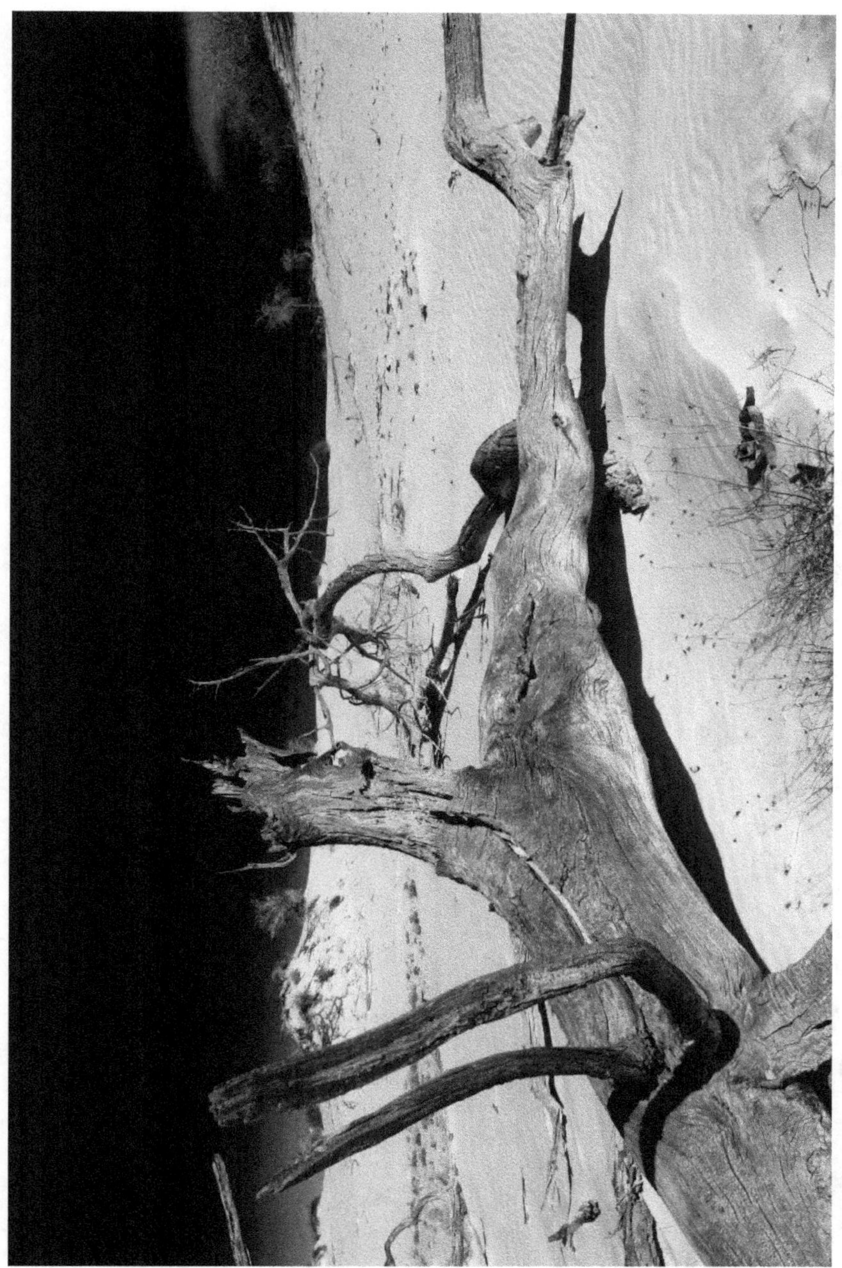

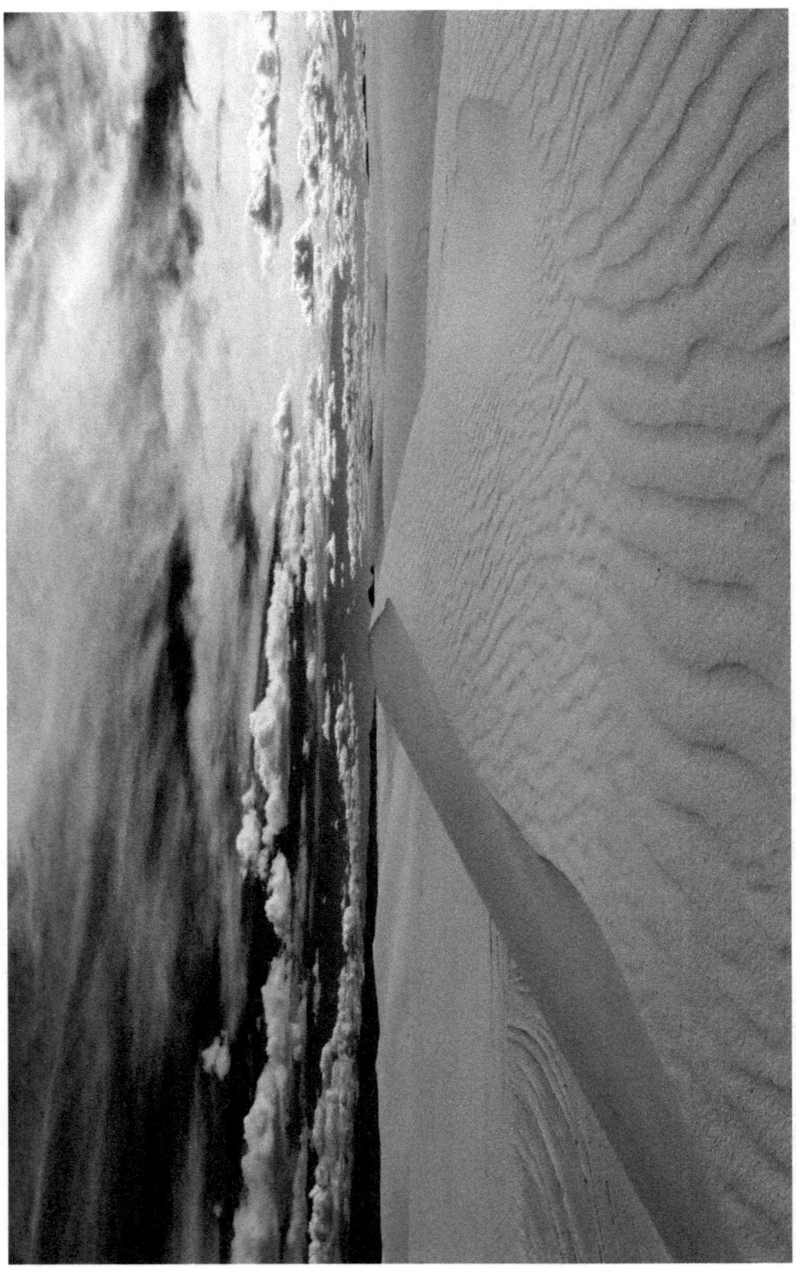

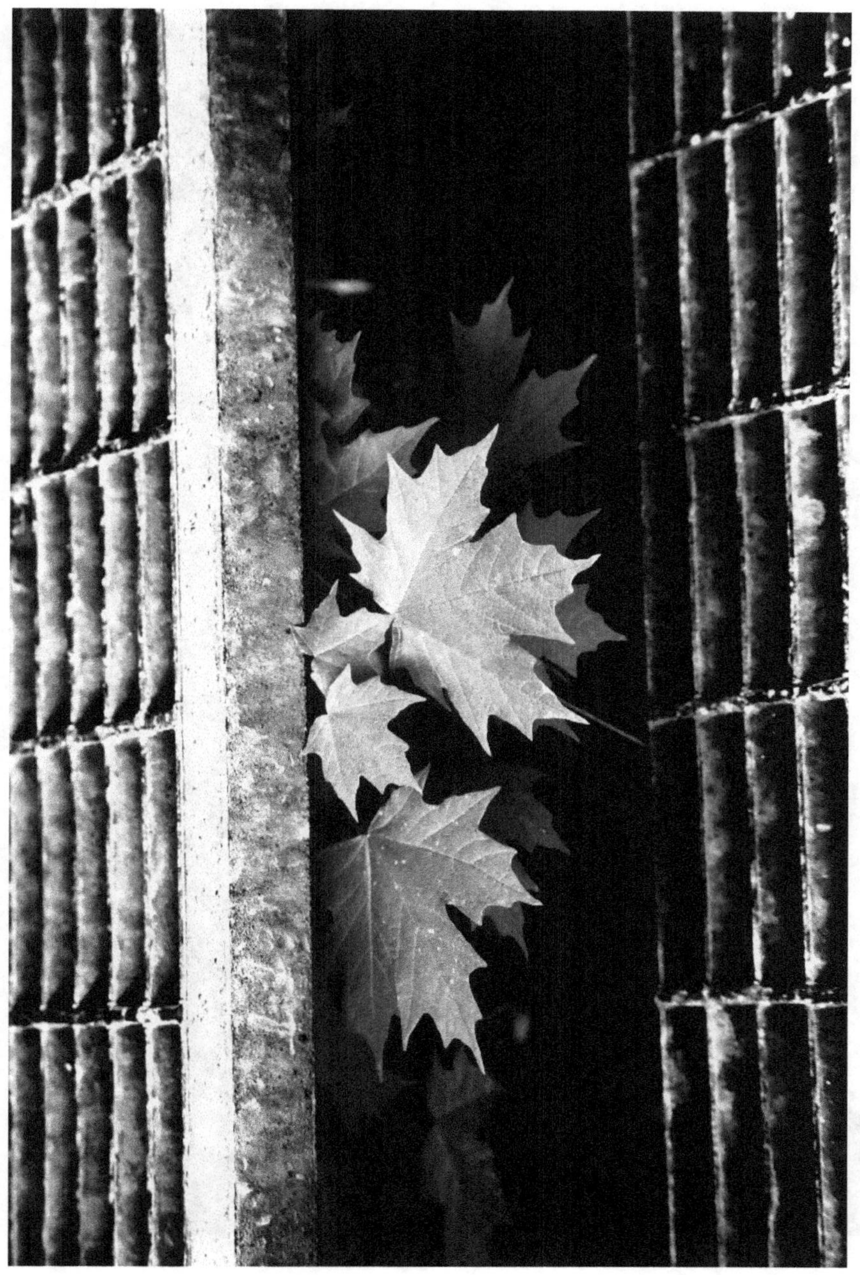

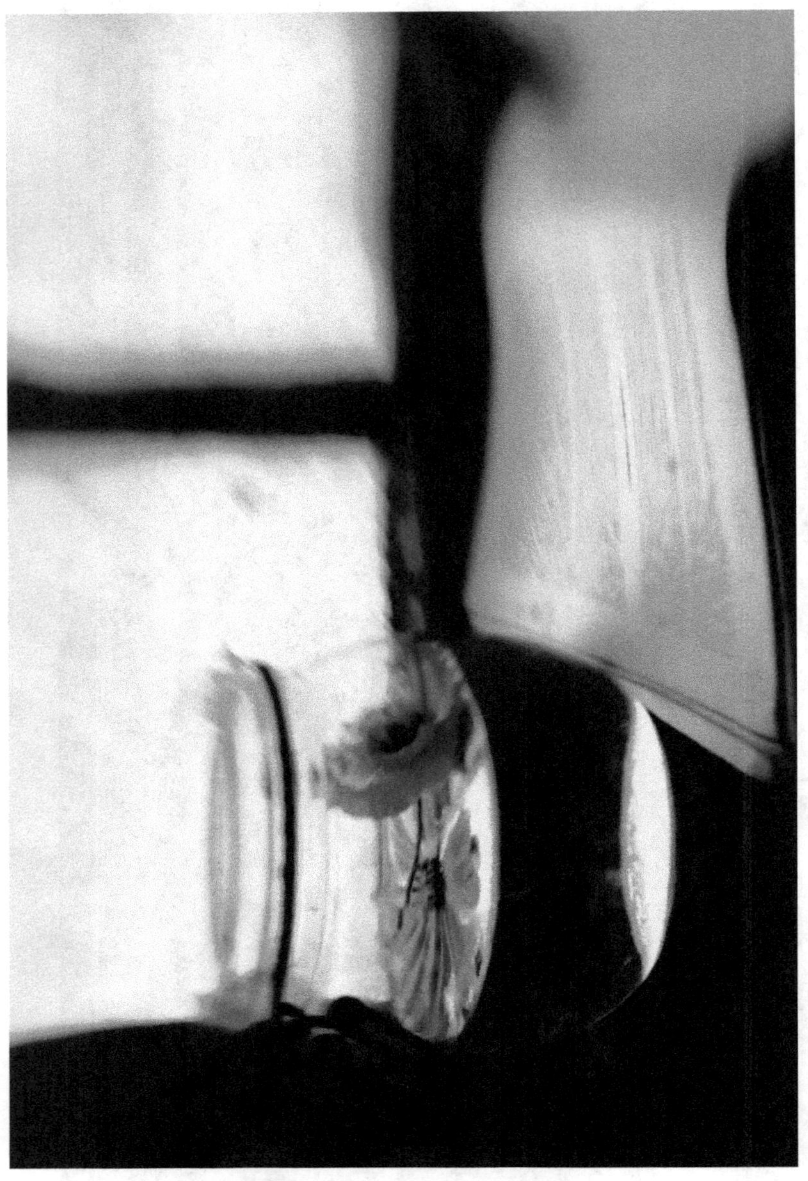

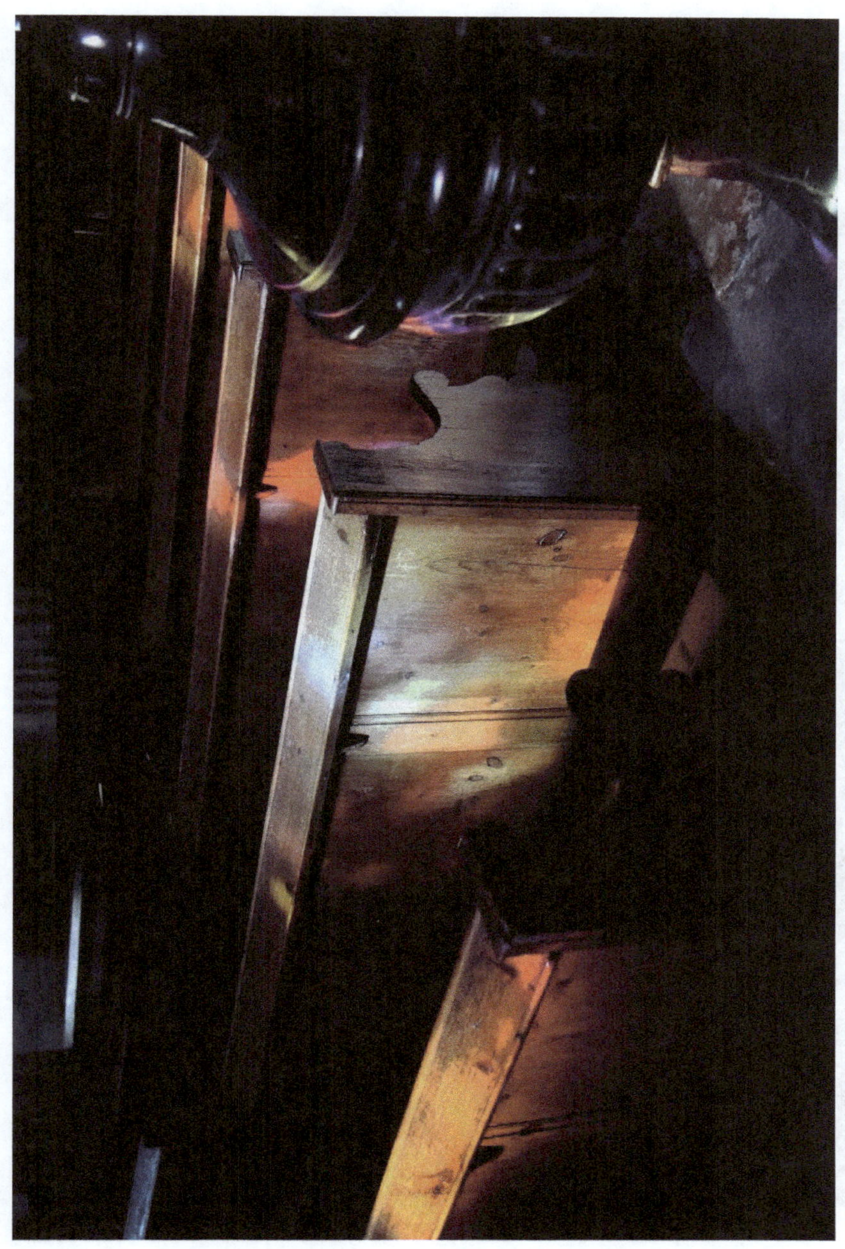

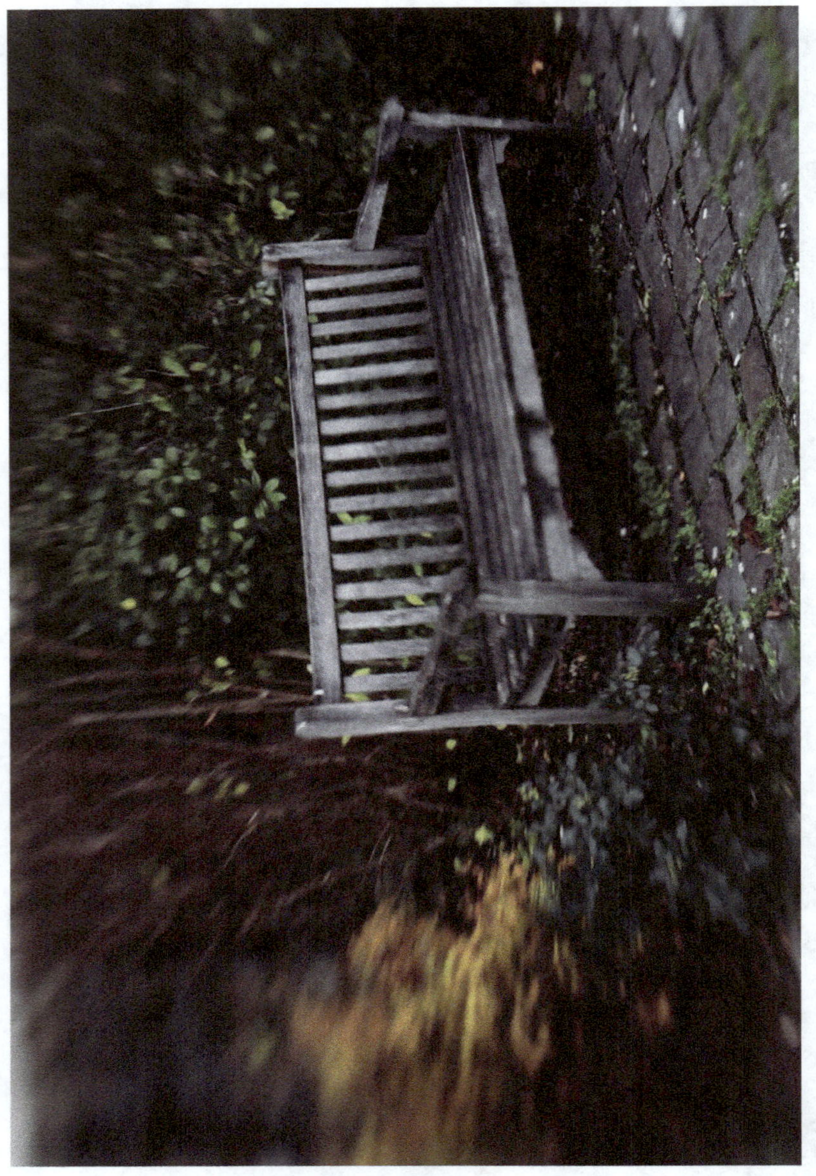

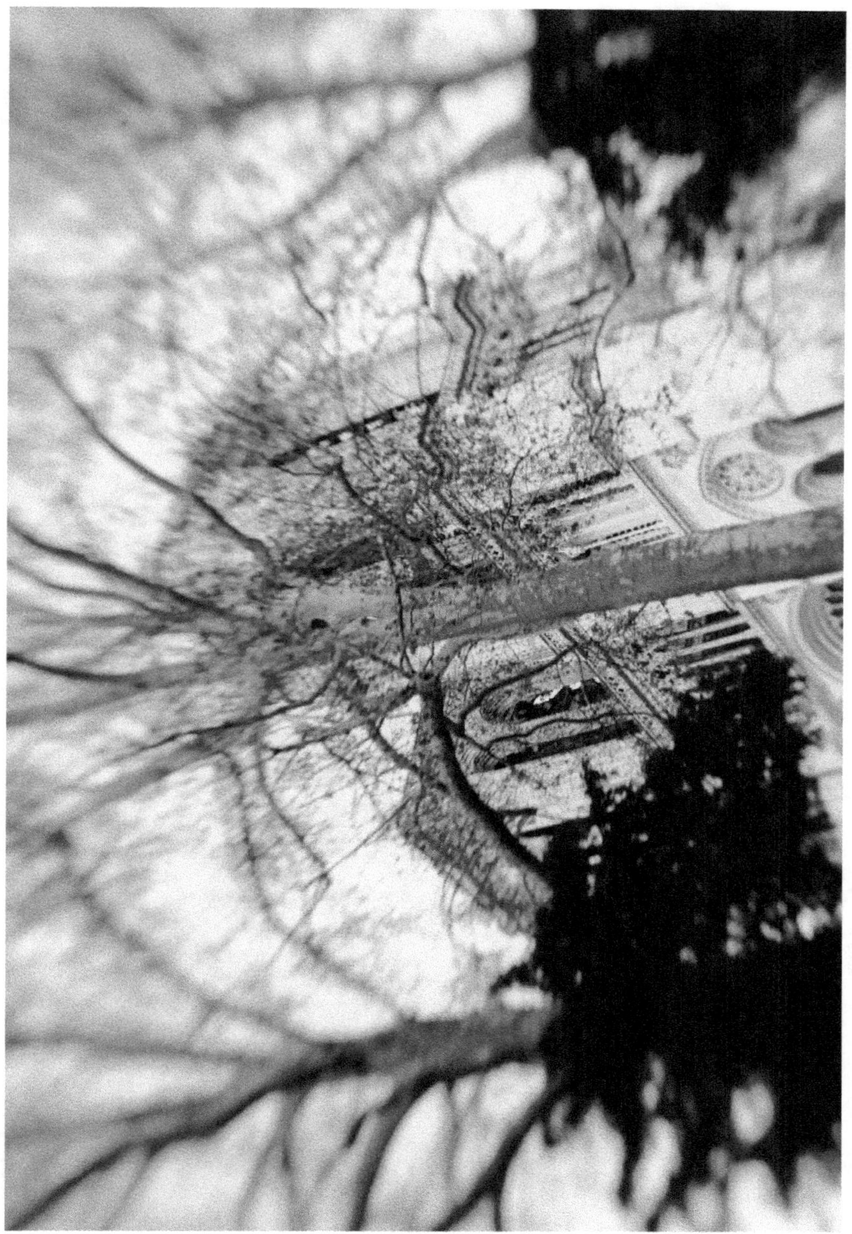

FABRICE POUSSIN PROFILE

Fabrice Poussin teaches French and English at Shorter Univer*sity in Rome, Georgia. Over and above being a photographer extraordinaire he is also the Author of novels and poetry. His work has appeared in "Kestrel", "Symposium", "La Pensee Universelle", "Paris", "The Chimes", "the Shorter University award winning poetry and arts publication", and other magazines.

His photography has been published in "The Front Porch Review", the "San Pedro River Review" as well as other publications.

Fabrice has published 5 books of poetry: "In Absentia"; "Half Past Life"; "If I Had a Gun"; "The Temptation of Silence" and his latest book of poetry is "Forgive Me For Dreaming".